"An illuminating study of metaphor in all its guises. . . . Required reading for anyone with even a passing interest in language."

—*Time Out London*

"Addictive. . . . Geary writes with clarity and power."

—*The Independent* (UK)

"You'll scarf down every page of *I Is an Other* and then ask for more."

—Michael Dirda, Pulitzer Prize–winning critic and author of *Book by Book* and *Classics for Pleasure*

"This book is a prism, refracting the white light of language into a kaleidoscopic celebration of its images and etymologies."

—Ben Schott, author of *Schott's Original Miscellany* and *Schott's Almanacs*

"This book is for everyone interested in the subtle operations of language and thought. *I Is an Other* is one of those 'must-read' books for this year, for any year. It deserves a wide audience, and it will find one."

—Jay Parini, Professor of English and Creative Writing, Middlebury College, and author of *Promised Land: Thirteen Books That Changed America*

"A fascinating excursion to the land of metaphor, with many delightful side trips selected by a knowledgeable and entertaining tour guide."

—Dr. Mardy Grothe, author of *I Never Metaphor I Didn't Like*

©Philip Hollis

About the Author

JAMES GEARY is the author of *Geary's Guide to the World's Great Aphorists* and the *New York Times* bestseller *The World in a Phrase: A Brief History of the Aphorism*.

I
Is an
Other

Geary's Guide to the World's Great Aphorists
The World in a Phrase: A Brief History of the Aphorism
The Body Electric: An Anatomy of the New Bionic Senses

I
Is an
Other

The Secret Life of Metaphor and
How It Shapes the Way We See the World

JAMES GEARY

HARPER  PERENNIAL

NEW YORK • LONDON • TORONTO • SYDNEY • NEW DELHI • AUCKLAND

HARPER ● PERENNIAL

A hardcover edition of this book was published in 2011 by HarperCollins
Publishers.

I IS AN OTHER. Copyright © 2011 by James Geary. All rights reserved. Printed in
the United States of America. No part of this book may be used or reproduced
in any manner whatsoever without written permission except in the case of brief
quotations embodied in critical articles and reviews. For information address
HarperCollins Publishers, 10 East 53rd Street, New York, NY 10022.

HarperCollins books may be purchased for educational, business, or sales
promotional use. For information please write: Special Markets Department,
HarperCollins Publishers, 10 East 53rd Street, New York, NY 10022.

FIRST HARPER PERENNIAL EDITION PUBLISHED 2012.

Designed by Cassandra J. Pappas

Library of Congress Cataloging-in-Publication Data is available upon request.

ISBN 978-0-06-171029-2 (pbk.)

12 13 14 15 16 OV/RRD   10 9 8 7 6 5 4 3 2 1

Contents

Reality is a cliché from which we escape by metaphor.
                                    —WALLACE STEVENS

I
Is an
Other

WHY I IS AN OTHER

In later life, Arthur Rimbaud was an anarchist, businessman, arms dealer, financier, and explorer. But as a teenager, all he wanted to be was a poet. In May 1871, the sixteen-year-old Rimbaud wrote two letters, one to Georges Izambard, his former teacher, and one to Paul Demeny, a publisher he was keen to impress.

Rimbaud waited around for Izambard every day, palely loitering outside the school gates, eager to show the young professor his most recent verse. He also peppered Demeny with copies of his work, accompanied by notes in which he effused about his poems and dropped heavy hints that he would not be at all averse to seeing them in print.

In these two missives, known together as the Seer Letters, Rimbaud outlined his vision for a new kind of poetry. "A Poet makes himself a visionary," he lectured Demeny, "through a long, boundless, and systematized disorganization of all the senses." Only that, Rimbaud argued, could create a language that "will include everything: perfumes, sounds, colors, thought grappling with thought."

Rimbaud's poetic program involved upsetting conventional orders of perception, deranging habitual ways of seeing, hearing, smelling, touching, and tasting, and rearranging them in novel combinations. Fresh, vivid, sometimes shocking images resulted when sense impression jostled sense impression, when thought grappled with thought.

"I got used to elementary hallucination," Rimbaud wrote in "A Season in Hell." "I could very precisely see a mosque instead of a factory, a drum corps of angels, horse carts on the highways of the sky, a drawing room at the bottom of a lake."

To achieve this systematized disorder, Rimbaud believed the poet needed to see similarity in difference and difference in similarity. Things are never just things in themselves; a visionary company of associations, correspondences, semblances always attends them. Everything can be seen—and, for Rimbaud, everything should be seen—as something else.

Rimbaud summarized his poetic mission, and his working method, in the phrase:

I is an other.

"I is an other" is more than just the Seer Letters' grandest dictum. It is metaphor's defining maxim, its secret formula, and its principal equation. Metaphor systematically disorganizes the common sense of things—jumbling together the abstract with the concrete, the physical with the psychological, the like with the unlike—and reorganizes it into uncommon combinations.

Metaphor is most familiar as the literary device through which we describe one thing in terms of another, as when the author of the Old Testament Song of Songs describes a lover's navel as "a round goblet never lacking mixed wine" or when the medieval Muslim rhetorician Abdalqahir Al-Jurjani pines, "The gazelle has stolen its eyes from my beloved."

Yet metaphor is much, much more than this. Metaphor is not just confined to art and literature but is at work in all fields of human endeavor, from economics and advertising, to politics and business, to science and psychology.

Metaphor conditions our interpretations of the stock market and, through advertising, it surreptitiously infiltrates our purchasing decisions. In the mouths of politicians, metaphor subtly nudges public opinion; in the minds of businesspeople, it spurs creativity and innovation. In science, metaphor is the preferred nomenclature for new theories and new discoveries; in psychology, it is the natural language of human relationships and emotions.

These are just some of the ways metaphor pervades our daily lives and daily minds. But there is no aspect of our experience not molded in some way by metaphor's almost imperceptible touch. Once you twig to metaphor's modus operandi, you'll find its fingerprints on absolutely everything.

Metaphorical thinking—our instinct not just for describing but for *comprehending* one thing in terms of another, for equating I with an other—shapes our view of the world, and is essential to how we communicate, learn, discover, and invent.

Metaphor is a way of thought long before it is a way with words.

Our understanding of metaphor is in the midst of a metamorphosis. For centuries, metaphor has been seen as a kind of cognitive frill, a pleasant but essentially useless embellishment to "normal" thought. Now, the frill is gone. New research in the social and cognitive sciences makes it increasingly plain that metaphorical thinking influences our attitudes, beliefs, and actions in surprising, hidden, and often oddball ways. Metaphor has finally leapt off the page and landed with a mighty splash right in the middle of our stream of consciousness. The waves rippling out from that impact are only just beginning to reach us.

Édouard Claparède, a Swiss neurologist and early investigator of memory who died in 1940, studied individuals with brain lesions and other neurological damage that affected their abilities to create new memories and recall old ones. One of his patients was a woman who had no short-term memory whatsoever. She had perfect recollection of the more distant past, including her childhood, but the recent past was a total blank. Unable to form any new memories, this woman saw Claparède every day at his clinic yet had no recollection of ever meeting him. Each time they met, it was as if for the very first time.

Claparède wanted to test whether some part of this woman's brain did indeed remember him. So one day he concealed a pin in his hand and, when the woman arrived for her next session, he shook her hand. The woman cried out in pain and withdrew her hand.

The following day, the woman arrived as usual for her appointment and, as usual, professed that she had never seen Claparède before. But when Claparède proffered his hand to shake, she hesitated, fearing another jab. The experiment proved that, on some unconscious level, the woman recalled the physical pain associated with Claparède's handshake. Therefore, Claparède concluded, some vestige of her short-term memory was still at work.

Like Claparède's handshake, metaphor slips a pin into the quotidian. By mixing the foreign with the familiar, the marvelous with the mundane, metaphor makes the world sting and tingle. Though we encounter metaphor every day, we typically fail to recognize it. Its influence is profound but takes place mostly outside our conscious awareness. Yet once metaphor has us in its grasp, it never lets us go, and we can never forget it.

ALL SHOOK UP

etaphor lives a secret life all around us. We utter about one metaphor for every ten to twenty-five words, or about six metaphors a minute.

Sound like a lot? Too many, perhaps? A quick look at some representative language samples shows just how popular metaphor is. Take this Australian weather forecast, for instance (the metaphors are in italics):

Perth is *in the grip* of a heat wave with temperatures *set to soar* to 40 degrees Celsius by the end of the week. Australia is *no stranger* to extreme weather. Melbourne was pummelled with *hailstones the size of golf balls* on Saturday. Long term, droughts, bushfires, and floods have all *plagued* large swathes of Queensland, New South Wales and Victoria.

That's five metaphors in an excerpt of fifty-eight words, or about one metaphorical phrase for every eleven words. These are all classic metaphors, too, in which one thing is described in terms of another: hailstones are described in terms of golf balls; extreme weather conditions are described in terms of biblical plagues.

Still, maybe we innately resort to metaphor when talking about meteorology. Would the metaphor-per-words ratio still hold for a presumably more exact science, like economics? Here are the headline and first line from a by no means atypical story about the economy, in this case Great Britain's:

> RISKS TO U.K. RECOVERY *LURK* BEHIND
> *CLOUDY OUTLOOK*
>
> Britain's recovery from the worst recession in decades is *gaining traction* but *confused* economic data and the high risk of a *hung* parliament could yet *snuff out* its momentum.

Six metaphors in thirty-seven words, or roughly one for every six words. Again, these metaphors describe one thing in terms of another: economic data is described in terms of confusion, a psychological state usually associated with the people who interpret the data rather than the data itself; economic growth prospects are described in terms of overcast skies.

These are both relatively trivial examples, however. We may well wax metaphorical when talking about the little stuff but surely we get seriously literal when talking about the big stuff. But that's not true, either. Here are the first line of Abraham Lincoln's Gettysburg Address and the fourth paragraph of Barack Obama's inaugural address (again, the metaphors are in italics):

> Four score and seven years ago, our *fathers brought forth*, upon this continent, a new nation, *conceived* in liberty, and dedicated to the proposition that "all men are created equal."

The words [of the presidential oath] have been spoken during *rising tides of prosperity* and the *still waters of peace*. Yet, every so often the oath is taken amidst *gathering clouds* and *raging storms*. At these moments, America has carried on not simply because of the skill or vision of those in high office, but because We the People have remained faithful to the ideals of our forebears, and true to our founding documents.

There are two main metaphors in Lincoln's opening line of thirty words (one metaphor for every fifteen words), both of which describe America in terms of conception and birth. Indeed, Lincoln's entire speech, which is only 243 words in length, is a single extended metaphor about how individuals and nations are conceived, born, fight, and die.

There are seventy-four words and four main metaphors in the fourth paragraph of Obama's speech (one metaphor for every eighteen or so words). He describes prosperity in terms of tides, peace in terms of becalmed water, and political trouble in terms of adverse meteorological events. Maybe there is something inherently metaphorical about the weather, after all . . .

If you're still skeptical about metaphor's ubiquity, just listen carefully the next time you or anyone else opens their mouth. You'll find yourself in the middle of a metaphorical blizzard.

To demonstrate this, I cite one of our greatest philosophers, the reigning king of the metaphorians, a man whose contributions to the field are so great that he himself has become a metaphor. I am, of course, referring to none other than . . . Elvis Presley:

She touched my hand, what a chill I got.
Her lips are like a volcano that's hot.
I'm proud to say that she's my buttercup.
I'm in love; I'm all shook up.

"All Shook Up" is a great love song. It is also a great example of how, whenever we describe anything abstract—ideas, feelings, thoughts, emotions, concepts—we instinctively resort to metaphor. In "All Shook Up," a touch is not a touch, but a chill; lips are not lips, but volcanoes (technically, any formulation involving the word "like" is a simile—as in, "Her lips are *like* a volcano that's hot"—but a simile is just a metaphor with the scaffolding still up); she is not she, but a buttercup; and love is not love, but the state or condition of being all shook up.

In describing love this way, Elvis follows Aristotle's classic definition of metaphor as the process of "giving the thing a name that belongs to something else." This is the mathematics of metaphor, the simplest equation of which can be written like this:

$$X = Y.$$

This formula works wherever metaphor is present. Elvis uses it in "All Shook Up":

lips = volcano.

Rimbaud uses it in his metaphor manifesto:

I = other.

And Shakespeare uses it in his famous line from *Romeo and Juliet*: "Juliet is the sun." In the mathematics of Aristotle's poetics, the line is written:

Juliet = sun.

Here, Shakespeare gives the thing (Juliet) a name that belongs to something else (the sun). This is a textbook example of meta-

phor. Indeed, this line turns up in almost every academic treat-
ment of the subject. In literary parlance, the "thing" is called the
metaphor's "target" and the "something else" from which it takes a
name is called its "source."

The terminology fits well with the etymology of the word "metaphor" itself. Derived from the Greek roots *meta* (over, across, or
beyond) and *phor* (to carry), the literal meaning of metaphor is "to
carry across." A metaphor carries across a name from the source to
the target. Rhetoricians throughout history have recognized metaphors as linguistic hand-me-downs, meanings passed on from an
old word to a new thing. In *De Oratore*, Cicero observed:

> When something that can scarcely be conveyed by the proper term
> is expressed metaphorically, the meaning we desire to convey is
> made clear by the resemblance of the thing that we have expressed
> by the word that does not belong. Consequently, the metaphors in
> which you take what you have got from somewhere else are a sort
> of borrowing.

In his treatise on rhetoric, *The Mysteries of Eloquence*, Abdalqahir Al-Jurjani also described metaphor as a sort of borrowing. In
fact, the Arabic word for metaphor is *isti'ara*, or "loan."

But when we lend a thing a name that belongs to something
else, we lend it a complex pattern of relations and associations, too.
We mix and match what we know about the metaphor's source
(in Shakespeare's case, the sun) with what we know about its target (Juliet). A metaphor juxtaposes two different things and then
skews our point of view so unexpected similarities emerge. Metaphorical thinking half discovers and half invents the likenesses it
describes.

The "Juliet is the sun" metaphor allows us to understand Juliet much more vividly than if Shakespeare had taken a more

literal approach, such as "But, soft! What light through yonder window breaks? It is Juliet, applying her luminous restorative night cream."

Metaphor is, however, much more than a mere literary device employed by love-struck poets when they refer to their girlfriends as interstellar masses of incandescent gas. Metaphor is intensely yet inconspicuously present in everything from ordinary conversation and commercial messaging to news reports and political speeches. Metaphor is always breathing down our necks.

Look no further than the common expressions we use every day to convey our feelings. Whether you're *down in the dumps* or *riding high, on the straight and narrow* or *at a crossroads, cool as a cucumber* or *hot under the collar,* you are fulfilling the classic Aristotelian definition of metaphor by giving the thing (your emotional state) a name that belongs to something else (waste storage facilities, well-paved thoroughfares, refrigerated vegetables).

Even the simplest, most unassuming words are capable of a bewildering variety of metaphorical mutations. Take "shoulder," for instance. You can give someone the *cold shoulder* or a *shoulder to cry on.* You can have a *chip on your shoulder* or be constantly *looking over your shoulder.* You can stand *on the shoulders of giants,* stand *shoulder to shoulder* with your friends, or stand *head and shoulders above the rest.* Wherever you turn, you can't help but *rub shoulders* with one of the word's multitude of metaphorical meanings.

Metaphor is present in proverbs (*A bird in the hand is worth two in the bush, Let sleeping dogs lie*), in idioms (*shoot the breeze, kick the bucket*), in compound phrases (*forbidden fruit, red herring*), and in formulaic expressions (*in the zone, the last straw*).

Ordinary conversation is so rife with figurative phrases because metaphor is about more than just words. We *think* metaphorically. Metaphorical thinking is the way we make sense of the world, and every individual metaphor is a specific instance of this imaginative process at work. Metaphors are therefore not confined to spoken or written language.

Visual metaphors abound in advertisements and other types of popular imagery, such as the lightbulb that appears above someone's head to signify a *bright* idea. But metaphors are not merely symbolic; they have implications for—and impacts on—the "real" world. In one study, for instance, participants exposed to a bare illuminated lightbulb performed better at spatial, verbal, and mathematical problem solving than those exposed to shaded lightbulbs or fluorescent lighting. Brightness, it seems, facilitates insight.

A common metaphorical gesture is the "thumbs-up" sign, in which we indicate our state of general well-being by closing the fist and extending the thumb upward at a 90-degree angle. Visual metaphors like these also follow Aristotle's definition. The only difference is that the thing is given an image or a gesture rather than a name that belongs to something else.

Metaphor is so essential that it is impossible to describe emotions, abstract concepts, complex ideas, or practically anything else without it, as art historian and connoisseur of metaphor Nelson Goodman wrote in *Languages of Art*:

> Metaphor permeates all discourse, ordinary and special, and we should have a hard time finding a purely literal paragraph anywhere. This incessant use of metaphor springs not merely from love of literary color but also from urgent need of economy. If we could not readily transfer schemata to make new sortings and orderings, we should have to burden ourselves with unmanageably many different schemata, either by adoption of a vast vocabulary of elementary terms or by prodigious elaboration of composite ones.

Shakespeare's description of Juliet is a marvel of metaphorical economy. On the surface, Juliet is nothing like the sun.

Nevertheless, she shines. Romeo is inexorably drawn by her gravitational pull. She is the center of his universe. She radiates heat. And her brightness can, of course, burn. In these particulars at least, she is indeed the sun. Shakespeare's schematic transfer tells us everything we need to know about Juliet—and Romeo's feelings for her—in just four simple words.

After hundreds of years of constant use, this comparison has become something of a cliché. But the metaphorical thinking that enabled the equation to be made in the first place is the essence of creativity in the sciences as well as the arts. Whenever we solve a problem, make a discovery, or devise an innovation, the same kind of metaphorical thinking takes place.

Scientists and inventors compare two things: what they know and what they don't know. The only way to find out about the latter is to investigate the ways it might be *like* the former. And whenever we explore how one thing is *like* another, we are in the realm of metaphorical thinking, as in this comparison, another academic staple, from Scottish poet Robert Burns:

My love is like a red, red rose.

By drawing our attention to the similarities between the object of his affections and a perennial flowering shrub of the Rosaceae family, Burns exquisitely—and economically—tells us about the unknown (his love) by comparing it with the known (a red, red rose). We can therefore be reasonably sure that the beauty of Burns's beloved is flush and full (and fleeting), her perfume is sweet, and she can be very prickly. And we know all this without ever having laid eyes on her.

The paradox of metaphor is that it tells us so much about a person, place, or thing by telling us what that person, place, or thing is not. Understanding a metaphor (like reading a book about that process, in fact) is a seemingly random walk through a deep, dark forest of associations. The path is full of unexpected twists and turns, veering wildly off into the underbrush one minute and abruptly disappearing down a rabbit hole the next. Signposts spin like weather vanes. You can't see the wood for the trees. Then, suddenly, somehow, you step into the clearing. A metaphor is both detour and destination, a digression that gets to the point.

Aristotle identified the mastery of metaphorical thinking as "a sign of genius, since a good metaphor implies an intuitive perception of the similarity in dissimilars." French mathematician Henri Poincaré found an ingenious metaphor for metaphorical thinking in the theories of one of Aristotle's predecessors, Epicurus.

According to the Greeks, the world was made up of just two basic things: atoms and the void. "Atoms are unlimited in size and number," wrote Democritus, the fourth-century B.C.E. philosopher who formulated ancient Greece's version of atomic theory, "and they are borne along in the whole universe in a vortex, and thereby generate all composite things—fire, water, air, earth; for even these are conglomerations of given atoms."

To the Greeks, the physical universe was, quite literally, an atomic shower, a steady downpour of tiny, indivisible particles falling through empty space. All the objects in the world—all the things we see, hear, smell, touch, and taste—were made up of atoms combining and recombining in every conceivable way.

In some of the wilder expositions of the theory, thinkers imagined a distant time when the body parts of every living thing tumbled through the void. The early universe was a cascade of arms and legs, feet and paws, fins and wings, hands and claws. Every limb connected randomly with every other until it met its corresponding shape and clicked into place. Through this process of trial and error, the world as we know it was made.

But Epicurus, who was born around 341 B.C.E., spotted a flaw in the theory. In order to meet its match, an atom could not simply fall through the void like rain. It must veer from the vertical path and waft its way down like a feather. Otherwise, he reasoned, it would never bump into any other atoms and thus never form the conglomerations Democritus described.

So Epicurus came up with the *clinamen*—the unpredictable moment during which each atom deviates from its course, creating the opportunity for a chance encounter with another atom. It was only through these "clinamactic" collisions, Epicurus believed, that change, surprise, and variety entered the world.

Like most ancient Greek philosophers, Epicurus left behind very few of his own words and even less about his own life. We know about the *clinamen* largely thanks to the first-century C.E. Roman poet Lucretius, whose epic poem *On the Nature of the Universe* is an encyclopedic exposition of Epicurean philosophy.

Not much is known about Lucretius, either, except that, according to Saint Jerome, he was driven insane by a love potion and killed himself at the age of forty-four. Whether his love resembled the sun, a red, red rose, or something else entirely, we do not know.

Still, for a love-crazed, suicidal poet, Lucretius summed up Epicurus's ideas quite lucidly. Without the *clinamen*, he wrote, "No collision would take place and no impact of atom upon atom would be created. Thus nature would never have created anything." Some 2,000 years after the composition of Lucretius's poem, Poincaré used Epicurean atomic theory to explain the nature of mathematical discovery and, by extension, the nature of metaphorical thinking.

Born in Nancy, France, in 1854, Poincaré was a cross between a dandy and a distracted professor. He was "short and plump, carried an enormous head set off by a thick spade beard and splendid moustache, was myopic, stooped, distraught in speech, absent-minded and wore pince-nez glasses attached to a black silk ribbon." He was also intensely interested in the sources of creativity.

In *The Foundations of Science*, Poincaré set out his general theory of ingenuity. Based on his own experience as well as his interrogations of other mathematicians, Poincaré concluded that great creative breakthroughs occur unexpectedly and unconsciously after an extended period of hard, conscious labor. He invoked an Epicurean analogy to explain this. Poincaré described ideas as being like Epicurus's atoms, writing:

> During the complete repose of the mind, these atoms are motionless; they are, so to speak, hooked to the wall . . . During a period of apparent rest and unconscious work, certain of them are detached from the wall and put in motion. They flash in every direction through the space . . . as would, for example, a swarm of gnats . . . Their mutual impacts may produce new combinations. What is the role of the preliminary conscious work? It is evidently to mobilize certain of these atoms, to unhook them from the wall and put them in swing. After this shaking-up imposed upon them by our will, these atoms do not return to their primitive rest. They freely continue their dance.

Poincaré's atomic two-step is a deft analogy for how mathematical creativity—indeed, all creativity—lies in the dance of metaphorical thought, the tumultuous tango that ensues when idea rubs up against idea, when thought grapples with thought.

Metaphor is the mind's great swerve. Creativity don't mean a thing if it ain't got that clinamactic swing.

This same idea is contained in the three most famous words in all of Western philosophy, Descartes's "Cogito ergo sum." This phrase is routinely translated as:

I think, therefore I am.

But there is a better translation.

The Latin word *cogito* is derived from the prefix *co* (with or to-gether) and the verb *agitare* (to shake). *Agitare* is the root of the English words "agitate" and "agitation." Thus, the original mean-ing of *cogito* is "to shake together," and the proper translation of "Cogito ergo sum" is:

I shake things up, therefore I am.

Metaphor shakes things up, producing everything from Shake-speare to scientific insight in the process.

The mind is a plastic snow dome: most beautiful, most inter-esting, and most itself when, as Elvis put it, it's all shook up. And metaphor keeps the mind shaking, rattling, and rolling long after Elvis has left the building.

LANGUAGE IS FOSSIL POETRY

When Elvis appeared on *The Ed Sullivan Show* for the first time, on September 9, 1956, his pelvic undulations on other programs had already unsettled television executives and nervous parents across the country. Elvis performed two sets that night. For the first, the camera remained fixed above his waist. For the second, it pulled back far enough for the world to see the gyrations that earned him the moniker, Elvis the Pelvis. The uproar occasioned by Elvis's early TV appearances is not unlike that which has periodically attended metaphor. Elvis was condemned for promoting immorality and licentiousness; metaphor has been condemned for promoting deception and subversion.

Historically, metaphor has often been considered a devious use of language, an imprecise and vaguely suspicious linguistic trick employed chiefly by charlatans, faith healers, snake oil salesmen, and poets. Many philosophers regarded metaphorical language as at best a harmless diversion and at worst a deliberate and potentially dangerous obfuscation. As a result, not many serious thinkers took metaphor at all seriously.

In *Leviathan*, Thomas Hobbes classified metaphor as one of the "abuses of speech" and accused people of lying when they "use words metaphorically; that is, in other sense than that they are ordained for; and thereby deceive others . . . Reasoning upon [metaphor] is wandering amongst innumerable absurdities; and their end, contention and sedition, or contempt."

The Anglo-Irish philosopher George Berkeley advocated going cold turkey to protect against the errors of metaphorical thinking. "A philosopher should abstain from metaphor," he urged.

In *An Essay Concerning Human Understanding*, John Locke was equally unsympathetic:

> If we would speak of things as they are, we must allow that all the art of rhetoric, besides order and clearness; all the artificial and figurative application of words eloquence hath invented, are for nothing else but to insinuate wrong ideas, move the passions, and thereby mislead the judgement; and so indeed are perfect cheats.

As Hobbes, Berkeley, and Locke plunged the dagger of reason into metaphor's cheating heart, they were presumably unaware that the weapon they wielded was, in fact, metaphor itself.

Hobbes, in his brief denunciation, repeatedly abuses speech by using words in senses other than that for which they were ordained. The meaning of the word "ordain," for example, comes from roots that mean "to set in order," not "to designate," "to decree," or even "to admit to the Christian ministry." Similarly, "deceive" literally meant "to catch or ensnare" before it meant "to make a person believe what is not true."

And can we really construe the phrase "wandering amongst innumerable absurdities" as anything other than a seditious, contemptible deployment of figurative language when perfectly rational language would do? After all, how can one wander amongst absurdities? The idea itself is absurd.

Berkeley shamelessly indulged in metaphor by using the word "abstain," which is derived from the Latin verb *tenere* (to hold) and literally refers to anything untenable, anything that cannot be held—such as a mistaken opinion about metaphor.

Even Locke's seemingly innocuous choice of "insinuate" harbors a hidden metaphor. The word comes from the Latin *sinus*, meaning "a bay, gulf, or cove"; only much later was it used to describe the introduction of a thought or a thing through a winding, circuitous route, as seafaring smugglers shift contraband by hugging the shore.

Metaphor got up so many philosophical noses because it seemed so imprecise. Comparing your beloved to a red, red rose might be fine if you're writing a poem, but these thinkers believed more exact language was needed to express the "truth"—a term, by the way, distilled from Icelandic, Swedish, Anglo-Saxon, and other non-English words meaning "believed" rather than "certain."

The truth is, metaphor is astonishingly precise. Nothing is as exact as an apt metaphor. Even the most mundane metaphors contain finely detailed descriptions, hidden deposits of knowledge that a quick dig into a word's etymology will turn up.

Open a dictionary at random; metaphors fill every page. Take the word "fathom," for example. The meaning is clear. A fathom is a measurement of water depth, equivalent to about six feet. But fathom also means "to understand." Why?

Scrabble around in the word's etymological roots. "Fathom" comes from the Anglo-Saxon *fæthm*, meaning "the two arms outstretched." The term was originally used as a measurement of cloth, because the distance from fingertip to fingertip for the average man with his arms outstretched is roughly six feet. This technique was later extended to sounding the depths of bodies of

water, since it was easy to lower a cord divided into six-foot incre-
ments, or fathoms, over the side of a boat. But how did fathom
come to mean "to understand," as in "I can't fathom that" or "She's
unfathomable"? Metaphorically, of course.

You master something—you learn to control or accept it—when
you embrace it, when you get your arms around it, when you take
it in hand. You comprehend something when you grasp it, take its
measure, get to the bottom of it—fathom it.

Fathom took on its present significance in classic Aristotelian
fashion: through the metaphorical transfer of its original meaning
(a measurement of cloth or water) to an abstract concept (understanding). This is the primary purpose of metaphor: to carry over
existing names or descriptions to things that are either so new that
they haven't yet been named or so abstract that they cannot be
otherwise explained.

This ferrying back and forth happens all the time. What accounts for the amazing acceleration of a sports car? Horsepower.
What happens to an economy when growth falls and unemploy-
ment rises? A depression. What do you see when you switch on
a computer? A desktop. These are all metaphors, names taken
from one thing and applied to a completely different thing because
someone somewhere once noticed a resemblance.

The English literary critic, philosopher, and evangelical etymologist Owen Barfield picked up Aristotle's definitive insight when
he wrote in *History in English Words*:

> When a new thing or a new idea comes into the consciousness of
> the community, it is described, not by a new word, but by the name
> of the pre-existing object which most closely resembles it.

Look at and listen to the language around you and you will discover a moveable feast of metaphor. Let me *run* this idea by you;

ideas do not have legs (neither do tables or chairs, by the way) but "run" is used metaphorically to request a brisk consideration of a proposal. Similarly, combs do not have teeth; books do not have spines; and mountains do not have feet.[1]

The markets are *jittery* today; markets don't get the jitters, investors do, but the phrase metaphorically expresses the reigning uncertainty.

I *see* what you mean; you "see" absolutely nothing when you say this, but you do convey quite clearly that you understand what someone else is saying.

Etymologies make perfect poetic sense. The word "emotion," for example, comes from the Latin verb "to move," *movere*. How do we describe the emotional state occasioned by a poignant encounter, a beautiful film, or a powerful piece of music? We are *moved*. Movement is even visibly ensconced in the word "*emotion*" itself.

Even the word "literal"—derived from the Latin *litera*, meaning "letter"—is a metaphor. "Literal" means "according to the letter"; that is, actual, accurate, factual. But *litera* is, in turn, derived from the verb *linire*, meaning "to smear," and was transferred to *litera* when authors began smearing words on parchment instead of carving them into wood or stone. The roots of *linire* are also visible in the word "liniment," which denotes a salve or ointment. Thus, the literal meaning of "literal" is to smear or spread, a fitting metaphor for the way metaphor oozes over rigid definitional borders.

It is impossible to pinpoint the first use of most words as metaphors. It happened far too long ago and, in most cases, long before reading and writing were commonplace. But it is possible to pinpoint the metaphorical debuts of some words, thanks to the *Oxford English Dictionary.*

---

[1] Notes do not have feet, either, just as lines do not have heads. The words "footnote" and "headline" are metaphors for the text that appears at the bottom and the top of a page, respectively, thereby occupying positions analogous to the corresponding body parts.

The first recorded literal use of the word "hot," for example, occurred in 1000, according to the *OED*. Its first recorded metaphorical use in relation to taste (a *hot*, or spicy, food) occurred in 1390, to sound (a *hot* musical passage) in 1876, and to color (a *hot* red) in 1896. The first literal meaning of the word "bridge" dates back to the eleventh century, but the common figurative use of the word (to *bridge* our differences) didn't occur until the middle of the eighteenth century.

Often, the most common phrases have the most intricate etymologies. When someone does something *beyond the pale*, they are not pushing the boundaries of pigmentation. They are venturing outside the limits of the acceptable by going beyond the wooden stakes ("pale" comes from the Latin *palus*, meaning "pole" or "stake," as in the English word "impaled") that marked the edge of a settlement in the Middle Ages. Fences made of wooden pales often surrounded medieval towns and villages, demarcating the point beyond which it was considered unsafe—or unacceptable—to go.

Similarly, during the American Civil War, the word "deadline" referred to the perimeter around a prison camp beyond which any wayward prisoner would be shot. Now, it commonly refers to the precise time and date beyond which an author or journalist will be executed for not handing in a finished manuscript.

When you take a *parting shot* at someone, flinging one last insult before you depart, you are reenacting a battlefield technique perfected by the ancient Parthians. The Parthians, who lived near the Caspian Sea around the first century B.C.E., were expert archers and horsemen. They lured enemies into the open by feigning retreat. Then, as their opponents advanced in *hot* (a metaphor for angry or impassioned) pursuit, they turned in their saddles and picked them off with their arrows, a practice known as the Parthian shot.

As archaeologist A. H. Sayce, who specialized in deciphering ancient languages, observed in *The Principles of Comparative Philology*:

Our knowledge grows by comparing the unknown with the known, and the record of that increase in knowledge grows in the same way. Things are named from their qualities, but those qualities have first been observed elsewhere. The table like the stable originally meant something that "stands" but the idea of standing had been noted long before the first table was invented . . . Three-fourths of our language may be said to consist of worn-out metaphors.

These "worn-out metaphors" are incredibly durable, and many of them are consistent across a diverse range of times and places. The use of the verb "to see" to mean "to understand" is an example of how identical seams of etymological meaning run under the crust of very different languages and cultures.

The "seeing is knowing" metaphor is present throughout the Indo-European language group. The Indo-European root *weid, meaning "to see" became *oida (to know) in Greek, *fios (knowledge) in Irish, and words like "wit," "witness," "wise," and "idea" in English, all of which originally connoted some sense of understanding as vision. In Aristotle's metaphorical mathematics, the equation is written:

Seeing = knowing.

Other examples of the "seeing = knowing" link include the words "intuition," derived from the Latin in (at) and tueri (to look), and "speculate," from the Latin speculari (to watch, examine, or observe). This etymological root also surfaces in common expressions like "I'm in the dark," "Your argument is transparent" (or murky or opaque), "The explanation is crystal clear," and "That really sheds light on the problem."

The same thing has happened with the verb "to grasp," which means "to understand" in English, French, Italian, German, and

Polish, among many other languages. Other consistently cross-cultural metaphors include the association of anger with heat, happiness with altitude, and importance with size.

In Japanese, anger is equated with hot stuff just as it is in English, Arabic, and the Sotho languages spoken in South Africa, though the locus of the combustion is different. English speakers with bad tempers are *hotheads*, while angry Tunisian Arabic speakers say their *brains are boiling*. In the Sotho languages, angry people are described as *hot-blooded* but in Japan they have *boiling intestines*. Even in American Sign Language, anger is depicted as a fire or an explosion in the abdomen.

Languages as different as Chinese and English both describe positive emotional states using phrases that suggest height, as in "He is in *high spirits*" and "I feel really *up* today." Even Hungarian, a language that, along with Finnish, developed independently of the Indo-European group, employs familiar metaphors like "I'm *on cloud nine*" to convey extreme happiness.

The equation of size with significance—as in "It was a *big* deal" and "It is her *big* moment"—is present in Zulu, Hawaiian, Turkish, Malay, and Russian as well as English, while the use of the sense of smell to indicate suspicion—as in "I *smell* a rat" and "He's been *sniffing around* the premises again"—is universal, too, active even in a geographically isolated non-Indo-European language like Basque. Whenever we use words or phrases like these, we are using ancient comparisons or, as linguist Joseph Grady has called them, primary metaphors: "low-level metaphorical associations between concepts, based directly on experiential correlation." And people from vastly different times and places always seem to converge on the same figurative correlations.

Etymology is often said to be the final resting place for dead metaphors, figurative uses of language that we no longer consciously recognize as figurative. But these metaphors are still very much alive and well. Few people may be consciously aware of the etymological origins of common words and phrases, but the essential metaphor-making process of comparing the unknown with the known is still vital and ongoing. This process is the way meaning was, is, and ever shall be made.

A better way to describe the relative animation of metaphors would be to classify them like volcanoes. (Elvis would no doubt approve.) Active metaphors are those still bubbling with figuration, as in early twentieth-century artist and author Wyndham Lewis's definition:

Laughter is the mind sneezing.

Dormant metaphors, which tend to petrify into clichés, are those whose figurative nature slumbers just below the surface, as in the expression:

We're getting in over our heads.

Extinct metaphors are those whose metaphorical magma will never rise again, as in the phrase:

I see what you mean.

One of the ironies of etymology is that the less conscious we are of a metaphor as a metaphor, the more literal it becomes, a paradox observed by Nelson Goodman: "With progressive loss of its virility as a figure of speech, a metaphor becomes not less but more like literal truth. What vanishes is not its veracity but its vivacity."

Barfield, always preternaturally aware of buried etymological meanings, neatly mapped out the geology of metaphor when he wrote:

Every modern language, with its thousands of abstract terms and its nuances of meaning and association, is apparently nothing, from beginning to end, but an unconscionable tissue of dead, or petrified, metaphors . . . A man cannot utter a dozen words without wielding the creations of a hundred named and nameless poets.

These named and nameless poets are still active, busy wherever new advances, insights, or discoveries require new designations. After the advent of the Internet, for example, we needed a word to describe electronic messages. The old word, mail—from the French *malle*, meaning a "bag, sack, or wallet"—had served us well, so we just put the word "electronic" in front it. Hence, e-mail, a surprisingly accurate term since an e-mail is essentially a tiny sack of electrons encoding information.

The new designations coined by metaphorical thinking can also be applied retroactively to things that already have names but can be even better described. Hence, once e-mail was in circulation, the ancient word "prayer"—which comes from the same etymological root as "precarious"—became *knee-mail*.

Scientists are also prolific recyclers of terminology. Louis de Broglie won the Nobel Prize in Physics in 1929 for his theory of electron *waves*, a term he borrowed from acoustics. De Broglie loved chamber music, and he imagined atoms as musical instruments that emitted different tones with different wavelengths, just as each instrument in an orchestra transmits sound in different wavelengths.

Even economics—the driest of all the sciences, a parched landscape of jagged flow charts and desiccated statistics—is drenched in metaphors, many of which describe money in terms of fluid dynamics.

Liquidity is the ability to quickly convert assets into cash. A firm is *solvent* when it has plenty of *liquid assets*. *Cash flow* occurs at the confluence of *revenue streams*. A company *floats* shares in an initial public offering. *Dark pools* are platforms that allow share trading without revealing prices, even to the participants, until the trades are completed.

Banks get *bailed out* when they are too big to fail. Governments *prime the pump* by *pouring* money into the economy. When you need money, you can *tap* a friend, *sponge off* relatives, *dip* into savings or—if you're prepared to be unscrupulous—*skim* a little something off the top. When growth is *buoyant*, a rising tide lifts all boats. When options are *underwater*, though, checking your investment portfolio feels like snorkeling into a shipwreck.

The word "broker" is a fluid metaphor, too, derived from the Anglo-French *brokur* (or broacher), the person in a tavern who tapped kegs of wine or beer. Today, brokers are still in the business of tapping liquidity for clients or, perhaps just as often, draining it from them.

The blandest words, the ones we think about the least, invariably have deep, twisted etymological roots. The term "stock" is a case in point. In the thirteenth century, the English Exchequer needed some method of tracking payments to the Treasury. The receipt had not been invented yet, but without proof of debits and credits there was no way to settle disputes.

So Treasury officials came up with tally sticks, narrow strips of hazel wood that were notched to indicate various amounts of money. A notch about the width of a man's thumb, for example, represented £100; a notch about the width of the little finger represented £20; and, in what has to be one of the most poetic of all financial phrases, a notch about "the width of a swollen barleycorn" represented £1.

After a tally stick was appropriately notched, it was split down its length into two halves, each of which bore corresponding markings. One half of the stick, known as "the stock," was given to the person who deposited the money with the Exchequer. Treasury officials retained the other half of the stick, known as "the foil."

Whenever an account was audited, the sundered halves of the stick were matched up again to see if they tallied. Our use of the term "stock" is derived from this practice, as is the term "teller," or "tallier," which comes from the Latin *talea* and originally referred to a plant cutting or a thin piece of wood.

Ralph Waldo Emerson, an avid amateur etymologist, once said that money was "as beautiful as roses." In his essay "The Poet," Emerson described language itself as a kind of etymological artifact, or "fossil poetry." But before language was fossil poetry, it was fossil metaphor, as Emerson wrote:

> The poets made all the words, and therefore language is the archives of history, and, if we must say it, a sort of tomb of the muses. For though the origin of most of our words is forgotten, each word was at first a stroke of genius, and obtained currency because for the moment it symbolized the world to the first speaker and to the hearer. The etymologist finds the deadest word to have been once a brilliant picture. Language is fossil poetry. As the limestone of the continent consists of infinite masses of the shells of animalcules, so language is made up of images or tropes, which now, in their secondary use, have long ceased to remind us of their poetic origin.

The metaphors entombed in even the simplest words are not mere etymological curiosities. These fossils still breathe, exerting a potent but largely unnoticed influence on us. We don't normally feel the long, slow grinding of Earth's tectonic plates, but still the ground shifts beneath our feet. Economics is one of the places where the secret life of metaphor breaks the surface, and where its ruptures and ructions can have powerful aftershocks.

HOW HIGH CAN A DEAD CAT BOUNCE?

Stocks do the most amazing things. They soar, surge, climb, leap, and perform all kinds of other superheroic statistical feats. Sadly, they also plummet, slide, plunge, drop, and fall, subject as they are to gravity and similar dismal laws.

Flick on the business news and you're in for a smorgasbord of financial metaphors. Gasp in horror as the *bear market* grips Wall Street in its hairy paws; then cheer as fearless investors *claw back* gains. Watch in amazement as the NASDAQ *vaults* to new heights; then cringe as it *slips*, *stumbles*, and *drops* like a stone. Wait anxiously to see if the market will *shake off the jitters, slump into depression*, or *bounce back*.

Finance and economics are the ultimate numbers games, yet commentators from Helsinki to Hong Kong instinctively use metaphors to describe what's going on. Here are just a few of the more outlandish ones you might have come across in the financial news:

Stock prices took a rollercoaster ride and ended up in the subway.

Optimists saw the makings of a baby bull, but nay-sayers warned it could be a bum steer.

The question every trader will be asking himself this week is: Just how high can a dead cat bounce?

"Dead cat bounce" is the term used to describe the feeble, temporary uptick in share prices that can follow a sudden, precipitous fall. The etymology of this particular metaphor is unclear, but one hopes it did not involve dropping an actual cat from a great height and measuring its rebound after impact. Still, this and other examples of the figurative language commonly used in economics (*boom*, *bust*, or *bubble* anyone?) demonstrate that metaphor is at work in this seemingly most stolid of disciplines.

According to Deirdre N. McCloskey in *The Rhetoric of Economics*, "The most important example of economic rhetoric . . . is metaphor. Economists call them 'models.' To say that markets can be represented by supply and demand 'curves' is no less a metaphor than to say that the west wind is 'the breath of autumn's being.' "

Pundits and prognosticators don't use just any old figurative language, though. When describing the stock market, they consistently use specific types of metaphors for specific types of price movements. Psychologist Michael W. Morris and collaborators studied a slew of financial commentaries and identified two primary market metaphors.

What they call "agent metaphors" describe price movements as the deliberate action of a living thing, as in "the NASDAQ *climbed* higher" or "the Dow *fought* its way upward." In contrast, "object metaphors" describe price movements as non-living things subject to external forces, as in "the NASDAQ *dropped* off a cliff" or "the Dow *fell* like a brick." The researchers found that "agent metaphors tend to be evoked by uptrends whereas object metaphors tend to be evoked by downtrends." An interesting correlation, perhaps, but what does it have to do with the price of tea in China?

Morris and his colleagues observed that agent and object metaphors have very different effects on those exposed to them: "Agent metaphors imply that the observed trend reflects an enduring internal goal or disposition and hence it is likely to continue tomorrow . . . Object metaphors do not imply that it reflects an internal force that will manifest itself again tomorrow."

To human beings, "agents"—anything to which we attribute human feelings, motives, and motivations—are special, so special, in fact, that attributing agency to stock price movements through agent metaphors can actually affect our financial decisions.

Because a metaphor like "the NASDAQ *climbed* higher" suggests a living thing pursuing a goal—after all, only something that is alive, and determined, can climb—people expect the upward trend to continue. If, for example, house prices are relentlessly described as *climbing* higher and higher, homeowners might unconsciously assume that the steady ascent is unstoppable. They might feel confident in, say, taking out mortgages they really can't afford in the expectation that *soaring* property values will eventually make unsustainable debt look like a smart investment. If prices have minds of their own, they can continue to rise through sheer willpower alone. This kind of thinking helped trigger the 2007 subprime mortgage crisis.

Something entirely different is suggested by object metaphors like "the NASDAQ *dropped* off a cliff." When something drops off a cliff, it tends to keep falling. And when it hits bottom, it usually remains exactly where it landed. So, if stock prices are described in passive terms as *dropping*, *plunging*, or *plummeting*, investors might be unconsciously prompted into panic selling, imagining that the decline is irreversible. This kind of thinking pushes investors to sell en masse when prices fall, at precisely the time when logic dictates they should be buying since stocks are becoming cheaper. This is exactly what happened during the Great Recession of 2008–2009.

Morris tested the influence of agent and object metaphors by asking a group of people to read a clutch of market commentaries and then predict the next day's price trend. The researchers controlled whether participants were exposed to agent metaphors for rising prices or object metaphors for falling prices. Sure enough, those exposed to agent metaphors had higher expectations that the price trends they read about would continue the next day.

Economists call this phenomenon expectancy bias. Once we spot what we think is a trend—a steady increase in house prices, for example—we involuntarily expect that trend to continue, an expectation aided and abetted by agent metaphors. This bias originates in the brain regions that are active whenever a stimulus repeats itself. These modules are largely responsible for our ability to detect patterns, an ability crucial to our physical survival—and to the evolution of metaphorical thinking.

Our brains are always prospecting for pattern. Behavioral studies show that, when exposed for just a few minutes to alternating visual stimuli on the left and right sides of a display, infants as young as two months old instinctively shift their eyes to the next expected spot in the sequence. By the age of three months, infants are able to anticipate far more complex patterns.

Studies of adults show that even when presented with random stimuli, and explicitly informed that the stimuli are random, people still claim to be able to find patterns in the sequences. The brain is so fanatical about pattern that it will gladly generate patterns even where none exist. Look at the figure below.

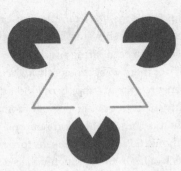

There are no overlapping triangles in this image; the brain's pattern recognition circuits create them. *Image courtesy of Adam Somlai-Fischer, Prezi.com.*

Three wayward Pac men and three pointy brackets are all that is actually printed on the page. What we see, however, are two overlapping triangles. Where patterns are incomplete, or even nonexistent, the brain is happy to fill in the blanks. Some researchers suggest that there is even a specific brain module, called the "interpreter," that is tasked with sifting out patterns from the slurry of information continuously flowing through our skulls.

From an evolutionary perspective, pattern recognition is essential. The brain's pattern recognition circuits take raw data from the senses, sort through it for apparent patterns, and use those patterns to determine a response. The ability to accurately predict the future based on recurring patterns is crucial to everything from hunting and gathering (snakes with cylindrical heads are mostly harmless; snakes with triangular heads could kill me) to mate selection (animals with the most symmetrical, or highly patterned, features tend to be the fittest, and hence the most popular sexual partners).

Once a pattern has repeated itself long enough, it starts to influence behavior. Because lush meadows were found to reliably surround lakes and streams, for example, our brains came to associate green grass with fresh water. Using this type of analogical reasoning, we also began comparing situations to decide whether a new object or environment was sufficiently *like* a previous object or environment to ensure a steady supply of food and water. Survival depends on having the fittest pattern recognition circuits.

The brain contains some 100 billion neurons, each of which is linked to tens of thousands of other neurons through a vast network of synapses. A fleck of brain tissue roughly the size of a match head sports about a billion connections, according to neurobiologist and Nobel Prize–winner Gerald Edelman. He estimates that the number of possible connections in the typical human brain totals somewhere in the region of ten followed by millions of zeroes, a number far in excess of the number of particles in the known universe.

In *Second Nature: Brain Science and Human Knowledge*, Edelman theorizes that the human brain's astonishing interconnectivity produces consciousness and, because of the astronomical number of associations our brains are capable of making, pattern recognition is the basis not just for metaphorical thinking but for all thinking:

> Brains operate . . . not by logic but by pattern recognition. This process is *not* precise, as is logic and mathematics. Instead, it trades off specificity and precision, if necessary, to increase its range. It is likely, for example, that early human thought proceeded by metaphor, which, even with the late acquisition of precise means such as logic and mathematical thought, continues to be a major source of imagination and creativity in adult life.

Pattern recognition is so basic that the brain's pattern detection modules and its reward circuitry became inextricably linked. Whenever we successfully detect a pattern—or *think* we detect a pattern—the neurotransmitters responsible for sensations of pleasure squirt through our brains. If a pattern has repeated often enough and successfully enough in the past, the neurotransmitter release occurs in response to the mere presence of suggestive cues, long before the expected outcome of that pattern actually occurs. Like the study participants who reported seeing regular sequences in random stimuli, we will use almost any pretext to get our pattern recognition kicks.

Pattern recognition is the most primitive form of analogical reasoning, part of the neural circuitry for metaphor. Monkeys, rodents, and birds recognize patterns, too. What distinguishes humans from other species, though, is that we have elevated pattern recognition to an art. "To understand," the philosopher Isaiah Berlin observed, "is to perceive patterns."

Metaphor, however, is not the mere detection of patterns; it is the creation of patterns, too. When Robert Frost wrote,

A bank is a place where they lend you an umbrella in fair weather and ask for it back when it begins to rain

his brain created a pattern connecting umbrellas to banks, a pattern retraced every time someone else reads this sentence. Frost believed passionately that an understanding of metaphor was essential not just to survival in university literature courses but also to survival in daily life.

In "Education by Poetry," a lecture delivered at Amherst College in 1930, Frost said, "I have wanted in late years to go further and further in making metaphor the whole of thinking." He argued that, without a proper education in metaphor, students could not examine and evaluate the claims made by historians or scientists, newspaper editorialists or political campaigners. People "don't know when they are being fooled by a metaphor," he warned:

Unless you are at home in the metaphor, unless you have had your proper poetical education in the metaphor, you are not safe anywhere. Because you are not at ease with figurative values: You don't know the metaphor in its strength and its weakness. You don't know how far you may expect to ride it and when it may break down.

Knowing how far to ride a metaphor—and getting off before it breaks down—is fundamental when dealing with the figurative language of finance. Evolution may have made our pattern recognition abilities instinctive and involuntary, but it did not make them infallible.

The trouble starts when we detect patterns that are not really there, as in the stock market. The brain evolved to detect patterns of immediate significance in do-or-die, fight-or-flight situations. The financial markets generate oceans of data: tens of thousands of stocks, each traded thousands of times a day by tens of millions of investors in dozens of markets around the world. By random chance alone, apparent trends will appear everywhere.

But while the stock market is filled with transitory patterns, the vast majority of them are meaningless, at least in the short term. The hourly variance of a stock price, for example, is far less significant than its annual variance. If you're in the habit of checking your portfolio every hour on the hour, the noise in those statistics drowns out any real patterns. Still, people insist on making decisions based on these supposed patterns, even when explicitly told the patterns do not exist.

Oh, how quickly we're deceived when we a bogus pattern do perceive.

Perhaps no other creature has had its pattern recognition abilities plumbed in such depth as the humble frog. And the frog's gullibility in going after false patterns is a sobering analogy for the way we can be fooled by misleading financial metaphors.

The frog does not have a very discerning palate. In fact, a frog will try to eat anything you put in front of it, as long as the object is about the size of an insect and moves around in jerky, staccato bursts. If it looks like a fly and acts like a fly, frogs think, it must be a fly. Warren S. McCulloch, a neurophysiologist and early contributor to the field of cybernetics, and a group of colleagues proved this back in the late 1950s when they performed a meticulous study of the frog's visual apparatus.

McCulloch and his collaborators placed an aluminum hemisphere before some prostrate frogs. Objects were attached to this metal plate by magnets and, like puppeteers at a children's show, the researchers moved the objects across the frog's visual field by moving the magnets on the back of the plate. As they did so, they recorded the electrical traffic along the frogs' optic nerve, enabling them to detect which nerve fibers fired in response to which visual stimuli. In this way, they learned a lot about what and how the frog sees.

One of the team's most important discoveries was that, by the time a visual image reaches a frog's brain, it is already to a large extent classified and interpreted. So, for example, when a frog sees an object about the size of an insect moving around in jerky, staccato bursts, it does not delay, debate, or deliberate. The frog immediately shoots out its tongue to grab it. The researchers called the fibers that respond in this way "bug perceivers."

The scientists put on quite a show for their captive amphibian audience. They displayed "not only spots of light but things [the frog] would be disposed to eat, other things from which he would flee, sundry geometrical figures, stationary and moving about." No matter what was put before them, though, the frogs always focused on the zooming, buzzing confusion of the presumed fly's flight path. The frogs weren't interested if the object didn't move, or if it moved only in a straight line. So, the authors observed:

The frog does not seem to see or, at any rate, is not concerned with the detail of stationary parts of the world around him. He will starve to death surrounded by food if it is not moving. His choice of food is determined only by size and movement. He will leap to capture any object the size of an insect or worm, providing it moves like one. He can be fooled easily not only by a bit of dangled meat but by any moving small object.

The experiments showed, McCulloch concluded, "that the eye speaks to the brain in a language already highly organized and interpreted, instead of transmitting some more or less accurate copy of the distribution of light on the receptors."

This way of seeing makes a lot of evolutionary sense. Flies typically trace erratic patterns in the frog's natural habitat. They buzz about, alight for a moment, then zigzag off again on their tipsy trajectories. The frog's chances of snaring a meal are vastly increased if it simply snaps at any object that moves in this way, rather than investing a lot of time and brain power in trying to analyze the object's shape and color, too.

Among pond life, he who hesitates starves to death.

When it comes to stock price movements, we, too, take a frog's eye view. We rely on implied trajectories, suggested in part by agent and object metaphors. If it looks like a pattern and acts like a pattern, we think, it must be a pattern. This passion for pattern clouds our judgment whenever numbers or probabilities are involved, as when picking stocks—or playing basketball.

A team of researchers, including Amos Tversky who, along with Daniel Kahneman, founded the field of behavioral economics, which uses insights from the social sciences to inform theories of how people make financial decisions, investigated the notion of the "hot hand" in basketball. The "hot hand" theory is the belief that a player's chances of hitting a shot are greater following a basket than following a miss on the previous shot.

The researchers studied detailed shooting records of the Philadelphia 76ers and the Boston Celtics—and even conducted a controlled experiment with the men and women of Cornell University's varsity teams—and concluded that the outcomes of previous shots influenced predictions about players' chances but not their actual performance.

Tversky's group found that more than 90 percent of fans believed that a player has "a better chance of making a shot after having just made his last two or three shots than he does after having just missed his last two or three shots." Yet the probability of a hit was actually lower following a basket—51 percent—than following a miss—54 percent.

The researchers attributed the widespread belief in the "hot hand" to "a general misconception of chance . . . If random sequences are perceived as streak shooting, then no amount of exposure to such sequences will convince the player, the coach, or the fan that the sequences are in fact random. The more basketball one watches and plays, the more opportunities one has to observe what appears to be streak shooting."

As on the basketball court, so in the stock market, where the same confusion between pattern and chance makes people think they're on a winning streak.

Our brains greedily seek patterns in everything, even in the chaos of stock prices and other financial statistics. As soon as we spot anything that looks like a pattern, we latch onto it as quickly as frogs snatch at anything that looks like a fly. Investors regularly chase *hot* stocks and *hot* funds, trying to invest in them before they go *cold*. This is especially true when agent metaphors are at work, because agents pursue goals—and that makes them special.

We make agents out of objects, given even the slightest provocation, by imputing the characteristics of living things to them. These attributions are often based on nothing more than the fact that the behavior patterns of non-living things look *like* the behavior patterns of living things. Psychologists Fritz Heider and Mary-Ann Simmel memorably demonstrated this back in the mid-1940s. They showed subjects a simple animated film involving basic geometric shapes—a big triangle, a smaller triangle, a circle, and a large rectangle that opened and closed on one side—moving around on a plain white background.

Asked to describe what they saw, participants invariably reported dramatic stories in which the circle and the smaller triangle were in love, the bigger triangle was trying to steal away the circle, but the circle and the smaller triangle managed to trap the bigger triangle in the large rectangle and so live happily ever after. Personification like this involves the same kind of metaphorical thinking involved in attributing agency to stock price movements.

This anthropomorphic instinct is the jumping-off point for many a literary flight of fancy. Known in the jargon of cognitive psychology as "physiognomic perception," it operates whenever we endow the inanimate with emotional or expressive qualities. *Angry* thunderclouds, *smiling* sunbeams, and *plaintive* melodies are all metaphors of physiognomic perception. A related phenomenon, physiognomic projection, takes place whenever we address the inanimate as animate. You are physiognomically projecting every time you scold your computer for crashing, cajole your car for stalling, or have feelings (of affection or aggression) for your in-car GPS voice.

Brian Scholl of the Yale Perception and Cognition Laboratory has made films starring simple geometric shapes similar to those of Heider and Simmel. In one film, two small squares are situated across from one another. Square A moves in a straight line toward

Square B. But as soon as Square A gets close to Square B, Square B moves quickly away from Square A until it is several inches from it. The pattern repeats, and observers inevitably interpret it as a classic chase scene. "You see A *cause* the motion of B," Scholl wrote in a paper describing the experiments. "You see A and B as *alive*, and perhaps as having certain intentional states, such as A is wanting to catch B, and B trying to escape."

Of course, there is no chase scene in Scholl's film. It's simply some geometric shapes moving around on a screen, just as Heider and Simmel's circle and smaller triangle are not in love and three wayward Pac men and three pointy brackets do not two overlapping triangles make. Nevertheless, we perceive living physiognomies in these non-living things, inserting patterns where none exist.

Why are we so promiscuous with pattern, so profligate with personification? For the same reason frogs leap at anything that moves like a fly: it is essential for survival.

From an evolutionary perspective, it is far safer to automatically attribute agency to inanimate objects that behave like living things than it is to mistake a living thing for a seemingly inanimate object. That swaying in the trees may just be a breeze or it could be a wild beast, coiled and ready to strike. You can misperceive the breeze as a beast or the beast as a breeze. Which mistake would you rather make? And if you were an early hominid, which mistake would be more likely to ensure that you would survive long enough to reproduce?

Non-human primates share some of our pattern detection abilities. Starting in the late 1970s, psychologists David Premack, Guy Woodruff, and their collaborators taught Sarah, an African-born chimpanzee, to use and comprehend a simplified visual language. Sarah's vocabulary consisted of colored plastic tokens of various shapes, sizes, and textures. She learned to arrange these into simple sentences, such as "Apple is red."

Premack and Woodruff taught Sarah how to use tokens for "same" and "different" and then showed her two sets of objects—geometric shapes (triangles and crescents) that differed in size, color, or markings and ordinary household objects that differed in function (locks and can openers). The first set was designed to test Sarah's perceptual matching abilities (large triangles are "the same" as large crescents) and the second was designed to test her functional matching abilities (can openers have "the same" function as keys). Children are given similar tests to evaluate their metaphoric competence.

Sarah consistently spotted the right analogical patterns, correctly indicating that a large and a small triangle were "the same" as a large and a small crescent. She chose the "different" symbol when presented with a large and small triangle and two small crescents. In the test of her functional matching ability, Sarah chose the "same" symbol for a picture of a lock and a key and a picture of a can and can opener, demonstrating her understanding that unlocking a lock is the same kind of activity as opening a can.

The agent and object metaphors of economics tap into this primal urge for pattern. Agents are special because only agents move of their own volition; only agents move with a purpose. And pattern recognition evolved in large part to predict the purpose of living things. According to Morris and his collaborators, "Uptrend stimulus trajectories should automatically trigger schemas for animate action and downtrends should trigger schemas for inanimate motion, regardless of whether the trajectories are encountered on sand dunes or stock charts."

Decades of statistical analysis suggest the *random walk* metaphor is still the most accurate way to describe price movements in the stock market. Yet people insist on dragging bulls and bears into it. When it comes to spotting price trends, we all have amphibian brains. "People making sense of stock charts may be in a predicament something like that of the frogs," the Morris team wrote of McCulloch's research, "victims of their automatized responses to trajectory."

Morris observed that expectancy bias was at its height when information was presented in trajectory-like graphs. It was lower when financial information was presented in tables of numbers. They speculated that this is because graphs, such as those showing future growth projections, work much like visual metaphors, often depicting a trend heading inexorably in one direction. One way to tamp down expectations raised by agent metaphors is to display information as tables of numbers rather than in graph format.

Another way to limit expectancy bias is to mind your metaphors. The next time you hear "the NASDAQ *climbed* higher" or "*dropped* off a cliff," remember this simply means that the NASDAQ increased or decreased, terms that don't trigger such powerful metaphorical associations. "Unexamined metaphor is a substitute for thinking—which is a recommendation to examine the metaphors, not to attempt the impossible by banishing them," McCloskey wrote in *The Rhetoric of Economics*. "Metaphors evoke attitudes that are better kept in the open and under the control of reasoning."

Given the proliferation of financial commentary in print, online, and on TV, we might do well to pry our tongues from the price graphs on our plasma screens or, as Robert Frost warned, risk being taken for a ride by metaphor.

IMAGINING AN APPLE IN SOMEONE'S EYE

Rebecca arrives for our appointment, at a London café near the Thames, clutching a newspaper clipping. The headline reads:

BELT TIGHTENING LIES AHEAD

"What does that mean?" she asks.

This is a fascinating headline because, taken as a whole, it is an obvious metaphor. But each word in the headline is a metaphor, too. "Belt tightening" is a conventional metaphor for how households reduce spending because of dwindling amounts of disposable income. The phrase has become so familiar that it is now a cliché. Few people would spot it as a metaphor anymore.

But the word "lies" is also a metaphor, because it metaphorically locates the abstract act of belt tightening (budget cutting) in physical space. The word "ahead" is a metaphor, too, because it metaphorically conveys that the belt tightening will take place in the future by situating the constriction in the physical space in front of the reader. In this simple set of four words, there are three distinct metaphors at work.

Rebecca (not her real name) has no idea what this headline means. The use of "lies" in this context she can just about grasp, since similar usages have been explained to her in the past. But "belt tightening"? "I don't wear a belt," she notes matter-of-factly. On first reading the headline, she says she pictured lots of belts and lots of people tightening them. "Is the article about a new fashion trend? Or a new diet craze?" Rebecca hasn't got a clue.

Almost anyone else, of course, immediately understands that this headline refers to how a recession weakens consumer confidence, prompting households to cut back on spending. Rebecca, however, needs to read the entire article to understand this. And even then, the link between the economy and an article of clothing that holds up your pants still eludes her.

This failure to understand metaphor happens to Rebecca, who is working toward a doctorate in mathematics education, all the time. During one particularly animated classroom discussion, for example, a student nonchalantly referred to *the elephant in the room*. Alarmed, Rebecca quickly looked around to see if she could find the beast.

After a series of clashes with other staff at her first teaching job, Rebecca was called into the office of the headmaster, who kicked off the conversation by observing, "So you've been *burning bridges* again." Rebecca became indignant, convinced he had accused her of arson, and stormed out of the room.

Rebecca has Asperger's syndrome, a form of autism characterized by impaired social communication, interaction, and imagination. She was diagnosed with the condition in 2007, when she was twenty-seven years old. Asperger's and other autism spectrum disorders (ASD) affect about 1 percent of the population and are found much more commonly in males than in females. The causes of ASD are unknown, though genetic factors are almost certainly involved.

People with Asperger's syndrome are typically highly functioning and of average or above average intelligence. Rebecca already has degrees in mathematics and educational research methods. But the difficulties those with ASD have understanding the world and communicating with others can lead to perceived behavioral problems, which can interfere with social relationships.

It can be difficult for individuals with ASD to express emotions, to initiate and sustain relationships, and to understand common social cues like gestures and facial expressions. When shown the Heider and Simmel film, for example, most people with ASD won't attribute intentions or motivations to the animated geometric shapes. Everything tends to be interpreted in strictly literal terms. As a result, those with Asperger's and other ASDs typically have enormous difficulty understanding metaphor.

Mark Haddon deftly explored the angst and alienation this causes in his novel *The Curious Incident of the Dog in the Nighttime*, in which the main character, Christopher Boone, a young boy with ASD, is bewildered by routine social situations. Christopher finds people confusing because they use so many metaphors, like: "I laughed my socks off. He was the apple of her eye. They had a skeleton in the cupboard. We had a real pig of a day. The dog was stone dead."

Christopher muses on metaphor, describing it in classic Aristotelian fashion as "when you describe something by using a word for something that it isn't." He ultimately concludes (like Hobbes, Berkeley, and Locke) that metaphors are both deceptive and dangerous:

I think it should be called a lie because a pig is not like a day and people do not have skeletons in their cupboards. And when I try and make a picture of the phrase in my head it just confuses me because imagining an apple in someone's eye doesn't have anything to do with liking someone a lot and it makes you forget what the person was talking about.

Individuals with ASD tend to find socialization and communication so difficult because so many of our daily interactions—everything from etiquette to gossip to business negotiations—are mediated by metaphor. It was only after her diagnosis that Rebecca "recognized how much I didn't recognize," she says. Before that, she thought everybody was just as confused as she was by figurative language. Her condition can turn the simplest social situations into frightening and embarrassing experiences.

When Rebecca joined her university's climbing club, the instructor welcomed her to the first class by warmly greeting her and saying she would send someone over to *show you the ropes.* "I know what a rope is," Rebecca thought to herself, "and why you need one in a climbing club. Why do they need to show me those?" She completely failed to get the social meaning of what the instructor was saying; namely, "I will send someone over to familiarize you with the way we do things around here." "You look very odd when someone says something and you don't get it," Rebecca explains.

When someone used the phrase "he's *a big fish in a small pond*" in conversation, she thought it was a reference to a shark in a goldfish pond. This amused the people she was with, but embarrassed Rebecca.

"It separates you from people," she says, "and so you start to avoid situations that cause difficulty, which in turn causes even more isolation. If I feel I missed something important, it is very upsetting. I worry about the future of my career, how I will be able to work with people, to have a normal social life."

Rebecca feels the metaphor deficit in all aspects of her life. She doesn't read poetry and has trouble with novels, too; the metaphors mean nothing to her. She finds it hard to get emotionally involved in films, since she can't pick up the verbal and physical hints that reveal a character's feelings. She prefers the clarity and precision of mathematics.

Rebecca is learning to recognize phrases that contain figurative language, but she can't always decipher them. Sometimes, she can understand the meaning of a metaphor if it is explained to her. But, more often than not, she can't.

She has a number of coping strategies. If she encounters a phrase she doesn't understand during class, she Googles it when she gets home. That doesn't always help, however. She still can't figure out how the story of the Trojan horse relates to computer viruses. The more unusual the metaphor—the more distant the source from the target—the more difficult it is for her to grasp.

Rebecca, like individuals without ASD, has no problem using or comprehending simple extinct metaphors, such as "I *see* what you mean." But in trying to comprehend active and dormant metaphors, Rebecca automatically visualizes them in literal representations, as she did with the "belt tightening" headline. This is, in fact, a sensible interpretative technique, since the best metaphors invite us to picture astonishing events like laughter propelling socks from feet, apples lodged in eyeballs, and skeletons capering in closets.

"The test of a true metaphor," the eighteenth-century English essayist, poet, and politician Joseph Addison observed, "is whether or not there is sufficient detail for it to be painted." People consistently rate metaphors with vivid, concrete imagery as most memorable, in part because most people recall pictures much better than words. Cicero, too, remarked on the visual aspect of metaphor:

Every metaphor, provided it be a good one, has a direct appeal to the senses, especially the sense of sight, which is the keenest . . . Metaphors drawn from the sense of sight are much more vivid, virtually placing within the range of our mental vision objects not actually visible to our sight.

So it's logical that a reference to an important issue no one wants to discuss will set off Rebecca on an elephant safari. When she doesn't find the animal, though, she cannot make the leap to the figurative meaning. Then she wonders what people are talking about. If it seems important, she plays it over and over in her mind, obsessing about it until it crowds out everything else. "It interferes with everything," Rebecca says. "Other people just think I'm being strange, a bit odd."

The oddity other people often notice about individuals with ASD has to do with the lack of what researchers call "theory of mind," the ability to understand—or *read*—the mental states of others and to predict their behavior based on social cues such as body language, facial expressions, and figures of speech.

Most of us can easily read other people's minds. We do it all the time. Say, for example, you're chatting pleasantly with someone who has his arms firmly crossed across his chest. You instinctively note the disconnect between that person's posture and what he is saying. The person's body language belies his speech, leading you to conclude that (unless he's chilly) he may not be as happy as he seems. We call this intuition; autism researchers call it mindreading; those with ASD cannot do it.

Individuals with ASD tend to be easily flummoxed by social situations in which other people's feelings must be inferred from ambiguous clues. In one study, people with ASD were shown a series of illustrations depicting a burglar making his getaway after robbing a house. A policeman happens to stroll by, unaware that a crime has just been committed. The policeman sees the burglar drop a glove and shouts, "Stop!" The burglar puts his hands in the air, turns around, and gives himself up.

Participants in the study did not get the irony of the story because they were unable to read what was in each character's mind. The burglar thought he had been caught red handed, but the policeman was just trying to return his glove. The individuals studied were unable to attribute different beliefs to the different characters. They could not put themselves in someone else's shoes.

Yet putting ourselves in other people's shoes is exactly what the protocols of social life require us to do. We understand other people's intentions and states of mind by understanding the physical cues of body language and the verbal clues of figurative language. Social language "is riddled with figurative phrases that require one to compute the speaker's unspoken meaning or intention," writes Simon Baron-Cohen, director of the Autism Research Centre in Cambridge in the United Kingdom, in *Mindblindness: An Essay on Autism and Theory of Mind*. "In decoding figurative speech (such as irony, sarcasm, metaphor, or humor), mindreading is even more essential."

The ability to mind-read enables us to understand that what people do is not always what they think; how people act is not always how they feel; and what people mean is not always what they say, a process akin to pretend play, another activity in which people with ASD have difficulty engaging.

In pretend play, two people both know that a specific scenario is not literally the case—and they both know that the other person knows this, too. A child knows, for example, that when an adult touches a toy teacup and withdraws his hand in pain, the teacup is not really hot. The same principle is at work in metaphor. Unlike Rebecca, most people do not think that the headline "Belt Tightening Lies Ahead" introduces a fashion article.

In the 1980s, psychologist Alan Leslie set out to understand how pretend play works in the brain and why people with ASD have difficulty pretending. He started his investigation by posing the somewhat surreal question: "How is it possible for a child to think about a banana as if it were a telephone?"

The ability to pretend, and to understand pretense in others, usually develops between the ages of twelve and twenty-four months. To be able to think about a banana as if it were a telephone, you must first be able to hold two different ideas in your mind at the same time. The child knows that if she picks up the banana, she will not hear a dial tone. But just as Robert Burns's love is, in some respects, like a red, red rose, the banana is, in some respects, like a telephone. They both have roughly the same size and shape, both fit into the hand in the same way, and both cradle snugly between shoulder and chin.

Researchers call this ability to hold two ideas about one thing in the mind at the same time "double knowledge," and it becomes pronounced around the age of two when children begin to play "make-believe" games and use their first words.

In children, just as in the pattern recognition experiments with the chimpanzee Sarah, the two sides of double knowledge are normally linked either through functional similarity (a shoe can double as a teacup because both can hold liquid) or perceptual similarity (a banana looks like a telephone).

Developmental psychologist Jean Piaget observed this kind of double knowledge at work in his own daughter, Jacqueline, who once said of a bent twig, "It's like a machine for putting in petrol." Piaget called this phenomenon "syncretism," describing it as a "condensation by which several disparate images melt into one . . . and transference by which the qualities belonging to one object are transferred to another." We discover—or invent—these functional and perceptual similarities using our pattern recognition abilities.

According to Leslie's theory, a make-believe game requires a primary representation (the thing itself as it actually is, i.e., the banana) and a second-order representation (the thing as it imaginatively is, i.e., the banana-phone). In pretend play, Leslie suggested, the child takes her primary representation of the banana and copies it to make a second-order representation.

She now has two bananas in her mind, the real one and its copy. The child can introduce imaginative changes to the second-order representation that transform it into a telephone while leaving the primary representation intact. The literal truth of the banana is "quarantined," as Leslie put it, so that the imaginative truth of the banana-phone can emerge.

Make-believe games are therefore "not representations of the world but representations of representations," or metarepresentations. "Pretence is an early manifestation of what has been called theory of mind," Leslie concluded.

Metarepresentations are not a million miles away from metaphors. Take the relatively straightforward metaphor

My job is a jail.

From a cognitive point of view, saying "My job is a jail" is a lot like pretending that a banana is a telephone. In both cases, there are primary representations (my actual job, the actual banana) and second-order representations (my job-jail, the banana-phone). By grafting certain characteristics of jails—a confined space, soul-crushing routine, no chance of escape—onto my idea of my job, I create a metarepresentation of my job while leaving the primary representation of my job intact. I select only those features of jails that I regard as relevant to my job and ignore the rest.

This process is exactly what happens in pretend play. The shape of the banana is relevant for my telephonic purposes, so I include that in my second-order representation; the banana's squishiness is not, so I ignore it. At no time do I mistake the banana for an actual phone, just as when I say "My job is a jail," few people will take me literally—unless, of course, I happen to be employed in a prison. Both the speaker and the listener know that my job is not a real jail, and they both know that the other person knows this, too.

Leslie suggested that people with ASD have difficulty with pretend play because they are unable to make metarepresentations, an inability that may also hamper their comprehension of metaphor. To understand metaphors, literal truth must be quarantined so metaphorical truth can emerge. Some research suggests that individuals with ASD find it difficult to quarantine literal truth because of malfunctioning brain cells known as mirror neurons.

Mirror neurons (note the metaphor in the name!) were first discovered in the mid-1990s, in the premotor cortex of monkeys. Since then, they have been discovered in human brains, too. These neurons are active whenever an animal performs an action (reaching for a banana, for example) and whenever the animal observes that same action performed by another animal.

Mirror neurons also kick in during emotional responses. The same neurons that fire when we wrinkle our noses and stick out our tongues in response to foul smells also fire when we see someone else wrinkle her nose and stick out her tongue. The same thing happens with pain; neurons active when we observe someone in pain are also active when we are in pain ourselves. By reflecting the actions of others in our own brains, mirror neurons may enable us to feel empathy, to intuit other people's emotions, and to guess other people's motivations. Mirror neurons may be the neurological shoehorn that allows us to slip into other people's shoes.

Studies show that the mirror neuron system in people with ASD does not function properly. In one experiment, two groups of twelve-year-olds—one with ASD and one without—were shown pictures of faces displaying various emotions, such as fear, anger, or happiness. The children were asked to either observe the faces or to imitate them. In both cases, brain scans of typically developing children showed activity in sites identified with mirror neuron properties; scans of children with ASD did not.

There may yet turn out to be cracks in the mirror neuron hypothesis, but the correlation between mirror system dysfunction and ASD suggests that these brain cells may provide a neurological basis for both theory of mind and metaphor. "To mind-read, or to imagine the world from someone else's different perspective, one has to switch from one's own primary representations . . . to someone else's representation," Baron-Cohen writes. "Arguably, empathy, dialogue, and relationships are all impossible without such an ability to switch between our primary and our second-order representations."

This inability to switch between primary and second-order representations, between the literal and the figurative, may also help explain the metaphor deficit ASD brings with it. Yet not all forms of metaphorical thinking are inaccessible to those with ASD.

In his memoir *Born on a Blue Day*, Daniel Tammet, who has Asperger's and is a so-called autistic savant, describes how his mind works by association, a prime characteristic of metaphorical thought: "A chance word or name in the middle of a conversation can cause a flood of associations in my mind, like a domino effect . . . The sequence of my thoughts is not always logical, but often comes together by a form of visual association."

Like Rebecca, Tammet uses visual imagination to understand abstract or metaphorical terms. The word "complexity," for example, calls up in his mind an image of braided or plaited hair. He imagines the metaphor "fragile peace" as a glass dove.

Tammet has extraordinary mathematical and linguistic abilities. He once recited the number pi from memory to 22,514 digits

in just over five hours. For the past several years, he has been inventing his own language, called Mänti.

Tammet builds Mänti in a way that would please über-
etymologist Owen Barfield: he makes new words from the pre-
existing words that most closely resemble what he is trying to
describe. Thus, tardiness is *kellokült* (*kello*, meaning "clock," and
kült, meaning "debt") and telephone is *pullo* (derived from *puhe*,
"to speak," and *kello*, "bell").

Rebecca has a way with words, too. She loves puns—and jokes
in which the punch line is a pun—a passion, she says, that at times
can try the patience of friends and family. Some of her favorites:

> Why do statisticians never have friends?
> Because they're mean people.

> What did the Dalai Lama say when he got an electric
> shock?
> Ohm.

> What color is the wind?
> Blew.

Puns like these share important characteristics with metaphors.
Both involve a kind of double knowledge, in which speaker and
hearer understand that what is literally said is not what is figuratively meant. To "get" puns, alternative word meanings must be
accessed, just as with many metaphors.

Unlike metaphors, however, puns can be logically figured out,
just like a mathematical problem. "Puns are just different meanings
of a word or different words that sound the same," Rebecca says,
"rather than something being used to mean something it isn't."

Rebecca also has no trouble with analogical reasoning, even

using an analogy to describe the difficulty she has with metaphor. When Rebecca encounters a non-literal phrase, she says she can learn it and its figurative translation word for word, just as she would memorize a phrase in an obscure foreign language. If she saw that exact phrase again, she would know what it meant because she had memorized it.

The trouble is, metaphor is a moving target. "People are annoying in that they don't use metaphors consistently—changing words, using two phrases together, mixing them up or simply making up their own," Rebecca says. "This means I do not recognize the phrases, or work out far too late what they mean."

This process is analogous, she explains, to encountering a foreign phrase containing some of the words she has memorized but with new ones thrown in. Even though she can recognize certain words, she cannot translate the phrase as a whole. Knowing the exact meaning of one phrase doesn't help in guessing the meaning of others.

To help her translate the foreignness of figurative language, Rebecca often travels with a copy of *The Asperger Dictionary of Everyday Expressions*. The book contains over 5,000 phrases (which, as the compiler admits in the introduction, represents only a fraction of the metaphorical expressions in common use) and functions as a kind of tourist's dictionary for strangers in the strange land of metaphor.

With help from the *Asperger Dictionary*, Rebecca was able to understand what it means to play *devil's advocate*, defined as presenting "the argument for the opposite case without necessarily believing it." The metaphor is derived from the title given to the cardinal at the Vatican assigned the task of finding evidence against a person being considered for sainthood.

However, Rebecca still doesn't get the meaning behind "to give someone the *cold shoulder*," which the *Asperger Dictionary* defines as "to be made to feel unwelcome." The expression derives from the medieval habit of giving an unwanted guest unappetizing cold shoulder of mutton, suggesting they had outstayed their welcome.

Rebecca's experience, as well as that of others with ASD, reveals just how riddled with metaphor daily life is. The way individuals with ASD process and try to cope with figurative language provides important clues about how metaphorical thinking works in the brain, offering a fleeting glimpse of what goes on in our minds when imagining an apple in someone's eye.

IMAGINARY GARDENS WITH
REAL TOADS IN THEM

W hat kind of smoke are you?

That question may sound as nonsensical as asking how it is possible to think about a banana as a telephone, but in the 1950s members of the Iowa Writers' Workshop regularly played a game called "Smoke" designed to answer it.

Intended as a warm-up exercise for workshop participants, Smoke was a more literary version of the old television game show *What's My Line?*, in which celebrity panelists interrogated contestants in order to guess their (typically somewhat unusual) occupations.

In Smoke, one player thinks of a person with whom the other players are familiar and provides a general clue about that person's identity, such as "I am a living American" or "I am a dead European." The other players then try to guess who that person is by asking offbeat, evocative questions like "What kind of smoke are you?" or "What kind of weather are you?" The player answers these questions as if the person really is a specific kind of smoke or weather.

If the person in question is, say, Marlon Brando, the smoke might be from a fire in an empty oil drum on a desolate, rain-soaked dock; the weather would be sultry, smoldering, with dark clouds brooding.

The aim of the game is to demonstrate how figurative language adds depth to characterization in fiction, as the novelist John Gardner, a member of the Iowa Writers' Workshop in the 1950s and an avid Smoker, explained:

> No one can achieve profound characterization of a person (or place) without appealing to semi-unconscious associations. To sharpen or intensify a characterization, a writer makes use of metaphor and reinforcing background—weather, physical objects, animals—details which either mirror character or give character something to react to . . . The game proves more dramatically than any argument can suggest the mysterious rightness of a good metaphor.

The mysterious rightness of metaphor is, of course, essential to arts other than fiction. Successful advertisements depend almost entirely on metaphors that resonate with the target audience. Advertising executives, copywriters, and graphic designers are, in many respects, professional metaphor-makers.

In devising campaigns, marketers regularly ask themselves and their focus groups questions like "If Product X was an automobile, what kind of automobile would it be?" and "If Product Y was an alcoholic drink, what kind of alcoholic drink would it be?" In fashioning commercial messages from answers to these kinds of questions, advertising executives are doing more than just blowing smoke up our assessments of consumer goods. They are searching for metaphors that tap into the emotional associations that motivate purchasing decisions.

The metaphorical technique of personification is one of the primary ways to achieve this. After all, if we eagerly attribute human traits to Heider and Simmel's animated geometric shapes, why wouldn't we do the same for brand name products and corporations? Consumer surveys show this is exactly what we do.

Absolut vodka, for example, has been personified as a cool twenty-five-year-old, while Stolichnaya has been considered a more conservative older man. Cars are routinely imbued with human personalities (Explorer, Monarch, Warrior) or animal instincts (Mustang, Bronco, Cougar). Jennifer Aaker, a professor of marketing at the University of California, Los Angeles, has even defined five core elements of "brand personality": sincerity, excitement, competence, sophistication, and ruggedness.

The influence of these kinds of semi-unconscious associations on decision making is known as the "affect heuristic." Decisions are easily influenced by our affective state, which can be determined by everything from the images we see to the words we read.

Affective states can be swayed by the seemingly innocuous, such as simply asking consumers about their buying intentions. In one study involving some 40,000 participants, asking people whether they intended to purchase a car increased actual purchases by 35 percent. Another study found that those asked if they intended to avoid eating fatty foods in the coming week consistently chose a low-fat snack (a rice cake) over a high-fat snack (a chocolate chip cookie) in a taste test.

Researchers have observed that simply placing a "Limit 12 per customer" sign above a stack of tomato soup cans influences sales. Shoppers read the sign, and the word "limit" immediately raises associations of value and scarcity. That tomato soup must be pretty good, we think, otherwise the store would not have to restrict purchases. Better stock up while supplies last.

We may have had no intention whatsoever of buying tomato

soup when we walked into that shop—we may not even like tomato soup—but the associative wisps rising from that sign create a
persuasive affective state. For potential dieters and car purchasers,
questions regarding intent immediately trigger thoughts like "You
know, I really should cut out the snacks" and "Come to think of it,
a new car would be nice."

The same thing happens when a salesperson tries to sell an extended warranty. Not long ago, I bought a digital camera for around
$200. After studying all the brands on offer, I was pretty pleased
with my choice. My mood changed abruptly when I brought the
camera to the checkout and the salesperson asked, "Do you want
an extended warranty with that?"

To be honest, the idea of purchasing an extended warranty had
never occurred to me. When I walked into that electronics shop,
I was blissfully unaware of the many and varied risks to my new
digital camera. But to make me suddenly and painfully conscious
of everything that could possibly go wrong, all the salesperson had
to do was say "extended warranty." My affective state had been
dramatically altered.

The affect heuristic affects all of us, even supposedly sophisticated consumers who might be expected to know better.

Decision-making researcher Paul Slovic and colleagues asked
business students in a securities analysis course to evaluate industry groups represented on the New York Stock Exchange. The
students saw imagery and affective evaluations for each industry
group and then reported whether they would invest in companies
associated with each group. Groups with the coolest, most alluring
affective profiles (the computer and technology sectors) received
the most investments, even though they were among the poorest
actual performers.

Image trumps information.

Social psychologists suggest that affective language and imagery nudge us into mental states that subtly influence our subsequent decisions. A specific picture or specific phrase activates a field of unconscious correlations, and the influence of these associations prompts us into behavior that is largely outside our control or awareness. Advertising uses metaphor to create clouds of connotation designed to put us in a buying frame of mind.

The associations conjured up by advertisements can't be screened out. They start to work as soon as they are perceived, whether we want them to or not. "Representations of objects and events in people's minds are tagged to varying degrees with affect," Slovic and his coauthors concluded. "People consult or refer to an 'affective pool' (containing all the positive and negative tags associated with the presentations consciously or unconsciously) in the process of making judgments."

Gerald Zaltman of the research and consulting firm Olson Zaltman Associates has spent the past few decades plumbing the depths of this affective pool. He has surfaced with what he calls "deep metaphors," universal orientations that structure and guide consumer attitudes toward products. He's even patented a method—the Zaltman Metaphor Elicitation Technique (ZMET)—for identifying these metaphors. Though the ZMET sounds as if it might require participants to don electrode-studded helmets, it is actually a rather gentle process, kind of like taking a Rorschach test administered by Carl Jung.

Both Jung and Hermann Rorschach studied with Eugen Bleuler, an early supporter of Freud's ideas. Bleuler encouraged staff at the Burghölzli Psychiatric Hospital at the University of Zurich in Switzerland, where he was director, to investigate the unconscious. Jung and Rorschach were fascinated by Freud's technique of "free association" and they both created new ways to use free association in their own practices.

During a psychoanalytic session, Freud often asked patients to say the first thing that popped into their minds—to free-associate— and then follow the trail of associations, which Freud believed would eventually lead to insights about issues that patients could not otherwise consciously access. While Freud worked with words, Rorschach asked his patients to free-associate with inkblots.

As a child, Rorschach played a lot of "klecksography," an activity popular among Swiss children at the time that involved dripping ink onto a sheet of paper and then folding the paper so that the ink smudges produced a recognizable shape, like a flower, a bird, or a butterfly. Rorschach, a talented artist, was so good at this that he was nicknamed Klecks, Swiss German for "inkblot."

Rorschach retained his fascination for inkblots well into adulthood, developing a set of images that worked as a visual variation on Freud's verbal technique. The process is simple. Individuals look at Rorschach's inkblots and tell researchers what they see. Different people see different things, and researchers analyze the significance of the different associations.

Rorschach's method is a form of physiognomic perception, yet another example of the human brain's determination to find patterns in absolutely everything. Even when presented with images with few or no recognizable features, we still find patterns in them—animal shapes in cloud formations, human faces in Martian craters, figures of the Virgin Mary in grilled cheese sandwiches, and butterflies in inkblots.

Jung also devised a visual free-associative technique, "active imagination," that involved mental rather than inkblot images. Active imagination evolved from Jung's work with dreams. He often asked patients to embellish a dream image or association through drama, dance, drawing, writing, or talking. In this way, Jung believed, archetypes—innate, universal prototypes of human experience lurking in the collective unconscious—could be coaxed to the surface. "When we concentrate on an inner picture and when we are careful not to interrupt the natural flow of events," he wrote, "our unconscious will produce a series of images which make a complete story."

A ZMET study combines a Rorschach-like analysis of imagery with a Jungian search for archetypes to help advertisers construct the most complete—and the most effective—commercial stories.

A full-blown ZMET study involves about a dozen people and focuses on a specific product or sector such as, say, kitchenware. Participants each have an individual ZMET session, but before attending they spend about a week collecting eight to ten images that in some way represent their thoughts and attitudes about the product or service under investigation. The only instruction: the images should be metaphorical rather than literal depictions.

So if the topic is kitchenware, participants are discouraged from bringing in pictures of knives and forks or pots and pans. Instead, ZMETicians want people to free-associate, to bring in pictures that illustrate their ideas, feelings, and other semiconscious associations about kitchenware. If you associate kitchenware with domestic life, for example, images of happy families would be appropriate; if you associate kitchenware with fine food, then pictures of succulent cuts of meat would fit.

After collecting his or her images, the subject attends a two-and-a-half-hour interview with a ZMET practitioner. During this session, the interviewer asks detailed questions about each picture. Why did you select this picture? What feelings do you associate with the picture? How do the different pictures relate to one another?

After the interview, each person creates a collage of his or her selected imagery with the help of another ZMET staffer. The starting point is a single central image that most strongly represents that person's feelings about the product or service in question. The ZMET staffer then blends in the other pictures under the subject's supervision, gradually working toward a composite depiction of his or her overall attitudes and associations.

The collages and interview transcripts are then analyzed to extract common themes. The result: a dozen product-related Rorschach blots and actively imagined Jungian embellishments.

After conducting more than 12,000 ZMET sessions for more than one hundred clients in over thirty countries, Zaltman has identified seven recurring motifs that, like Jungian archetypes, bubble up again and again from the depths of the consumer unconscious—balance, connection, container, control, journey, resource, and transformation. These, according to Zaltman, are the guiding metaphors of the marketplace.

In Zaltman's taxonomy, the deep metaphor of balance refers to social and psychological equilibrium, expressed in phrases like "I am *centered*" and "It feels slightly *off*." Connection involves the sense of belonging ("a *team player*" or "a *loose cannon*"). Container describes psychological or emotional states ("*in* a good mood" or "*out* of your mind"). Control implies mastery of events ("It's *out of my hands*" or "We're *on the same page*"). Journey suggests movement toward or away from a goal ("We're *on course*" or "We got *waylaid*"). Resource references basic necessities such as food, family, friends, and finances ("*bread and butter* issues" and "My job is my *lifeline*"). Transformation encompasses physical or psychological change ("He turned over a *new leaf*" or "She's *a different person* now").

Jung theorized that a small set of basic archetypal patterns generates all our psychological and emotional complexity, usually without our conscious knowledge. Indeed, Jung wrote, "Those people who are least aware of their unconscious side are the most influenced by it." Zaltman theorizes much the same thing about the influence of metaphor on consumer behavior.

Some market research supports this thesis. StrategyOne, a marketing consultancy, polled about a thousand Americans, trawling for their deep metaphors about life. People often use metaphors to describe their lives, the StrategyOne survey stated, before going on to ask:

"Which one of the following do you think best describes your life?"

Respondents could choose from about a half dozen metaphors, such as "life is a journey," "life is a battle" and "life is a play." Most people, 51 percent, chose the "life is a journey" metaphor. Eleven percent felt life was a battle; 8 percent said life was a novel; 6 percent said it was a race; and 4 percent were sure it was a carousel. The pollsters found few differences when the results were grouped by age, gender, or region. The only real disparity: those with annual incomes lower than $35,000 were three times more likely to describe life as a battle than those who earned more.

"Deep metaphors are enduring ways of perceiving things," Zaltman writes in *Marketing Metaphoria: What Deep Metaphors Reveal about the Minds of Consumers*, "making sense of what we encounter, and guiding our subsequent actions." By understanding the affective associations that structure customers' thinking, Zaltman suggests marketers can use these metaphors as selling tools in product design, shopping environments, and advertising campaigns. Deep metaphors are, for Zaltman, the ultimate hidden persuaders.

To explore my own deep metaphors, I had a private ZMET session with Richard Smith, associate director of the marketing consultancy firm Business Development Research Consultants (BDRC) in London, which uses the ZMET in its work.

When I did my interview, the Great Recession of 2008–2009 was in full swing. Some of the world's biggest banks teetered on the verge of collapse; pundits routinely proclaimed (using object metaphors, naturally) that the economy was falling off a cliff; the value of homes, investments, and pensions (including my own) was evaporating faster than spit on a griddle. So I chose the financial services industry as the focus of my session.

I spent the week before the meeting collecting images. My central figure was the poster from *Man on Wire*, the 2008 documentary about Philippe Petit's high-wire walk between the tops of the World

Trade Center's Twin Towers in 1974. The promotional image was a close-up of Petit's foot on the tightrope, with a dizzying view of the vertiginous 1,300-foot drop to the streets of New York.

My other imagery included photos of a man standing on a melting ice floe and a man standing beside his car, which was submerged up to its wheel wells in river water. Both images represented my feeling that the recession was a kind of natural disaster, on the scale of the climate crisis, that affected the whole planet.

I also brought along an image of a volatile stock price chart (a financial EEG displaying the world economy's not-very-vital signs), a dollar bill consumed by flames (an almost literal depiction of what was happening to my kids' college funds), and an agonized, ecstatic marathon runner reaching the finish line (my hoped for goal: financial security).

My ZMET collage of the financial services industry, circa 2008–2009. *Image by Noleen Robinson; courtesy of Business Development Research Consultants, London.*

Smith, a genial man with the reassuring air of a family physician, ushered me into BDRC's magnificently nondescript conference room. He explained the process and asked if I had brought the images. I spread the pictures out on the table one by one, and Smith started asking me questions.

"What does it feel like to be on the wire?"

"It scares me shitless," I admitted. (The "scared shitless" metaphor derives from the physiological fact that animals in stressful situations—an antelope pursued by a lion, for example—involuntarily defecate to shed excess weight, thus speeding their flight.)

"Where are you going?"

I was walking from one safe place to another, but the only way to get there was along this perilous path across an abyss. My present position was about in the middle of the tightrope, halfway between the relative security of early adulthood (a time of few financial responsibilities and no kids) and late middle age (a time of paid-off mortgages and empty nests).

I was midway through this journey, with two decades of school fees ahead of me and the industries by which I earned my living (journalism and publishing) seemingly headed toward extinction. I was completely exposed. One false step and I was finished.

"What does the picture mean for you on a practical level?"

The shift from figurative to fact unsettled me. Suddenly, the man on the wire felt all too real. I realized the images I had been nonchalantly tearing out of magazines and printing from the Web for the past week revealed a lot about me.

Like a lot of people, I was genuinely terrified by what was happening to the economy. Having already experienced job loss once, I was scared that I would lose my sources of income again, that I would not be able to pay my kids' tuition, that our home would be at risk. Along with these primal fears came memories of my parents' money habits—my mother's caution and frugality, my father's breezy Micawberian confidence—and the fragility of their finances in later life. I was anxious that at any moment the financial rug could be pulled out from under me, that I would fall, and in falling fail my family.

I hadn't expected my financial free associations to dredge up quite such troubling issues. After my session ended, I felt worried—and very wobbly.

My collage clearly tapped into at least three of Zaltman's deep metaphors—balance, control, and journey—and I had no trouble thinking of formative commercial messages from my childhood that played off these associations.

Allstate's classic tagline "You're in good hands with Allstate," accompanied by the picture of a lovely suburban home carefully cupped in a pair of strong hands, is all about control and security. Prudential's "Get a piece of the rock," and the accompanying image of a Gibraltar-like promontory, is rooted in ideas of balance and stability. The fact that both of these ads have stuck in my mind since the 1970s testifies to the fact that they hit a deep archetypal target.

Certain archetypal marketing images are used so often that they become visual clichés. Acorns are symbols of long-term growth; clocks are symbols of regularity and reliability; hearts are symbols of love and affection. Everything from chocolates to automobiles to beer has been advertised as nestled in an oyster shell, playing off the ancient metaphor of a pearl signifying anything of great price.

One study even found that people are more likely to respond to symbols that have once been widely known—even if they are not consciously familiar with that particular symbol and the symbol itself originated in an unfamiliar culture. Researchers created two sets of twenty images: one consisting of actual symbols from a variety of cultures (flags, trademarks, emblems) that were once popular but are now forgotten, and one consisting of variations on those symbols created especially for the experiment. In fifteen of the twenty cases, participants selected the original symbol as more familiar and appealing. These kinds of tired images persist and are revivified "because they contain an essential truth that appeals to our collective sense of myth and form," graphic designers Philip Thompson and Peter Davenport wrote in *The Dictionary of Visual Language*. In other words, they tap into deep metaphors.

If I had been part of an actual ZMET study, Smith would have collated my comments with a dozen or so other interviews and compared my collage with a dozen or so other collages. Transcripts of each interview would have been fed into a software program that extracts all the associations made by at least four people. These associations would have been compiled into a "consensus map" representing a snapshot of consumer attitudes toward the financial services industry. The consensus map would then be used to plot a marketing campaign or a new product launch.

One ZMET study, conducted for a major agricultural corporation, prompted a complete rethinking of advertising strategy. Ads for crop seeds typically stress things like disease resistance and higher yields. But in their ZMET sessions, farmers brought in highly emotive pictures and talked about farming as a multigenerational journey, a vocation inherited from their parents that they hoped to pass on to their own children.

As a result, the seed firm shifted its message from functional to familial. One print ad depicted a farmer and his father out in the fields studying a soil sample. The tagline: "Which came first, the chicken or the egg? Neither. The Farmer." By cultivating a paternal rather than a practical image, the company hoped it could grow sales.

For many mass-market goods, there are few profound or even discernible differences between an individual product and its competitors. One kind of cereal, deodorant, or running shoe is pretty much like every other kind. Product differentiation—the Holy Grail of "iconic" brand status—therefore involves creating unique Smoke-like associations. Advertisers don't promote breakfast cereal; they promote the "breakfast experience." To stand out from the crowd, companies sell the metaphor as much as the merchandise.

Sometimes, the merchandise itself embodies metaphor. Philips's Senseo coffeemaker, for instance, is designed as a sleek, black arc that conjures up the image of a bow-tied waiter bending over a café table to set down a steaming cup of fresh espresso. The Hourglass coffeemaker is designed in the shape of, well, an hourglass. The Hourglass doesn't use heat or electricity to brew coffee, a process that results in less acidity but takes about twelve hours. Users start making coffee before they go to bed, and it's ready by the time they wake up in the morning. The coffeemaker's hourglass shape is a visual reminder that all good things—or at least, a good cup of coffee—come to those who wait.

In her classic *Decoding Advertisements: Ideology and Meaning in Advertising*, Judith Williamson dissected the way ads construct affective associations. An avid reader of both Karl Marx and glossy women's magazines, Williamson would make the perfect ZMET subject. Her interest in advertising began as a result of her habit of tearing out ads from publications such as *Vogue* in order to study their effect on her. That effect, she concluded, is achieved through affect, the transference of human qualities and characteristics to consumer products.

In any advertisement, Williamson argues, there are always two meanings at work: the product itself and its host of semi-unconscious associations. Advertising works through metaphor—by transferring meanings back and forth. Ads, Williamson writes, "provide a structure which is capable of transforming the language of objects to that of people, and vice versa . . . Once the connection has been made, we begin to translate the other way and in fact to skip translating altogether: taking the sign for what it signifies, the thing for the feeling."

Thus, a breakfast cereal is not a breakfast cereal, but an aspect of domestic bliss. A seed is not a seed, but the bearer of a family's farming legacy. An insurance company is not an insurance company, but a rock of stability in turbulent times. An ad is a metaphor in which the product is the target and a set of affects—imagery, associations, archetypes—is the source.

The BDRC's Smith compares interpreting a ZMET study to interpreting a poem: the art lies not in understanding what the words literally describe but what they emotionally realize. Williamson, too, links advertising with poetry, invoking the idea of the "objective correlative" as an explanation for the way ads achieve iconic status in our minds.

T. S. Eliot defined the objective correlative in his essay "Hamlet and His Problems":

> The only way of expressing emotion in the form of art is by finding an "objective correlative"; in other words, a set of objects, a situation, a chain of events which shall be the formula for that *particular* emotion; such that when the external facts, which must terminate in sensory experience, are given, the emotion is immediately evoked . . . The artistic "inevitability" lies in this complete adequacy of the external to the emotion.

Williamson suggests that ads create objective correlatives for mass consumption. A product becomes linked to a highly emotional state—the desire for everything from status, sex, and wealth to intimacy, community, and security—through powerful affective associations and archetypes. Once these connections are made, " 'Objective correlatives' end up by *being* . . . the very indefinable qualities they were used to *invoke*," Williamson writes.

Thus, a deodorant does not just mask odors but confers a whiff of sexual potency; a car does not just convey you from one place to another but endows you with prestige and power. The effect of affective associations like these is subtle yet far-reaching, with impacts that are felt well beyond the specific products advertised.

McDonald's "golden arches," the Coca-Cola logo, and Colonel Sanders, the face of KFC, are among the most instantly recognizable symbols in the world. And ads for these types of products, which routinely depict fast food as fun, are very effective. One study on the impact of television advertising on food consumption found that children consumed 45 percent more snacks when exposed to ads for high-calorie, low-nutrient foods. Moreover, the ads increased consumption of all kinds of food, not just the kind featured in the commercials, regardless of whether participants reported being hungry or not. The researchers also concluded that ads depicting food as exciting and upbeat—can I interest you in a McDonald's "happy meal"?—prompted the most snacking. Ads such as these clearly access Zaltman's "connection" and "resource" metaphors.

But ads influence more than just what we eat. Another study, this one on the subliminal influence of fast-food logos, found that exposure to the corporate imagery of major fast-food chains increased people's feelings of impatience and reduced their willingness to save money.

Researchers subliminally exposed participants to either McDonald's and KFC logos or the logos of two diners offering similar food at similar prices. Those who saw the fast-food logos completed a reading task faster than those who saw the diner logos, even though there was no time limit set for the task. The fast-food group was also much more likely to accept an immediate but small cash payment rather than a larger sum in a week's time, suggesting they were less able to delay gratification, even though by doing so they would end up with more money.

The research team concluded that exposure to fast-food logos not only made people eat more but also made them engage in more behaviors associated with fast food: impatience, hurry, and a desire for immediate gratification. In these experiments, participants took the signs for the qualities signified.

In her poem "Poetry," Marianne Moore insisted that poets should be "literalists of the imagination," presenting "imaginary gardens with real toads in them." Ad makers are accomplished imaginative literalists, too, supplying the ultimate objective correlatives: real objects that evoke and satisfy our deepest emotions—by encouraging us to spend money.

I was on the verge of buying that extended warranty for my digital camera until I thought, "Wait a minute, do I really need this?" The idea that something could go wrong made me feel vulnerable. But I didn't know anyone who had ever had problems with a digital camera. In fact, the devices seemed amazingly sturdy. And even in the unlikely event that the camera did break down, was it really worth $20—10 percent of the purchase price—to make sure I got a new one? The chances of that happening seemed slim. So I decided to forgo the reassurance of an extended warranty. The camera works like a charm.

Decoding the objective correlatives in advertisements and sales pitches doesn't defuse them. Rather, recognizing the deep metaphors in commercial messages enables us to insert a moment of conscious choice into our purchasing decisions. Do I want to buy this product? If so, am I buying it because I need it or want it or because it has tapped into some powerful, though possibly completely irrelevant, affective associations?

Metaphors, whether in poems or advertisements, only work with our active collusion. Metaphors are born plotters and we are their eager co-conspirators. They need us, as readers and consumers, to complete the link between deodorant and sexual prowess, fast food and immediate gratification, real toads and imaginary gardens. By stepping outside the constant commerce of imagery and affect, we can allow our actual needs and desires to surface.

Smoke may always get in our eyes, but where there is smoke there is not always fire.

BRIGHT SNEEZES AND
LOUD SUNLIGHT

Which is brighter, a cough or a sneeze? Which is louder, sunlight or moonlight?

These queries may seem as strange as asking, "What kind of smoke are you?" or "How can a child think about a banana as a telephone?" But Lawrence E. Marks, a professor at the Yale School of Public Health, asked people these very questions and found that adults invariably equate brightness with loud, high-pitched sounds. When queried about the relative brightness of coughs and sneezes, those surveyed immediately and overwhelmingly said a sneeze was brighter. When asked about the comparative loudness of sunlight versus moonlight, they just as immediately and overwhelmingly said sunlight was louder. Even children as young as four associated high-pitched sounds with brightness and low-pitched sounds with dimness.

Bright sneezes and *loud sunlight* are examples of synesthetic metaphors. Synesthesia is the ability to perceive a stimulus in one sense organ through a different sensory system as well. Some synesthetes perceive tastes when they see shapes; others hear sounds when they see numbers; some experience powerful feelings when they come into contact with specific textures, such as denim or sandpaper. Colored hearing is probably the most common form of synesthesia, with perhaps as many as 1 in every 2,000 people seeing distinct and vivid colors when they hear or even think about the sound of words, letters, or numbers.

Many of the metaphors we use every day are synesthetic, describing one sensory experience with vocabulary that belongs to another. Silence is *sweet*; facial expressions are *sour*. Sexually attractive people are *hot*; sexually unattractive people leave us *cold*. A salesman's patter is *smooth*; a day at the office is *rough*. Sneezes are *bright*; coughs are *dark*. Along with pattern recognition, synesthesia may be one of the neurological building blocks of metaphor.

No one is quite sure how synesthesia works. Some researchers suggest that we are all born synesthetes, that synesthesia is the original way we experience the world. Newborn infants have an abundance of neural connections among the various sensory centers in the brain, connections that are gradually pruned back over time. According to this theory, synesthesia is the natural result of crosstalk among these massively interconnected neurons. Only after the age of about four months, when the cortex has sufficiently matured and the excess neural connections start to snap, does this innate synesthesia fade.

Synesthetic metaphors follow a remarkably consistent pattern: words derived from more immediate senses like touch, taste, and smell describe the experience of less immediate senses like sight and hearing. Touch, taste, and smell are "experience-based sensations," whereas sight and hearing are "object-based sensations." An unpleasant taste, for example, is experienced much more viscerally than an unpleasant color. The former is felt as if it is inside the body; the latter is felt as if it emanates from an external object.

In a synesthetic metaphor, the source tends to come from the more immediate sense and the target tends to come from the less immediate sense far more often than the other way around.

Some researchers suggest that this movement from less to more immediate parallels the physiological development of the senses themselves, thereby reflecting a basic mode of perception. Indeed, studies show that people find metaphors that follow this principle of directionality much easier to understand. Which may be why "sweet silence" (taste modifies sound) is common and "silent sweetness" (sound modifies taste) is not, and why "soft brightness" (touch modifies sight) makes sense and "bright softness" (sight modifies touch) does not.

Studies of nineteenth-century English, French, and Hungarian verse and twentieth-century poetry in Hebrew suggest that people from many different languages and cultures tune into the same sensory scale. The vast majority of metaphors studied in these texts point in the same direction—from more immediate to less immediate. In one experiment, graduate students at Tel Aviv University were asked to interpret forty synesthetic metaphors, which were derived from poems written in Hebrew and followed standard directionality, and those same synesthetic metaphors with the directionality reversed. Students found standard metaphors ("coarse whiteness" and "fragrant purple") far easier to interpret than nonstandard ones ("white coarseness" and "purpled fragrance").

The directionality of synesthetic metaphors follows the directionality of metaphor in general. Metaphorical thinking usually travels one way, appropriating concrete language—the words we use for everyday experiences and physical things and sensations— to describe abstractions like thoughts, feelings, emotions, and ideas. Juliet is the sun in ways that the sun is not and never will be Juliet. Stephin Merritt of The Magnetic Fields wrote a song about this—"Love Is Like a Bottle of Gin," which chronicles the many and varied ways love is similar to gin:

> *It makes you blind, it does you in*
> *It makes you think you're pretty tough*
> *It makes you prone to crime and sin*
> *It makes you say things off the cuff.*

But the final verse acknowledges metaphor's unidirectionality:

> *You just get out what they put in*
> *And they never put in enough*
> *Love is like a bottle of gin*
> *But a bottle of gin is not like love.*

Daniel Tammet is a synesthete as well as a savant. His memoir is titled *Born on a Blue Day* because his birthday—January 31, 1979—was a Wednesday and "Wednesdays are always blue, like the number 9 and the sound of voices arguing." Tammet has an especially rich type of synesthesia, in which he experiences individual numbers up to 10,000 as having specific colors, shapes, textures, movements, and even emotional tones. To Tammet, "Five is a clap of thunder or the sound of waves crashing against rocks. Thirty-seven is lumpy like porridge, while eighty-nine reminds me of falling snow."

Neuroscientist Vilayanur Ramachandran, who has studied Tammet's abilities, suggests that metaphor may have evolved from synesthesia. The visual and auditory pathways in the brain are anatomically very close together. Over the course of evolutionary time, stray visual neurons could have branched out into neighboring auditory regions to transmit visual signals in response to sounds.

Thus, every time the neurons encoding letter sounds were activated in someone with colored hearing, there would be a corresponding activation of the neurons encoding color. "Can it be a coincidence," Ramachandran asks, "that the most common form of synesthesia involves graphemes [letters, numbers, punctuation marks, etc.] and colors and the brain areas corresponding to these are right next to each other?"

We all retain some synesthetic abilities, as the German-American psychologist Wolfgang Köhler showed in 1929 with his discovery of what has come to be known as the "bouba-kiki effect."

Köhler is best known for his demonstration of tool use among chimpanzees. But while working with chimps on Tenerife in the late 1920s, he also conducted an experiment in which he showed islanders two shapes—one round and amoeboid, the other sharp and spiky—and asked them to associate the made-up words "takete" and "baluba" with the shapes. Participants overwhelmingly associated "takete" with the sharp, spiky shape and "baluba" with the round, amoeboid shape.

Which one is bouba and which one is kiki? *Image courtesy of Adam Somlai-Fischer, Prezi.com.*

Around eighty years later, Ramachandran and cognitive psychologist Edward Hubbard repeated Köhler's experiment, substituting the made-up words "kiki" for "takete" and "bouba" for "baluba." They achieved the same result: around 98 percent of subjects identified the curved shape as "bouba" and the jagged one as "kiki." They also found the same associations present regardless of language or culture. Other studies have shown that children as young as two and a half make the same choices. "This result suggests," Ramachandran concluded, "that the human brain is somehow able to extract abstract properties from the shapes and sounds—for example, the property of jaggedness embodied in both the pointy drawing and the harsh sound of kiki."

The bright sneeze/loud sunlight exercise is essentially a variation on the bouba-kiki test. We extract the property of brightness from a sneeze because it is higher in pitch than a cough; we extract the property of loudness from sunlight because it provides more intense illumination than moonlight.

In fact, both sneezes and sunlight occupy the upper bands of their respective frequency ranges. Similarly, in the bouba-kiki test, the amoeboid shape and the "bouba" sound share aspects of roundness, while the sharp shape and the "kiki" sound share aspects of spikiness. When making associations like these, we instinctively find—or create—patterns. These patterns, in turn, connect the disparate sensory descriptions in synesthetic metaphors.

These primal perceptual associations may be hardwired into our brains, since even very young children associate visual and auditory stimuli. In one study, infants listened to a pulsing tone until they became bored with it, as measured by a reduction in their heart rates. (Heart rates tend to decrease when we become habituated to a stimulus and tend to increase when we perceive a different, and therefore more interesting, stimulus.) Researchers then presented the infants with either a dotted line—the visual equivalent of a pulsing tone—or a continuous tone, and measured their heart rates again.

The infants' heart rates picked up in response to the continuous tone, suggesting that they perceived the dotted line as similar to the pulsing tone and therefore less interesting than the continuous tone. Some metaphors may thus derive from synesthetic pattern recognition abilities that precede language acquisition.

If synesthesia is the result of cross-connectivity among the brain's sensory regions, the same connectivity could explain why so many metaphors take the commonly shared world of physical sensation as their source and the private, abstract world of ideas, feelings, thoughts, and emotions as their target.

Take the mundane metaphors "She has a *warm* personality" and "He's as *cold* as ice." Warmth and cold are primal sensations, present even in the womb, that become associated over time with emotional states. The warmth of a mother's embrace is linked in an infant's mind with affection and security, the chill of its absence with rejection and fear. Warmth is such an essential sensation that non-human primate infants prefer heat to food. In one experiment, young macaque monkeys preferred a cloth surrogate mother (warmed by a 100-watt lightbulb) to an unheated wire surrogate mother, even when the wire surrogate was their only source of food.

Metaphor extends the vocabulary of these physical experiences to other circumstances that occasion the same kinds of feelings. Hence, we speak of friendly people as *warm* and unfriendly people as *cold*. There is evidence that these basic, universal physical experiences determine routine metaphorical associations.

In a classic study of how people form first impressions, social psychologist Solomon Asch gave two groups identical lists of character traits—except for one term. Half the participants received a list of adjectives including "intelligent," "skillful," "industrious," "determined," "practical," "cautious," and "warm"; the other half received the same list, except the word "cold" replaced the word "warm." Each group then wrote a brief sketch of the person thus described. Those whose list included the word "warm" formed far more positive first impressions of the person than those whose list included the word "cold."

Asch observed that the words "warm" and "cold" dramatically affected people's opinions, concluding that the associations emanating from these two little words are of special importance when assessing character. He also linked "warm" and "cold" to the formative role these sensations have in our early experience. "When we describe the workings of emotions, ideas, or trends of character, we almost invariably employ terms that also denote properties and processes observable in the world of nature," Asch wrote. "Every man deploys the language of naive physics when he is talking about psychological matters."

In a cleverly updated version of Asch's experiment, researchers casually asked participants to briefly hold a cup of hot coffee or a cup of iced coffee while en route to a room where they were meant to take a survey. After arrival, they each read a description of a fictitious person and answered questions regarding their judgments of that person's character. Both those who held the hot coffee and those who held the iced coffee read identical descriptions, but the hot coffee–holders described the person as more caring, generous, and friendlier (*warmer*) than the cold coffee–holders.

Another experiment showed that giving someone the *cold shoulder* can actually make that person perceive a reduction in temperature. In this study, participants recalled an experience of social exclusion and then estimated the temperature of the room in which they were sitting. A different group recalled an inclusive social experience and made the same estimate while sitting in the same room. Those who remembered an exclusion experience gave lower estimates of the room's temperature—about 3 degrees Celsius lower—than those who recalled an inclusion experience.

In a related experiment, the same team engaged participants in a virtual game of "catch." Subjects threw a ball around online, supposedly with three other people. In fact, a computer program controlled the throws, ensuring that after two catches subjects in the exclusion group didn't receive the ball for the rest of the game. Afterward, participants took an ostensibly unrelated marketing survey. Those who had been excluded from the game rated warm food and drink (hot coffee and hot soup rather than apples and crackers) as far more preferable than those in the control group, who had received the ball intermittently throughout the game.

Dispensers of icy stares, beware. You may actually make the target of your frosty glances feel colder.

This metaphorical effect is not limited to the laboratory, either. When Campbell's Soup revamped its packaging, the firm added steam above the previously steamless photos of cream of potato, chicken noodle, and tomato soup because consumers said they felt more emotionally connected to the product if it looked warm.

Warmth—and the affective steam it produces—is such a hot attribute in advertising that Conquest, a London-based marketing consultancy, devised a way to measure it via metaphor. To gauge the effectiveness of marketing campaigns, Conquest asks consumer panels to use online avatars to express their attitudes toward particular brands. So instead of asking "What do you think of Brand X?" Conquest instructs: "Move your avatar to show how you feel about Brand X." The closer the consumer moves the avatar, the "warmer" her feelings for the brand. And, according to Conquest, the affective warmth generated by an ad is predictive of its success in the marketplace.

Even something as apparently trivial as an object's weight can have a synesthetic impact on the perceived heft of an issue.

Many common metaphors equate weight with importance. We carefully *weigh* the pros and cons before making an important decision. When we're flippant in the face of adversity, we fail to appreciate the *gravity* of the situation. Someone of little ability occupying a position of great responsibility is a *lightweight*. Serious issues requiring lots of reflection and soul-searching are, like, *heavy*, dude.

Dutch researchers handed college students clipboards in order to fill out questionnaires in which they were asked about the estimated value of foreign currencies and whether they wished to be consulted by the university committee in charge of distributing financial grants. Some clipboards weighed significantly more (2.29 lbs) than others (1.45 lbs). Those with the heavier clipboards gave higher estimates of the foreign currency values and more often said that they should *weigh in* on the grant distribution. Participants with heavier clipboards judged the questions as *weightier* than participants with lighter clipboards, the researchers concluded, suggesting that physical weight prompts us to invest more cognitive effort when dealing with *heavy* things.

Similar studies have shown that people interviewing job applicants while holding a heavy rather than a light clipboard rated candidates as more important; people who handled rough jigsaw puzzle pieces described social interactions as more difficult than people who had handled smooth pieces; and people sitting on hard chairs were more rigid in price negotiations compared to people sitting in soft chairs. The metaphorical associations arising from these basic tactile sensations influenced participants' perceptions of social situations, the researchers found.

As Ramachandran's theory predicts, the associations observed in these kinds of studies typically involve brain regions that process both concrete and abstract information. The anterior insula, for example, is involved in the regulation of both body temperature (physical warmth) and interpersonal experience (psychological warmth). Ramachandran himself has identified the angular gyrus as an area that may be essential to certain forms of metaphorical thought.

Ramachandran and his team asked four patients, each of whom had impaired functioning in the left angular gyrus as a result of a stroke or a tumor, to explain the meaning of about two dozen proverbs and metaphors. The angular gyrus processes the senses of sight, hearing, and touch, among other functions. Presented with sayings like "The grass is always greener on the other side of the fence" and "An empty vessel makes more noise," the patients interpreted the phrases literally.

When asked to explain the proverb "All that glitters is not gold," for example, one participant said it was a warning "to be very careful when buying jewellery." As a control, the researchers tested patients with damage to other brain regions; they interpreted the proverbs correctly. The four left angular gyrus patients also failed a version of the bouba-kiki test, while a group of people with intact left angular gyri passed it. Ramachandran posits that the right angular gyrus, which processes spatial information, could also be critical to metaphors like "He has a *massive* ego" or "She has a *big* heart."

Philosopher Roger Scruton suggests that even something as immaterial as the appreciation of music depends on our experience of physical space. Citing musical terms like *high* and *low* notes and *rising* and *falling* tones, he argues that we can only understand music through spatial metaphors. "There lies, in our most basic apprehension of music, a complex system of metaphor," Scruton writes. "Take the metaphor away, and you cease to describe the experience of music."

Some experiments provide evidence that even mathematical thought may be at least partly based in the body. Researchers asked a dozen right-handed subjects to randomly recite forty different numbers between 1 and 30 and monitored their eye movements as they did so. They noticed that if participants looked up and to the right they were more likely to pick a higher number than the previous one; if they looked down and to the left they were more likely to pick a lower number than the previous one.

The research team concluded that even the disembodied realm of numbers is connected to the experience of our bodies in space. That connection may derive from basic physical facts we experience from birth, such as "more" generally equals "up," an observation that applies to everything from Lego bricks to skyscrapers. Thus, anything that is greater than something else, even numbers, becomes associated with height.

Similarly, the team concluded that right-handed people favor the right side of their bodies because they are more competent on that side. And since most people are right-handed, this preference could be the origin of metaphors like "*my right-hand* man" and the association of "left" with "evil" or "lesser" things, as in the word "sinister," which is derived from the Latin for "left."

The synesthetic link between music/space and numbers/height, like the correlations between sound/light, may be due to our ability to extract similar properties from dissimilar things. Just as we extract "depth" from a bass note because the sound is "low" in frequency, we extract "height" from a greater number because it is "more than" a lesser number.

In terms of neurobiological economy, the mix of physical and metaphorical makes sense. As we evolved to process not only concrete sensory information but also increasingly abstract thoughts, new neural circuits did not evolve to handle these tasks. Instead, in a proposed evolutionary process called "scaffolding," existing circuits were adapted to do double duty.

Thus, the brain module devoted to monitoring environmental temperatures branched out into monitoring emotional temperatures, too. The modules devoted to assessing physical space and weight started moonlighting as assessors of psychological space and weight as well. In this way, the concept of psychological warmth became scaffolded onto physical warmth and the concepts of psychological space and weight became scaffolded onto physical space and weight.

This synesthetic link between the abstract and the concrete may be the source of more than just metaphor, as cognitive psychologist Steven Pinker observed in *The Stuff of Thought*:

> If all abstract thought is metaphorical, and all metaphors are assembled out of biologically based concepts, then we would have an explanation for the evolution of human intelligence. Human intelligence would be a product of metaphor and combinatorics. Metaphor allows the mind to use a few basic ideas . . . to understand more abstract domains. Combinatorics allows a finite set of simple ideas to give rise to an infinite set of complex ones.

The theory that biological experience forms the basis for metaphorical thinking—or, indeed, for all thinking—is known as "embodied cognition," an idea given contemporary formulation by cognitive scientists George Lakoff and Mark Johnson. Lakoff and Johnson observed that the most common metaphors, the ones we use instinctively and unconsciously every day, are all deeply rooted in our physiology.

Expressions like "I'm feeling *up* today" and "I'm *high*," Lakoff and Johnson argue, derive from the metaphorical equation of happiness and height, while expressions like "I'm feeling *down* today" and "I'm *low*" derive from the metaphorical equation of dejection with depth. Why? Because we are literally up (i.e., vertical) when we are active, alert, and awake and we are literally down (i.e., horizontal) when we are sluggish, sleepy, or sick.

Ordinary language is filled with such elevated and depressed phrases. People who come across all *high and mighty* need to be *taken down a peg*. If you *put someone on a pedestal*, they often *sink to new lows*. You can *look up to* someone, at least until he *crashes and burns*.

All kinds of studies show the physical-psychological links between high and low. People recognize negative words faster in a low versus a high vertical position and positive words faster in a high versus a low vertical position. The taller the vertical lines on a company's organizational chart, the more powerful people judge that company's executives to be. People reporting symptoms of depression respond faster to objects in the lower rather than the higher portions of their visual fields. Even a physical action as mundane as moving marbles from a lower to a higher position correlates with the recall of positive memories, while moving marbles from a higher to a lower position correlates with the recall of negative memories.

The same synesthetic effect shows up in links between desirability and size. Study participants evaluate positive words more quickly when they are presented in larger font sizes and negative words more quickly when they are presented in smaller font sizes. This correlation lies behind common metaphorical expressions like "He has a *big* salary" and "She has a *small* mind," providing a physical grounding for the truism "bigger is better" and a plausible psychological clarification for the popularity of "super-sized" meals.

The "Belt Tightening Lies Ahead" headline that Rebecca had so much trouble with is another example of a synesthetic metaphor in which an abstract concept is described via a physical property. Phrases like "She's *out in front* on this issue" and "We're all *behind* you" conceal the spatial metaphors of front and back. Even the "seeing is knowing" metaphor is synesthetic, equating the concrete experience of vision with the abstract experience of understanding. But "seeing is knowing" only makes sense if you're a member of a species for whom vision is the primary source of information.

English author Olaf Stapledon wondered what metaphors might be used by a species whose primary source of information was a different sense. So in his visionary novel *Star Maker*, published in 1937, he invented a race of "Other Men" whose main sensory interaction with the world is taste. The "Other Men" have taste buds not just on their tongues and in their mouths but on their hands, their feet, and even their genitalia. And their synesthetic metaphors are similarly gustatory:

> Taste played as important a part in their imagery and conception as sight in our own. Many ideas which terrestrial man has reached by way of sight, and which even in their most abstract form still bear traces of their visual origin, the Other Men conceived in terms of taste. For example, our "brilliant," as applied to persons or ideas, they would translate by a word whose literal meaning was "tasty" . . . Many of our non-visual concepts also were rendered by means of taste. "Complexity" was "many-flavored," a word applied originally to the confusion of tastes round a drinking pool frequented by many kinds of beasts.

Lakoff and his collaborators have identified scores of what they call "conceptual metaphors," figurative phrases that describe fundamental abstract concepts using the language of physiology and physical experience. Expressions like "Your claims are *indefensible*" and "He *shot down* all of my arguments," for example, are instances of the conceptual metaphor ARGUMENT IS WAR; "This relationship is *a dead-end street*" and "We'll just have to *go our separate ways*" are examples of LOVE IS A JOURNEY; "This plan is *half-baked*" and "Let me *chew it over* for a while" exemplify IDEAS ARE FOOD.

Without conceptual metaphors like these, Lakoff and other advocates of embodied cognition believe, we would have no way of talking about—or even thinking about—abstractions like love, beauty, suffering, and joy. According to Lakoff and Mark Turner, another cognitive scientist:

> Basic conceptual metaphors are part of the common conceptual apparatus shared by members of a culture . . . We usually understand them in terms of common experiences. They are largely unconscious, though attention may be drawn to them. Their operation in cognition is mostly automatic. And they are widely conventionalized in language, that is, there are a great number of words and idiomatic expressions in our language whose interpretations depend upon those conceptual metaphors.

There may even be a neurological basis for some conceptual metaphors. Back in the late 1960s, Polish neurophysiologist Jerzy Konorski identified what he called "gnostic neurons," brain cells that fire in response to images of specific people or objects. These neurons later came to be known as "grandmother cells" because of an experiment in which researchers observed that specific brain cells responded to pictures of participants' grandmothers. More recent work has shown that these neurons respond not only to physical representations but also to the concepts behind those representations.

Researchers showed eight epileptics, each of whom had electrodes implanted in their brains to identify areas responsible for their seizures, a series of pictures of famous people or places. The team then recorded which neurons fired in response to which pictures. They found that specific neurons were activated in response to specific images.

Some neurons responded only to pictures of Bill Clinton, for example; others responded only to pictures of The Beatles or basketball star Michael Jordan or characters from *The Simpsons*. The same neurons even responded to a person's name. One participant had "Halle Berry neurons" that fired in response to pictures of the actor as well as the words of her name, suggesting that these cells were responding not just to the image of Halle Berry but to the idea of Halle Berry, too.

The researchers believe gnostic neurons may be crucial in forming long-term memories as well as enduring concepts, which may arise from the repeated association of specific physical stimuli with specific abstract representations. Experiments with monkeys, for example, show that certain neurons respond to correlations among objects. When a monkey is repeatedly shown unrelated objects, different neurons encode each object. But when those objects are presented together or in a recurring temporal sequence, the same neurons encode the objects. A neural link is thus formed among distinct things. In humans, this may be how metaphorical associations are formed.

Some scientists speculate that such brain cells might also encode behaviorally important features of the environment, allowing us to toggle back and forth between physical space and conceptual space. If that suggestion is correct, these cells would have evolved, or been scaffolded, to perform exactly the kind of double duty needed to process literal and metaphorical thought. If a single cluster of neurons can encode the concept of Halle Berry, why not LOVE IS A JOURNEY or IDEAS ARE FOOD as well?

Most conceptual metaphorical expressions have long ago petrified into cliché. Yet that is not to say the synesthetic connections and grandmotherly cells that may have occasioned them in the first place also lie dormant. As cognitive linguist Zoltan Kovecses has pointed out, "The 'dead metaphor' account misses an important point; namely, that what is deeply entrenched, hardly noticed, and thus effortlessly used is most active in our thought."

Synesthesia creates the experience of one sense in the context of another. Metaphorical thinking creates a kind of conceptual synesthesia, in which one concept is understood in the context of another. The abstract is understood in the context of the concrete, the metaphysical in the context of the physical, the emotional in the context of the biological. Through metaphor, body and mind are inextricably intertwined.

ANGER IS A HEATED FLUID
IN A CONTAINER

Time *flies*. The day *drags* by. The hours *crawl*. Spatial metaphors of movement like these are commonplace when describing time. But time, of course, does nothing of the kind. Each of these figurative phrases is, Lakoff and Johnson would argue, an instance of the TIME IS MOTION conceptual metaphor.

Time's physical flight is evident even in basic temporal terms like "then" and "when," which have etymologies rooted in space— "then" and "when" both come from a Germanic word indicating "from that place." Indeed, brain scans show that when we think about time, the regions devoted to motion and spatial relations are active as well. A simple experiment demonstrated just how embodied our concept of time actually is.

Participants looked at a drawing of a chair with a rope attached to it. Half of the subjects imagined pulling the chair toward themselves with the rope; the other half imagined sitting in the chair and pulling themselves forward along the rope. Both groups then read the statement "Next Wednesday's meeting has been *moved forward* two days" and were asked: What day is the meeting that has been rescheduled?

The statement about next Wednesday's meeting contains two metaphors of spatial movement: the first, the meeting itself is a physical object that can be moved; the second, rescheduling the meeting means moving it forward in space. The answer to the question "What day is the meeting that has been rescheduled?" is not obvious, because the concept of "forward" in the context of "the future" is ambiguous. When the meeting is rescheduled, does it move closer to you or do you move closer to it?

The answer depends on whether you metaphorically regard time as something in motion that approaches you or something in motion that carries you with it. In the former scenario, you remain stationary as time brings next Wednesday's meeting closer. In the experiment, this corresponds to pulling the chair toward you with the rope. In the latter scenario, you travel with time toward the stationary object of next Wednesday's meeting. This corresponds to sitting in the chair and pulling yourself forward along the rope. The researchers found that people's imagined positions in physical space affected their responses to the metaphorical movement of next Wednesday's meeting.

Participants who imagined pulling the chair toward themselves more often reported that the meeting had been moved to Monday, consistent with the metaphorical concept that time moves events toward them. Participants who imagined pulling themselves along the rope more often reported that the meeting had been rescheduled to Friday, consistent with the concept that an event is a stationary object toward which time moves them.

The same experiment was carried out with students waiting in line at a café and people on a moving train. In both cases, the results were the same. Those who had experienced the most forward motion—the students at the front of the line and the passengers nearest the end of their journeys—were more likely to say that the meeting had been moved to Friday, consistent with the metaphorical understanding of an event in time as a stationary object toward which we move.

These experiments demonstrate the conceptual synesthesia connecting our ideas of the concrete experience of space and the abstract experience of time. Our concept of physical motion through space is scaffolded onto our concept of chronological motion through time. Experiencing one—indeed, merely thinking about one—influences our experience of and thoughts about the other, just as the theory of embodied cognition suggests.

Metaphor grounds even the most abstract ideas in the physiological facts of our bodies. Through a process known as "priming," these physiological facts insensibly shape our beliefs and behavior.

Priming posits that, through a process of metaphorical association, the physical profoundly impacts the psychological, and vice versa. Sensations, objects, and experiences repeatedly occur together with internal states, thereby becoming linked in our minds. Proximity, for instance, occasions both bodily and emotional warmth. So over time, we come to connect the two, describing our loved ones as *near and dear* and our most intimate friends as *bosom buddies.*

A similar process takes place in the brain. The more often clusters of neurons respond together, the stronger the connections among them become. If specific neuronal groups respond repeatedly over time to the same stimulus—anything to do, say, with Halle Berry—the connections become fixed. In neuroscience, this is known as the "neurons that fire together wire together" axiom.

In priming, the physical fuses with the psychological. Once this rewiring takes place, as in the association of proximity with emotional warmth, traffic flows both ways: from mind to matter and from matter to mind. Our internal states determine whether we get *up close and personal* or remain *cold and distant*. But external circumstances determine our internal states, too. When primed by an associated cue—however trivial or irrelevant that cue might seem—we tend to think and act in ways consistent with the prime.

Thus, people asked to plot points on a line relatively far apart report weaker family bonds than those who plot points on a line relatively close together. People seated in an upright position report feeling more pride than when they are seated in a slouched position. In the former case, physical distance foreshadows psychological distance; in the latter case, physical posture stiffens psychological posture. Metaphors function as primes, too. People shown texts containing metaphors for speed ("on a *fast track* to success") read them faster than texts containing metaphors for slowness ("on a *slow path* to success").

In his famous studies of impression formation, Solomon Asch noticed how the physical correlated with the metaphorical. He compiled a list of adjectives that applied to both, including the pairs "warm" and "cold," "dull" and "bright," "straight" and "crooked," and "bitter" and "sweet." He then researched other, very different languages—Old Testament Hebrew, Homeric Greek, Thai, Malayalam (a language spoken in southwestern India), Hausa (spoken in West Africa), and Burmese, among others—and found exactly the same words used in exactly the same ways.

The word "sweet" gives a flavor of what Asch found. Eating something sweet, like chocolate, creates a pleasant physical sensation as well as a pleasant psychological state. These two things are so tightly linked that anything that occasions the psychological state becomes described in terms of the thing that occasioned the physical state. To paraphrase etymologist Owen Barfield, when a new psychological state comes into consciousness, it is described by the physical state that most closely resembles it.

So, ancient Hebrew features "sweet to the soul"; Greek has "sweet laughter"; Hausa speakers say "I don't taste sweetness" when they don't feel well; and the Chinese warn that "sweet words" can be deceiving, just as too much chocolate can make you sick. Words like these "do not denote exclusively the 'raw materials' of experience," Asch observed. "They are also the names of concepts."

These concepts tend to be universal because our experience of our bodies in the world is pretty much universal, too. Still, there is plenty of room (mind your step around the physical metaphor "room") for cultural variation in this kind of embodied cognition.

In the West, people typically gesture in front of themselves when talking about the future. In one study, participants contemplating the future even tended to lean forward, while those recalling the past tended to lean backward. It seems that we're not in a position to decline our inclination to regard the future as something in front of us.

In South America, however, speakers of Aymara gesture behind themselves when talking about the future. Why? In Aymaran culture, the past is ahead because it is already known and can therefore be seen. The future, in contrast, is unknown and can't be seen; therefore, it is located behind the speaker. Aymaran and Western embodied concepts of the past and future are contradictory, yet they are based on identical bodily metaphors.

Lera Boroditsky, the cognitive scientist behind (make way for "behind," yet another physical metaphor) the "Next Wednesday's meeting" experiment, also studied the different space-related metaphors that English and Mandarin speakers use to think and talk about time.

The horizontal metaphors of "front = future" and "back = past" are common in both languages. But Mandarin speakers also use vertical metaphors to refer to chronological sequences. Events occurring earlier in time are said to be "up" (April is *above* May), while events occurring later in time are said to be "down" (May is *under* April). English speakers use similar expressions—Her birthday is coming *up*; the watch was handed *down* from generation to generation—but far fewer than Mandarin speakers. Mandarin's vertical bias also shows up in the fact that the language is traditionally written from top to bottom in columns running from right to left.

Boroditsky exposed speakers of both languages to horizontal or vertical primes—a picture of a black worm in front of a white worm, with an arrow indicating direction, accompanied by the sentence "The black worm is ahead of the white worm" or a picture of a black ball on top of a white ball accompanied by the sentence "The black ball is above the white ball." She then asked participants temporal questions that did not involve spatial metaphors, such as "Is March *earlier* than April?" and "Is April *later* than March?" English speakers answered faster after horizontal primes; Mandarin speakers answered faster after vertical primes. Mandarin speakers answered faster after vertical primes despite the fact that they responded in English, suggesting that their preference for vertical primes was active regardless of the language in which they spoke.

Boroditsky even trained English speakers to use vertical metaphors when talking about time. They learned to say "cars were invented *above* fax machines," for example, and "Wednesday is *lower than* Tuesday." Like Mandarin speakers, English speakers trained in this way started answering earlier/later questions faster after vertical primes, suggesting to Boroditsky that "differences in talking do indeed lead to differences in thinking."

Boroditsky concluded that spatial metaphors affect how we think about time even when answering questions that contain no spatial metaphors. People "use spatial knowledge to think about time in a way that is consistent with (and encouraged by) the particular metaphors popular in their language," she wrote.

The same is true for all types of embodied metaphors. Just as we instinctively associate "up" with positive things and "down" with negative things, we associate "forward" with good things and "backward" with bad things. We routinely describe progress in difficult negotiations as "moving *forward*" and the return of unsavory personal practices as "going *back* to old habits." Similarly, we are happiest when the best is still *ahead* and the worst is already *behind* us.

These metaphors derive from the fact that our senses for the most part point in front of us. As a result, that is the direction from which our information about the world arrives. What is before us is clear and easily seen; what is behind us is obscure and inscrutable—unless, of course, you're Aymaran. Our hands and feet also work much better when we're going forward than when we're going in reverse.

If our bodies were different, though, our metaphors would be different, as Olaf Stapledon showed in *Star Maker*. Crabs walk sideways, for instance. If crabs could talk, they would undoubtedly describe progress in difficult negotiations as *sidling* toward agreement and express the hope for a better future by saying their best days are still *beside* them.

Our bodies prime our metaphors, and our metaphors prime how we think and act.

This kind of associative priming goes on all the time. In one study, researchers showed participants pictures of objects characteristic of a business setting: briefcases, boardroom tables, a fountain pen, men's and women's suits. Another group saw pictures of objects—a kite, sheet music, a toothbrush, a telephone—not characteristic of any particular setting. Both groups then had to interpret an ambiguous social situation, which could be described in several different ways. Those primed by pictures of business-related objects consistently interpreted the situation as more competitive than those who looked at pictures of kites and toothbrushes.

This group's competitive frame of mind asserted itself in a word completion task as well. Asked to complete fragments such as "wa_," "_ight," and "c__p___tive," the business primes produced words like "war," "fight," and "competitive" more often than the control group, eschewing equally plausible alternatives like "was," "light," and "cooperative." They also behaved less generously in a money-sharing game that rewards players the more equitably they dole out a small pot of cash.

Anger is another of priming's prime targets. "She's about to *blow her top*," "He's all *steamed up*," "She's a *hot head*," and "In the *heat* of the moment" are all variations on another Lakoff-Johnson conceptual metaphor—ANGER IS A HEATED FLUID IN A CONTAINER. In fact, figurative descriptions of anger display some of the clearest synesthetic links between metaphorical expression and physical experience.

The experience of physical heat is processed in the anterior insula, a brain region also active when anger-related concepts are in use and during the experience of emotional warmth. To find out if heat-related imagery triggered concepts of anger in people's minds, psychologist Benjamin M. Wilkowski and collaborators showed subjects a set of ten anger-related words ("angry," "annoyed," "furious") and a set of ten neutral words. Wilkowski wanted the neutral words to be as bland as possible, so he chose furniture-related terms like "armchair," "bench," and "bookcase."

Some subjects saw words presented along with imagery evocative of heat; flames flickered from the tops of letters, or words were displayed against the background of a campfire. Others saw words presented along with imagery evocative of cold; icicles dangled from some letters, or words were displayed partially concealed in snowdrifts.

ANGRY   **BOOKCASE**

ANGRY   **BOOKCASE**

Feel the heat? Subjects recognize anger-related words much
faster when they are accompanied by heat imagery than by cold
imagery. *Image courtesy of Benjamin M. Wilkowski.*

The participants' task was simple: distinguish the anger-related
words from the non-anger-related words as quickly as possible.
The subjects did this much faster when the anger-related words
were accompanied by heat imagery than by cold imagery. Even the
word "angry" itself was recognized as anger-related faster when it
was in flames than when it was covered in snow.

Subjects also more often mistook furniture- for anger-related
terms when the name of the piece of furniture was presented along
with heat imagery. Other studies have shown that subjects are
quicker to identify anger-related words after being primed with
heat imagery, such as a picture of a lava flow. Physical cues of heat,
Wilkowski and colleagues concluded, really do prompt mental
concepts of anger. And these metaphorical promptings have physical consequences, too.

After priming subjects with either anger-related or furniture-
related cues, Wilkowski and colleagues asked them to estimate the
current room temperature or the temperature in an unfamiliar city.
Those exposed to anger-related primes consistently gave hotter temperature estimates than those who were thinking about furniture.
A similar effect was observed with faces. People exposed to heat-
related imagery more often and more quickly categorized ambiguous facial expressions as angry, even though the expressions could

have just as easily—and just as accurately—been categorized as sad or neutral.

The correlations between our experience of heat and our concepts of anger, like the parallels between movement through space and passage through time, suggest that there is a link between the corporal and the metaphorical. We *flip our lids* when pent-up rage explodes, just as a boiling fluid overflows its container. We tend to lose our tempers more easily when we *feel the heat*, both physically and metaphorically.

Colors, too, have metaphorical significance as well as physical influence. We tend to routinely associate darker colors with strength and lighter colors with weakness, an association that holds across cultures.

In one study, participants rated teams in darker professional football and hockey uniforms as nastier than teams in lighter uniforms. The researchers wondered whether this association correlated with actual nasty acts, as measured by the number of penalties received. A review of penalties covering seventeen seasons, from 1970 through 1986, revealed that teams in darker uniforms committed more infractions than teams in lighter uniforms, and the penalties often involved prohibited aggressive acts, such as slashing.

During the 1979–1980 season, the Pittsburgh Penguins hockey team provided optimum conditions for the study; players wore blue uniforms for the first half of the season and black uniforms for the second half. The team's penalties averaged eight minutes when they wore blue and twelve minutes when they wore black. The players may have indeed committed more infractions while wearing black uniforms, or the referees may have merely been more wary and watchful of them in darker jerseys. Either way, the color's metaphorical associations triggered a physical response.

Red colors our judgments in different ways. Typically associated with aggressiveness, dominance, and sexual attractiveness, red often signals these very qualities in nature. A flushed face, especially among men, is associated with either anger or physical exertion. When we're angry, it seems, we really do see red.

An analysis of more than fifty seasons of an English soccer league showed that teams wearing red jerseys finished higher in the rankings and won more home games than teams in other colors. In another study, a static variation on the classic Heider and Simmel film, researchers showed volunteers differently colored circles and asked which would be most likely to prevail in a physical competition. And the winner was . . . red.

In economics, red does not have very positive connotations. Market indices universally portray downticks in securities prices in red, while gains are always in green. If you are losing money, you're *in the red* or *drowning in red ink*. Red is, of course, also the color of choice when correcting written work. Teachers use red pens to mark errors on student papers, and computer spell-check programs typically underline misspelled words in red. One study found that people using red rather than blue pens not only awarded lower grades when marking essays, but also came up with more error-related terms in a word completion task like the one used in the business priming experiment. The use of red pens, the researchers concluded, increased the accessibility of concepts related to failure and poor performance.

These associations may be due to red's effect on the autonomic nervous system, raising pulse and blood pressure, increasing muscle tension, and stimulating sweat glands. Red tends to promote involuntary subjective impressions of stress, leading people to make decisions under greater perceived pressure. Which is why some stock traders refuse to own or even touch a red pen, let alone write with one, and some Massachusetts school districts are issuing teachers pens with purple ink.

The connection between our bodies and our metaphors may be explained by the fact that the same brain areas that are active when carrying out an action are active when mentally simulating that action, as research on mirror neurons has shown. The neural systems responsible for physical disgust, for instance, overlap with those responsible for moral disgust.

Just as traders get stressed by seeing red, our heart and breathing rates accelerate when we see pictures of threatening objects as well as when we mentally visualize those objects. The brain's visual circuits respond regardless of whether we see something with our own eyes or in our own minds.

Researchers in one study, in which participants had to retrace a memorized path with their eyes closed, found that mental simulation was as effective as physical practice in walking the simplest routes. Even the duration of actual and simulated strolls tends to be roughly the same. When test subjects are asked to imagine walking specific distances, the time it takes them to reach the imagined goal is equivalent to the time it would take to actually walk that distance.

The upshot of all this research is: thinking is a kind of simulated interaction with the world, a metaphorical engagement that makes what we imagine more realistic. Mental images can have the same effect on the body and the mind as actual physical things. And metaphors are mental image makers par excellence (another physical metaphor, by the way, from the Latin *excellere* via French, meaning "to rise above," "to project from," or "to stick out"). Metaphors are experience's body doubles, standing in for actual objects and events.

To find out if we do understand figurative language by mentally simulating the physical actions alluded to in metaphor, psychologist Raymond Gibbs Jr. put participants in front of a computer screen on which various icons appeared. Each icon represented a simple bodily action, such as throwing, stamping, pushing, kicking, or grasping. Whenever an icon flashed on the screen, subjects had to perform the physical action displayed.

After that, a string of words appeared, half of which were conventional metaphors related to the action just performed. If subjects had just been asked to kick, for example, the words "*kick around* an idea" might appear. The other word strings were random combinations that made neither literal nor metaphorical sense. Participants had to decide as quickly as possible which was which. If physical actions matched metaphorical concepts, Gibbs theorized, then subjects should be able to verify phrases as meaningful faster when they first performed a related action. And that's exactly what he found.

The phrase "*kick around* an idea" was identified faster after subjects actually kicked. Similarly, people were faster to recognize "*grasp* the concept" after actually making grasping motions. "Performing an action facilitates understanding of a metaphoric phrase containing that action word," Gibbs and his team concluded, which suggests that the same skeins of neurons are involved in understanding a metaphor and performing a related movement. Other experiments have delivered corresponding results: performing an action not only facilitates the understanding of related metaphors, but also facilitates the accessibility of the concepts behind those metaphors. These findings build on research showing that the literal meanings of verbs like "kick" and "walk" activate neurons in the brain regions involved in the physical actions of kicking and walking. In the brain, the networks for language, action, and metaphorical thinking overlap.

Researchers asked participants to play the children's game rock-paper-scissors, a ruse to assess whether making a fist (the "rock" hand position in the game) made the concept of power more accessible. They found that subjects identified power-related words ("rule," "win," "mighty," "strong") faster when forming the "rock" position than when forming the "paper" or "scissors" positions. The concept of power, the team concluded, was more accessible to those who made a fist than to those who did not.

Gesture is, in fact, another area where metaphor and the body intersect. Shaking your fist at someone is a metaphorical warning as well as a physical threat. "If language was given to men to conceal their thoughts, then gesture's purpose was to disclose them," wrote historian of the hand John Napier in his aptly titled book *Hands*. A metaphorical gesture is worth a thousand words.

The "nose thumb"—placing the thumb against the nose and wiggling the fingers—means mockery or disrespect practically everywhere. Its earliest known use was in the fifteenth century, when it might have derived from the practice of making satirical wax effigies with elaborately elongated noses.

The "fingers crossed"—folding the middle finger over the index finger—is an invocation of protection or good luck, except in Corfu and Turkey, where it means the breaking of a bond of friendship. It may have originated as a disguised version of the sign of the Cross, a kind of secret handshake among Christians.

The "OK sign"—curling the thumb and forefinger into a ring with the other three fingers extended—has a more variable significance, meaning "everything is fine" except in places like Tunisia (where it's a threat), France and Belgium (where it means "zero"), and Germany and Brazil (where it's a bodily orifice–related insult). Emblems like these are visual metaphors in which a physical sign or gesture is the source and an abstract idea or state of mind is the target.

Metaphorical gestures regularly accompany speech. If someone asks you how you're feeling and you reply with a weak "Eh . . ." accompanied by a seesawing motion with the flat of your hand, you clearly signal that, as the Hausa would say, you do not taste much sweetness.

But gesture on its own is also richly metaphorical. When some-one gives you the finger, there can be little doubt about the senti-ment expressed, however metaphorically conveyed. This gesture's metaphorical connotation is so clear, and so clearly derisory, that the anatomical term for the middle finger—*impudicus*—is derived from it. Actions do sometimes speak louder than words.

David McNeill, an expert on the relationship between gesture and thinking, argues that gesture is not some physical grace note to the music of talk. Instead, gesture—metaphorical gesture, in par-ticular—is an indispensable part of speech. "Language is insepa-rable from imagery," he wrote in *Gesture and Thought*, and imagery is "embodied in gestures that universally and automatically occur with speech." Neuroscientists Giacomo Rizzolatti and Michael A. Arbib suggest that a vocabulary of basic metaphorical gestures formed the scaffolding for language itself.

Brain imaging studies show that a mirror neuron system for ges-ture recognition exists in monkeys and in humans. In humans, it is located in the same region as the brain's language center. And the language center, some studies suggest, is active during the ex-ecution of hand and arm movements as well as during the mental simulation of these movements. Mirror neurons seem to connect thinking and doing, so Rizzolatti and Arbib posit that the mirror neuron system is the missing link between gestural communica-tion and spoken language.

Rizzolatti and Arbib theorize that mirror neurons allowed early primates to match their own actions to the actions of oth-ers. Through the mirror neuron properties that endow us with our "mind-reading" abilities, early primates came to associate internal states with specific physical movements. So they knew, say, that extending the hands with the palms upward was likely to "mean" the same thing no matter who performed the gesture.

Through a process of associative learning and imitation, Rizzolatti and Arbib propose, a visual language of gestures was created. Then, as hands became more and more specialized for tool use, spoken language itself evolved from those same brain circuits. And language would have brought with it huge evolutionary advantages, such as the ability to cooperate, to share information, and to organize more complex social groups. "What made us human crucially depended at one point on gestures," Arbib wrote. "Gesture is not a behavioral fossil but an indispensable part of our . . . ongoing system of language."

The co-evolution of gesture and speech could explain why so much of our talk is accompanied by some kind of hand or facial movement and would provide further evidence that metaphor is not merely a matter of language alone but of thought itself.

As much as 90 percent of spoken description is accompanied by gestures of some sort, according to McNeill. The blind gesture during speech with the same frequency as the sighted. Sign language even translates some of the same linguistic spatial metaphors into physical action. In American Sign Language, for example, "communication" is depicted as an object moving from one person to another; "authority" is shown as height; and "affection" is visualized as proximity.

Metaphorical gestures routinely replace their corresponding linguistic expressions. After making a joke no one else gets (an inexplicably frequent occurrence in my experience), I quickly whisk my palm above my head while producing a whistling sound instead of saying, "I guess that went *over your head*," which is in itself another case of metaphor couched in the language of the body. Indeed, when adults have their limbs restrained during speech, they produce less vivid imagery than when their limbs are free to gesture.

But McNeill points out (note the gestural metaphor embedded in the verb!) that gestures have meanings of their own that don't depend on words. The physical motion of a metaphorical gesture already contains the significance it wishes to convey, he argues: "In a metaphoric gesture, an abstract meaning is presented as form and/or space . . . The gestures provide imagery for the non-imageable."

Many of the gestures that occur during talk seem to be derived from embodied conceptual metaphors. The linguist Cornelia Müller has documented the unconscious metaphorical gestures that accompany ordinary speech, creating a kind of gestural lexicon from one woman's description of her relationship with a former boyfriend.

The woman, speaking in German, described her former boyfriend as "depressive," a word derived in both German and English from the Latin verb meaning "to press down." Though she was unaware of the etymology of the word, the woman extended her hand with the palm downward and slowly moved it toward the ground as she spoke. Müller concluded that the conceptual metaphor "physically down = psychologically down" was active on some nonconscious level in this woman's mind.

Metaphorical gestures can vary by culture, just like metaphorical ideas about time. Describing the excitement of her first encounter with her boyfriend—on a bus during a school outing—the woman in Müller's study said it was as if an electric spark passed between them, using the words "It sparked" (*Es hat gefunkt*). In German, the phrase is a colloquialism for falling in love, similar to the English expression "It was love at first sight." As she uttered the word *gefunkt*, Müller observed, the woman brought her fingertips together and quickly released them, mimicking the flaring of an actual spark.

In northwestern Kenya, speakers of Turkana use a similar gesture to convey the concept of knowledge. In the West, knowledge is typically conceived as an object conveyed—or *passed on*—from one person to another. In the Turkana culture, however, knowledge is depicted as something plucked from the brow and released into the air. When talking about knowledge, Turkana speakers pinch their fingers and make a plucking motion at the brow, then quickly open the fingers as if releasing a butterfly into the air.

Metaphorical gesture, like metaphorical speech, opens a window onto the inner world of thought and feeling, a metaphysical world rooted firmly in physical experience. Abstract concepts only take flight when tethered to the language of the body.

FREEDOM FRIES AND
LIBERTY CABBAGE

Jacques Jean Lhermitte, a French neuropsychiatrist who died in 1959, is best remembered for his identification of "Lhermitte's sign," a painful sensation occurring when bending the head forward so that the chin touches the chest. The pain, often compared to the sensation of an electric shock, is a symptom of multiple sclerosis.

Lhermitte specialized in the study of neurological anomalies such as Lhermitte's sign as well as phenomena like visual hallucinations and demonic possession. He was also a student of some of the stranger side effects of strokes and, like Swiss neurologist Édouard Claparède, who gave patients surreptitious pinpricks, was partial to experiments that in some ways resembled practical jokes.

In one impromptu study, Lhermitte performed an early priming test by inviting to his apartment two patients who had suffered stroke-related damage to the prefrontal cortex in brain areas involving the planning and control of actions. As the patients milled about his rooms, Lhermitte casually mentioned the word "museum." The two patients suddenly behaved as if they were actually in a museum, carefully studying the paintings and posters on the walls and examining with great interest various objects on the tables. Neither patient thought their behavior odd.

Social psychologist John Bargh performed a variation on this experiment with university students, none of whom had any stroke-related brain damage. As part of an ostensible language test, participants read a list of words. One group read a list that included synonyms for rudeness; the other group read a list that included synonyms for politeness.

Bargh then instructed members of both groups to walk down the hall, where they ran into a staged situation to which they could respond in either a rude or a polite manner. Those who had read synonyms for rudeness tended to respond more rudely, while those who had read synonyms for politeness tended to respond more politely. None of the participants connected their behavior to the words they had read.

These experiments prove the power of suggestion, yet they also indicate something more. This persuasive power resides in the swirl of associations arising from even the most ordinary words, associations that can directly—and sometimes dramatically— affect our attitudes and behavior, usually without our conscious knowledge. No prefrontal cortex damage required.

In a separate experiment, Bargh assembled two groups, priming one with words stereotypical of the elderly, such as "gray," "bingo," and "Florida." He then again sent subjects in both groups down the hall for a stroll. Primed participants walked more slowly than control participants, just as actual elderly people do.

The same thing happened with other kinds of primes. Subjects primed with words relating to cooperation, for example, cooperated more on test tasks than those who were not primed; those presented with achievement-related primes performed better on tests than those not presented with those primes. Bargh's conclusion: the stereotypical associations and behavioral norms triggered by primes prompt people to think and act in line with those same stereotypes and norms.

Priming can even influence judgments intended to be objective, unbiased, and completely independent. A muster of German trial judges read the details of the same criminal case in which the defendant was found guilty. Researchers then told one group that the prosecutor demanded a two-month sentence and another group that the prosecutor demanded a thirty-four-month sentence. The judges were then asked for their recommendations.

The average sentence was nineteen months when judges were told that the prosecutor demanded two months and twenty-nine months when they were told that the prosecutor demanded thirty-four months. Judges even gave significantly longer sentences when they were told that the person demanding the thirty-four-month jail term was not a prosecutor but a first-semester computer science student.

Of course, prosecutors' demands—much less the demands of a first-semester computer science student!—should have no bearing whatsoever on the length of sentence. Yet the German judges were clearly swayed by calls for a comparatively harsh or a comparatively lenient prison spell. Merely weighing these demands, however irrelevant, and assessing them against the judges' own opinions influenced their actual decisions.

Percy Bysshe Shelley might have misstated the case when he declared, "Poets are the unacknowledged legislators of the world." It would be more accurate to say that metaphor is the unacknowledged legislator of the world, since it so pervasively primes so many of our opinions, attitudes, and beliefs. Shelley was on firmer ground, though, when he wrote:

Language is vitally metaphorical; that is, it marks the before unapprehended relations of things and perpetuates their apprehension, until words, which represent them, become, through time, signs for portions or classes of thought instead of pictures of integral thoughts.

Priming experiments are case studies in the vitality of metaphorical language. A metaphor occurs when someone apprehends previously unapprehended relations between things. The metaphor perpetuates this fresh apprehension until, through time, core associations form. These associations cling fast to words themselves, eventually becoming so routine that they continue to appear long after the original relation has ceased to be consciously apprehended. In this way, the word "museum" can mean "a building filled with precious things" while also signaling that category of places requiring an attitude of quiet reverence. The word "bingo" can mean "a kind of lottery game" while also signifying that class of track-suited retiree commonly found ambling along the palm-fringed streets of Florida.

A similar phenomenon, known as "arbitrary coherence," occurs during financial reasoning. Give people any number—a town's population, for example—and then ask something like, "What is the maximum amount you would pay for a house?" The answers will be influenced by the cited figure. Given a population figure of 500,000, people will quote amounts much closer to $500,000 than people given a population figure of 1 million, who will quote amounts much closer to $1 million. We're all influenced by the seemingly irrelevant.

The coherence of metaphorical priming is anything but arbitrary, though. Metaphorical primes cohere precisely because the patterns of association connecting the concept and the behavior interlock. Criminal sentencing decisions, like all decisions, should not be influenced by irrelevant details. But they are. This is vitally important to political debate because, as conceptual metaphor theorists Lakoff and Johnson observed, "The people who get to impose their metaphors on the culture get to define what we consider to be true."

Lakoff and Johnson's observation echoes Friedrich Nietzsche:

> What therefore is truth? A mobile army of metaphors, metonymies, anthropomorphisms: in short a sum of human relations which became poetically and rhetorically intensified, metamorphosed, adorned, and after long usage seem to a nation fixed, canonic and binding; truths are illusions of which one has forgotten that they are illusions; worn-out metaphors which have become powerless to affect the senses.

Psychologist Thomas Gilovich demonstrated the power of these worn-out metaphors to affect our judgments by asking a group of Stanford undergraduates to imagine that they were high-ranking officials in the U.S. State Department. He informed them that a small democratic country of no vital interest to U.S. national security had been attacked by a moderately powerful communist or fascist country and had asked the U.S. for help. What should the U.S. do—nothing, appeal to the United Nations, or intervene?

Gilovich then gave each student one of three different descriptions of this hypothetical foreign policy crisis, each of which contained a few minor associations and a few familiar names designed to trigger different historical analogies. One scenario featured allusions to World War II, another featured allusions to Vietnam, and the third was historically neutral.

In the World War II scenario, minorities were described as fleeing in boxcars on freight trains, while the State Department briefing was described as held in Winston Churchill Hall. In the Vietnam scenario, minorities were described as fleeing in small boats up the coast, while the State Department briefing was described as held in Dean Rusk Hall, named after President Lyndon Johnson's secretary of state during the Vietnam War.

These historical cues were, of course, entirely irrelevant to the decision participants had to make. Nonetheless, subjects given the World War II scenario made more interventionist recommendations than the other two. The Vietnam and control groups both tended to recommend a hands-off approach. Gilovich quizzed students afterward, and none was aware of the historical allusions embedded in the descriptions—and all denied that these associations could have influenced their decisions.

"When one must make a decision about a course of events, one draws analogies between existing circumstances and presumably informative past events," Gilovich observed. "This process, in itself, is not too surprising. What is surprising is that the specific associations or analogies formed in a given situation can be influenced by such transient, incidental factors . . . The manipulations used in these studies led subjects to make associations that once formed were difficult to ignore."

Metaphors are notoriously difficult to ignore, as shown by psychologist Sam Glucksberg in a clever variation on the classic experiment demonstrating the "Stroop effect."

The Stroop effect is named after John Ridley Stroop, a devout Christian preacher and professor of religion who in 1935 happened to publish one of the most widely cited studies in the history of cognitive psychology. Subjects look at the names of colors printed in variously colored inks and must name as quickly as possible the color of the ink in which a specific word is printed.

This task is easy when the word and the color of the ink are the same. People easily reel off, say, "green" when the word "green" is printed in green ink.

Things get trickier when the name of the color is different from the color in which the word is printed; for example, when the word "green" is printed in blue ink. Then, subjects are inclined to read the word "green" rather than to name the color "blue." It takes longer for subjects to state the correct ink color, indicating that the meaning of the word itself creates "cognitive dissonance" that interferes with the ability to name the color of the ink. (To take the Stroop test, go to http://www.at-bristol.org.uk/stroopeffect.html.)

Stroop's conclusion: it is impossible for us to ignore the literal meanings of words, even when the literal meaning produces the wrong answer. Glucksberg postulated that it is also impossible for us to ignore the metaphorical meanings of words. To prove it, he and his team carried out a Stroop test with metaphors, using literally false and metaphorically true statements.

The researchers listed four different types of sentences: literally true ("Some birds are robins"), literally false ("Some birds are apples"), metaphors ("Some jobs are jails"), and "scrambled metaphors," sentences with no ready interpretation ("Some jobs are birds"). Participants had to identify the literally false sentences as quickly as possible.

If subjects were able to ignore metaphorical meanings, Glucksberg reasoned, they should be just as quick to reject the metaphors as the scrambled metaphors since both are literally false. If, however, people involuntarily register metaphorical meanings, they should take longer to reject as false the metaphors than the scrambled metaphors, because the metaphors are figuratively true. Glucksberg believed that rejecting a metaphorically true statement as false would set up the same kind of cognitive dissonance as naming the color "blue" when the word "green" is printed in blue ink.

Glucksberg found that the Stroop effect is indeed at work with metaphors. Participants took longer to reject metaphors as false than they did to reject literally false statements or scrambled metaphors. They understood the sentence "Some jobs are jails," for example, as quickly and as effortlessly as the sentence "Some birds are robins."

Glucksberg found evidence of the Stroop effect even in cases in which the metaphor and the literally false sentence differed by just a single word. Participants quickly identified the statement "All surgeons are butchers" as literally false; they took longer to identify the sentence "Some surgeons are butchers" as literally false—because it is, unfortunately, metaphorically true. (It could be literally true, of course, if the surgeon in question happens to also sell meat.) "Metaphorical meanings are apprehended whenever they are available," Glucksberg concluded. "We can no more shut off our metaphor-understanding machinery than our literal-understanding machinery."

Perhaps it should not be surprising that our metaphor-understanding machinery is always on, that fleeting, irrelevant associations—like whether a briefing is held in Winston Churchill Hall or Dean Rusk Hall—can impact major decisions such as whether to go to war. After all, just before Romeo compares Juliet to the sun, Juliet herself famously asks, "What's in a name?" Apparently, quite a lot, when that name carries powerful political associations.

In March 2003, just before the U.S.-led invasion of Iraq, Republican Congressman Robert W. Ney, head of the committee in charge of the cafeterias in the House of Representatives, decreed that henceforth the fried potato slivers served in House eateries would be known as "freedom fries" and the fried slices of bread dipped in egg batter would be known as "freedom toast." France had refused to back military action against Iraq, and Ney said his decision was "a small but symbolic effort to show the strong displeasure of many on Capitol Hill with the actions of our so-called ally."

In making this bold declaration of culinary independence, Ney followed the lead of Neal Rowland, owner of Cubbie's, a North Carolina fast-food joint. Inspired by World War I euphemisms for German food—sauerkraut became "liberty cabbage," hamburgers became "liberty steaks," and frankfurters became "hot dogs"—Rowland struck French fries and French toast from his menu.

Such symbolic re-namings are common in times of conflict, and the obstreperous French often seem to be on the receiving end of them. In the late 1990s, after France resumed nuclear weapons testing in the Pacific, French bread became "Kiwi loaves" in New Zealand. Danish baked goods were also renamed in anger when cartoons of Muhammad, regarded as blasphemous by many Muslims, were printed in one of Denmark's leading daily newspapers. In response, some Iranians dubbed Danish pastries "roses of the prophet Muhammad."

Names matter because they prime us to respond in specific ways. Some argue that the term "global warming," for example, is far too mild, suggesting a relaxed and possibly pleasant condition rather than one that is urgent and potentially catastrophic. Instead, they suggest that terms like "climate crisis" or even "climate cancer" would be more accurate and more likely to motivate changes in behavior.

Metaphors matter when it comes to changing attitudes as well as behavior. Ask the average voter what he or she thinks about the government and the answer is likely to be a burst of derisive laughter. That's what Joe Grady and colleagues from the Providence, Rhode Island–based firm Cultural Logic discovered when they asked people this very question as part of a research project for a nonprofit involved in public service provision. Cultural Logic is a consultancy that uses insights from the cognitive and social sciences to advise nonprofits on how to effectively communicate issues of public interest. Grady, the linguist who coined the term "primary metaphor" and who has collaborated with conceptual metaphor theorist George Lakoff, co-founded Cultural Logic to devise more productive ways of discussing topics of political and social import. Metaphor is one of his tools.

"Many of our most important challenges—climate change, politics, the economic meltdown—are poor targets for human cognition," Grady says. "Expert explanations are complex and jargon-filled and often fail to engage or even inform the public. Yet public engagement and understanding are essential to finding solutions. Metaphor helps bridge that gap."

The term "greenhouse gases" is a case in point. Cultural Logic did hundreds of consumer interviews around the subject of climate change and hardly anyone spontaneously referred to greenhouse gases in their responses. When specifically asked about the term, few could explain how it related to global warming. Perhaps this should not come as a surprise, since few people have any direct knowledge of greenhouses these days. As a result, when prompted, subjects in the Cultural Logic study typically described green-houses as "nice places where plants live," according to Grady— hardly the right connotations for a discussion of global warming. Which suggested to the folks at Cultural Logic that "greenhouse gases" is an unhelpful metaphor. So they alighted on a more pro-ductive one—"carbon dioxide blanket," which has the virtue of explicitly naming the offending gas (CO_2) but the drawback of suggesting that its embrace is warm and cuddly.

In quizzing people about their views of government, Cultural Logic found (after waiting for the derisive laughter to subside) that most respondents operated according to an "us and them" meta-phor. The government (them) does things to the people (us) in the form of laws, taxes, regulations, etc., and we (the people) do things to them (the government) every four years or so in the form of voting. A consequence of this metaphor is that voters tend to per-sonalize government, focusing exclusively on high-profile elected officials as individuals (who can be greedy, venal, and feckless) rather than on other, equally valid aspects of government, such as the government's role in maintaining essential public services. One important casualty of regarding government in this way is the idea of the common good. "While most Americans have some sense of the common good," Grady says, "the 'us and them' metaphor does not give them a way of expressing or even thinking about this important idea." So, as in the climate change exercise, Cultural Logic came up with a better metaphor: "public structures."

As a deft and beautiful use of metaphorical language, "public structures" just can't compete with "Juliet is the sun" or "My love is like a red, red rose." But as a vehicle for introducing the idea of the common good into discussions of government, it has been very successful. Cultural Logic knows this because company co-founder Axel Aubrun is an anthropologist, so fieldwork is a central part of every project.

To test drive its metaphors in the real world, Cultural Logic plays a version of the children's game "Telephone." In Telephone, one person says something to another person, which that other person must then repeat as accurately as possible to another person, who then must repeat it to another person, and so on and so on and so on. When the game is played in a large enough group, the original message usually comes back to the initial speaker completely distorted and often unrecognizable. Cultural Logic calls its version of the game a "talkback chain." Talkback chains are good measures because effective metaphors tend to be easily remembered and retransmitted. This is, in fact, what enables them to become clichés.

Grady and colleagues recruited about 120 people to take part in public structures talkback chains based on paragraphs like the following:

Economists now agree that what has made America so successful is the effectiveness of our Public Structures. The Public Structures Americans have created—such as laws, highways, health and safety agencies, and schools and colleges—are the machines that produce American success and quality of life. Without them, it would be difficult or impossible to get lots of important jobs done. Developing countries may have many smart, hard-working individuals, but they don't have the Public Structures that are essential for overall prosperity.

Talkback testing showed that paragraphs like this one survived reasonably intact and that participants explicitly used the public structures metaphor to think about government in the context of the common good. The same people who laughed in researchers' faces at the mere mention of the word "government" gave thoughtful, deliberate answers to questions about public structures. For example, when asked to explain what public structures are, one respondent said: "Things that we need like the post offices and stuff that keep our country running . . . Without those things, we'd be relying on individuals to do things." When asked how public structures are maintained, another said: "Well, obviously taxes, but also a common belief by everybody that they should be maintained. An agreement by everyone. Traffic lights are Public Structures but if everyone didn't agree that red meant stop then they wouldn't function . . . So I think a combination of government funding and a common belief that they are necessary."

The original text, of course, never mentioned the word "government." Yet the public structures metaphor prompted respondents to focus on government's less visible but no less vital role of providing and maintaining public services—in other words, of working for the common good. The idea of public structures made people less likely to personalize government as "fat cats" or "the nanny state" and more likely to frame government as a collective undertaking with shared responsibilities. The public structures concept even generated consensus on the issue of taxes, regardless of whether participants identified themselves as Republican or Democrat, conservative or liberal. Of nineteen people who read a paragraph about government services that did not contain the public structures metaphor, 75 percent expressed negative or critical views about taxes. Of fifty subjects responding to the public structures text, 4 percent expressed negative or critical views about taxes.

To be successful, though, a metaphor should not be too, well, metaphorical. If the concept is too novel or the language too flowery, people tend to regard the metaphor as merely decorative, thereby depriving it of any explanatory power. This is why lofty political rhetoric can sound insipid as often as it sounds inspiring; without a practical connection to the real world, voters quickly conclude it's all just fancy words.

The best metaphors are sticky. Once attached to a particular idea, they start to work as an organizing principle through which everything pertaining to that idea is seen. Though the public structures metaphor might seem pretty pedestrian, it does effectively direct people's thinking toward less familiar and perhaps more valuable roles of government.

The surest sign of a successful metaphor is its ability to reproduce. In the Cultural Logic project, subjects routinely extended and embellished the public structures metaphor, spontaneously applying it to new aspects of government (post offices and traffic lights) and teasing out its implications for other areas of public life (taxes). Indeed, other research has shown that people not only remember metaphors better than the actual wording of texts but they also continue to use those metaphors when thinking further about the same topic.

In one study, participants read a short passage about the economy, either one that explicitly compared economic development to auto racing or one that did not. Subjects in the auto-racing group read "China and India have turbocharged ahead economically," for example, while those in the control group read "China and India have pulled ahead economically." Those who read the passage with explicit auto-racing metaphors continued to use auto-racing metaphors when they talked about the economy, even several days later when they could only vaguely recall the actual content of the original passage. The effect was most pronounced when the metaphor was signaled with a simile, such as "Economic development is like auto racing."

"Metaphor is an indispensable tool for informed decision-making," Grady says. Faced with massively complex issues like climate change and good governance, "it can be difficult to imagine what our responsibility could be. Metaphor helps by putting things on a human scale. Any metaphor is a distortion, but some are more constructive than others. The challenge is to find metaphors that do some good."

The Obama administration has discarded some metaphors it decided weren't doing any good. Soon after taking office, the White House announced it was decommissioning the term "war on terror." Around the same time, Gil Kerlikowske, head of the White House Office of National Drug Control Policy, said he was surrendering the phrase "war on drugs," too. "Regardless of how you try to explain to people it's a 'war on drugs' or a 'war on a product,' people see a war as a war on them," Kerlikowske told the *Wall Street Journal*. "We're not at war with people in this country."

States of war, in fact, tend to rally the metaphorical troops—and most of these metaphors have to do with football.

There are around 1,700 sports metaphors in common use. One study of the figurative language deployed during the Gulf War identified fifty-nine different football metaphors alone. Diplomats *fumbled* relations with Saddam Hussein before he attacked Kuwait. Opponents of the war *sat on the sidelines* as air strikes *kicked off* hostilities. President George H. W. Bush *huddled* with advisors while his generals worked out a *ground game* for the army's advance. General Norman Schwarzkopf ("Stormin'" Norman; hey, what's in a name . . .) told his troops, "Iraq has *won the toss* and *elected to receive.*"

Schwarzkopf described the strategy of sending his soldiers on a flanking maneuver around the Iraqi forces as a "Hail Mary pass." In football, the Hail Mary (the *long bomb*; what's in a name, indeed) is typically a last desperate attempt by the losing team to score before time runs out.

This was a peculiar choice of metaphor, since America's chances of actually losing the Gulf War were exceedingly slim. Iraqi forces did outnumber U.S. forces, and at the time there was real concern that Saddam might use chemical weapons, but the United States had vastly superior firepower and intelligence. Plus, a Hail Mary pass usually comes at the end of a game; Schwarzkopf used it at the beginning. However inaccurate, the metaphor was effective because it primed those who heard it to regard the United States as the underdog, thereby tapping into the instinctive sympathy we have for gutsy, tenacious teams that come from behind to win.

Comedian George Carlin remarked on the martial nature of football metaphors in his famous routine comparing gridiron clashes with baseball games. He noted that baseball has the "seventh-inning stretch" but football has the "two-minute warning." In football, you receive a "penalty" but in baseball you make an "error"—"Oops!"

"Baseball begins in the spring, the season of new life," Carlin observed. "Football begins in fall, when everything is dying . . . Football is concerned with 'downs'; What 'down' is it? Baseball is concerned with 'ups'; Who's 'up'?" Carlin concluded his compare-and-contrast exercise with a consideration of the games' fundamentally different objectives:

In football, the object is for the quarterback, otherwise known as the field general, to be on target with his aerial assault, riddling the defense by hitting his receivers with deadly accuracy, in spite of the blitz, even if he has to use the shotgun. With short bullet passes and long bombs, he marches his troops into enemy territory, balancing this aerial assault with a sustained ground attack which punches holes in the forward wall of the enemy's defensive line.

In baseball, the object is to go home and to be safe.

Metaphorical choices are no laughing matter, especially in politics. In addressing Iranian nuclear ambitions, for example, entirely different primes result from phrases like "axis of evil" (President Bush) and "If countries like Iran are willing to unclench their fist, they will find an extended hand from us" (President Obama). The word "axis" is a loaded term alluding to the warmongering Axis powers of Germany, Japan, and Italy during World War II, while the word "evil" encourages people to see things in black or white. Unclenched fists and extended hands, in contrast, invite associations of negotiation, compromise, and reconciliation. Political crises are not resolved simply by choosing alternate metaphors, of course. But, as the Gilovich experiment demonstrated, metaphors do skew the pitch by putting into play different associations and analogies that, in turn, prompt different attitudes and behaviors.

One of the most pervasive political metaphors is A NATION IS A BODY, popularized by none other than that scourge of metaphorical language, Thomas Hobbes. *Leviathan* even contains an image of the "body politic": a giant monarch whose body is populated by the much smaller bodies of his subjects. The "nation = body" metaphor often occurs in debates about that perennially contentious issue, immigration. If a nation is a body, this analogy goes, then it is vulnerable to infection and contamination from "foreign" bodies, too.

In the early 1920s, corporal metaphors were particularly conspicuous in newspaper stories and op-eds about proposed immigration restrictions and national origin quotas. One writer at the time urged passage of a law that would

> give America a chance to digest the millions of unassimilated, unwelcome and unwanted aliens that rest so heavily in her.

Current body political metaphors may be less crude than those from the 1920s, but they are no less influential.

In one experiment specifically designed to explore the priming effects of the "nation = body" metaphor, a group of participants read an article, ostensibly from a popular science magazine, describing airborne bacteria as ubiquitous and harmful to human health. Another group read a similar article describing airborne bacteria as ubiquitous but harmless to human health.

Both groups then read parallel articles about the history of U.S. domestic issues other than immigration. The only difference between the two articles was that one contained "nation = body" metaphors (e.g., "After the Civil War, the United States experienced an unprecedented *growth spurt*, and is *scurrying* to create new laws that will give it a chance to *digest* the millions of innovations") and the other did not (e.g., "After the Civil War, the United States experienced an unprecedented period of innovation, and efforts are now under way to create new laws to control the millions of innovations").

Both groups then answered two questionnaires. The first gauged their agreement with statements about immigration and the minimum wage (e.g., "It's important to increase restrictions on who can enter the United States" and "It's important to increase the minimum wage in the United States"). The second assessed their concerns about contamination (e.g., "To what extent did the article on airborne bacteria increase your desire to protect your body from harmful substances?"). Subjects who read the article describing airborne bacteria as harmful reported being more concerned about contamination. No surprise there.

But the same people also expressed more negative views about immigration when America was metaphorically described as a body. Those who read the more neutral description of U.S. domestic issues had more positive views of immigration, even though they also read the article describing airborne bacteria as harmful. Both groups' views about the minimum wage were about the same because, unlike immigration, the "nation = body" metaphor does not attend that issue. The researchers concluded that manipulating a person's attitude toward one issue (personal health) affects that person's attitude toward an entirely unrelated issue (immigration)—if the two issues are metaphorically linked.

If you increase a person's concern about contamination and then prime the "nation = body" metaphor, opinions about immigration change. More literal descriptions do not have this effect. And, like the subjects in the Lhermitte and Bargh experiments, people are not aware of the shift.

The body politic is a metaphorical battleground, with different conceptions of social issues vying to colonize public opinion. These metaphors tend to become more propitious, or more pernicious, the more they are repeated. In *The Woman in the Body: A Cultural Analysis of Reproduction*, Emily Martin chronicled historical metaphors of menstruation to reveal the hidden assumptions gestating in supposedly factual descriptions. Noting that men have written most of the medical textbooks on the subject, Martin cites one standard reference work as follows:

When fertilization fails to occur, the endometrium is shed, and a new cycle starts. This is why it used to be taught that "menstruation is the uterus crying for lack of a baby."

Martin argues that metaphors like this, repeated in textbook after textbook, frame menstruation in terms of failure—specifically, the failure to reproduce—and hence contributed to historically negative views of the process. The same was true for menopause since, if menstruation is the failure to reproduce once, menopause is the failure to reproduce forever.

Medical texts therefore described this stage in a woman's life as a pathological state rather than a natural part of aging. "At every point in the system, functions 'fail' and falter," Martin writes. "Follicles 'fail to muster the strength' to reach ovulation. As functions fail, so do the members of the system decline: 'breasts and genital organs gradually atrophy,' 'wither,' and become 'senile.'"

Susan Sontag made a similar point in her books dissecting the metaphors of cancer and HIV/AIDS, which, she noted, usually depict the diseases in terms of military invasions and alien contaminations. Sontag argued that the associations triggered by these metaphorical descriptions create an unhelpful and unjustified sense of fear. "Illness is not a metaphor," Sontag wrote. "The most truthful way of regarding illness—and the healthiest way of being ill—is one most purified of, most resistant to, metaphoric thinking."

But, as Glucksberg's Stroop test showed, metaphorical thinking is hard to resist, especially since so much of it takes place below the surface. Psychologists Gary Sherman and Gerald Clore conducted moral Stroop tests to demonstrate the influence of metaphorical associations on some of our most fundamental judgments.

Sherman and Clore showed subjects fifty words suggesting immorality ("greed," "cheat," and "liar") and fifty words suggesting morality ("honesty," "justice," and "virtuous"), each of which was randomly presented in either black or white. Participants had to name as quickly as possible the color of the ink in which the words were printed. Subjects were able to name the color faster when the immoral words were printed in black and the moral words were printed in white. Seeing the word "greed" in white ink, for example, created the same kind of cognitive dissonance as seeing the word "green" in blue ink.

In a variation on the experiment, some participants copied out by hand an unethical statement. Those who copied out the statement identified words in black faster than those who did not copy out the statement.

The researchers concluded that our moral judgments are closely linked to our concepts of darkness and light. This light-dark nexus is evident in metaphors like "She's pure as *the driven snow*" or "He's *whiter than white*." It shines through in clichés that describe periods of trouble and strife as "*dark* times" and periods of peace and prosperity as "*sunlit* uplands." It also explains why brides traditionally dress in white and why in fairy tales heroic knights inevitably arrive on white steeds.

A study involving participants from twenty different countries—including Japan, Germany, Afghanistan, and Thailand—consistently found that the color white had positive associations and the color black had negative associations. "Just as the word 'lemon' activates 'yellow,' so too do immoral words activate 'black' and moral words activate 'white,' " Sherman and Clore wrote.

Clore and a different research team performed another metaphorical Stroop test, this time varying the moral and immoral words by brightness. Participants identified the moral words more quickly when they were brighter and the negative words more quickly when they were darker. No surprise then that we see a *glimmer* of hope when the future looks *bright* and an aura of *gloom* surrounds those who've gone over to the *dark side*.

People automatically assume, the Clore group concluded, that bright objects are good and dark objects are bad. Studies even show that children tend to assume that black boxes contain negative objects and white boxes contain positive objects.

These associations carry over into our beliefs and behaviors, too. Priming studies show that people subliminally primed with black faces are more hostile during a competitive game than those primed with white faces. Dutch researchers performing a similar experiment found that whites subliminally exposed to black faces had more negative attitudes toward blacks than whites who were not exposed to faces of any color.

In another experiment, Emory University psychologist Drew Weston and other researchers produced two different versions of a putative campaign advertisement for Barack Obama. One version featured a light-skinned black family and the other featured a darker-skinned black family. Subjects who had seen the version with the darker-skinned family were less likely to express support for Obama than those who had seen the version with the light-skinned family.

Results like these correlate with statistics on discrimination. Stanford psychologist Jennifer Eberhardt, for example, has found that, in cases involving a black defendant and a white murder victim, jurors are influenced by the extent to which the defendant appears stereotypically black, defined as having a broad nose, thick lips, and dark skin. Darker-skinned African-American defendants are more than twice as likely to get the death penalty than lighter-skinned African-American defendants for equivalent crimes involving white victims.

Eberhardt and Aneeta Rattan, another Stanford psychologist, carried out research showing that white people primed to think about blacks, by reading a list of names regarded as stereotypically African-American, are more likely to notice a gorilla in a short video clip. The clip is based on a video (which can be seen at http://viscog.beckman.illinois.edu/flashmovie/15.php) of a group of students passing around basketballs. The viewer's task: count only the passes made by players in white shirts, excluding the passes made by players in black shirts. About halfway through the clip, a person dressed in a gorilla suit nonchalantly strolls through the middle of the group. Less than half of viewers, who are intent on counting the passes, typically tend to notice the gorilla. In the Eberhardt and Rattan experiment, though, white participants primed with stereotypically African-American names noticed the gorilla more often than those primed with stereotypically white names. The researchers concluded that metaphorical associations—even erroneous and offensive ones like that between African Americans and apes—can determine what we see and, if not countered, can work to reinforce nonconscious prejudices.

The "Macbeth effect" is another example of how metaphorical associations exert a kind of unconscious gravitational pull on our actions. In this experiment, participants read stories containing either moral or immoral scenarios. Those who read stories about immoral acts were more likely to buy cleaning products and to take an antiseptic wipe after the testing session ended. The researchers even found that the act of washing their hands alleviated some of the uneasiness subjects felt after reading stories about immorality. The simple act of hand cleaning has also been found to wash away regrets about past decisions. Thus, a perceived threat to moral purity can prompt actual physical cleansing, just as in Shakespeare's play Lady Macbeth tries in vain to scrub the stain of murder from her hands. And clean hands can promote a clean conscience, too, in contrast to Lady Macbeth's experience.

Researchers at the University of Toronto put undergraduates in a brand-new lab, asking half of them to clean their hands with an antiseptic wipe before touching a keyboard or mouse. They then asked all the participants to rate issues such as smoking, illegal drug use, and pornography on an 11-point scale, ranging from "very moral" to "very immoral." Those who had cleaned their hands rated the issues as more immoral than those who had not cleaned their hands, leading the research team to conclude that the metaphorical association between cleanliness and virtue primed participants who used an antiseptic wipe to deliver harsher moral judgments.

Another experiment, a kind of olfactory Stroop test, found that those exposed to citrus-scented cleaner not only identified cleaning-related words more rapidly but also kept their direct environment tidier during a subsequent snack break. Another study found that subjects in a room perfumed with citrus-scented Windex shared more of the money they won in an anonymous trust game than those in an unscented room.

Even the relative brightness of a room can influence actions. In one study, participants in a dim room cheated more often in the anonymous trust game than did participants in a brightly lit room, while participants wearing sunglasses behaved more selfishly than those wearing clear glasses.

Studies like these suggest that metaphors like "light = moral" and "dark = immoral" or "clean = good" and "dirty = evil" are more than just rhetorical devices. The associations that cluster around these concepts influence our judgments and behaviors. Darkness summons thoughts of immorality while also encouraging more immoral acts; clean smells make the concept of virtue more accessible while also prompting more virtuous behavior.

It is impossible to refrain altogether from metaphorical thinking, as Sontag so passionately urged. It is, however, imperative to carefully and consciously choose the metaphors we do use—and to be vigilant about those used by others. As Cultural Logic's work has shown, different metaphors can prompt very different attitudes and behaviors.

Metaphorical choices don't just reflect opinions and actions; they help shape them. So becoming aware of which metaphors are at work—and why—provides an essential reality check in political debate. Bringing metaphorical meanings to the surface enables us to evaluate them, and to decide for ourselves the extent of their influence.

George Orwell believed the political chaos that he felt characterized his time was connected to the decay of language. "If thought corrupts language," he wrote, "language can also corrupt thought." He had a particular aversion to political language, describing it as "designed to make lies sound truthful and murder respectable, and to give an appearance of solidity to pure wind."

The next time you feel yourself being blown away by a political slogan or borne aloft on a flight of impassioned rhetoric, take a moment to mull over the metaphors. After examining the motives behind the metaphor and the associations it raises, you may or may not be just as uplifted. Unlike the subjects in the Lhermitte and Bargh experiments, though, you will definitely know how the effect was achieved.

To stop the decay of language, and thereby help prevent politics from descending into chaos, Orwell urged us to heed Nietzsche's warning by taking Shelley's advice—keep political debate vitally metaphorical:

> A newly invented metaphor assists thought by evoking a visual image, while on the other hand a metaphor which is technically "dead" (e.g., iron resolution) has in effect reverted to being an ordinary word and can generally be used without loss of vividness. But in between these two classes there is a huge dump of worn-out metaphors which have lost all evocative power and are merely used because they save people the trouble of inventing phrases for themselves.

Worn-out political metaphors belong in the dustbin of history because language that saves people the trouble of inventing phrases for themselves also saves people the trouble of thinking for themselves. And that's the first step on the slippery slope to chaos. In confronting intractable political issues, it makes all the difference in the world whether the next step is sudden death or extra innings.

EXPERIENCE IS A COMB THAT NATURE GIVES TO BALD MEN

Giambattista Vico was born and lived most of his life in Naples. When he was seven years old, he fell headfirst from a ladder, injuring himself so badly that it took him three years to recover. During that time he was unable to attend school, so Vico's father undertook the young boy's education at home. Vico the younger eventually went on to graduate with a degree in law from the University of Naples, where he became professor of rhetoric. He died in 1744 at the age of seventy-six.

In *New Science*, Vico set himself the modest task of explaining all of human history, from the evolution of speech and writing to the rise and fall of empires. As a professor of rhetoric, Vico was particularly interested in language, and he believed that metaphor played a formative role not just in the evolution of language but also in the advance of civilization.

Vico identified three historical ages—the age of gods, the age of heroes, and the age of men. Each age had a specific form of language adapted to its specific stage of human development. The earliest language dated from a time "when pagan peoples had just embraced civilization," Vico wrote:

> We find that it was a mute and wordless language that used gestures or physical objects bearing a natural relationship to the ideas they wanted to signify. The second language used heroic emblems—such as similes, comparisons, images, metaphors, and descriptions of nature—as the principle lexicon of its heroic language, which was spoken in the age when heroes ruled. The third language was the human or civilized language which used vocabulary agreed upon by popular convention.

Vico noted the link between gesture and language long before mirror-neuron theorists Rizzolatti and Arbib, and he was also keenly sensitive to how ordinary speech is filled with figuration. "In all languages expressions for inanimate objects employ metaphors derived from the human body and its parts, or from human senses and emotions," he wrote, listing common examples such as the *lip* of a pitcher, the *neck* of a bottle, the *mouth* of a river.

Vico was also convinced that he had discovered the "universal principle of etymology . . . Words are transferred from physical objects and their properties to signify what is conceptual and spiritual." His views anticipate much of the conceptual metaphor and embodied cognition theories prevalent today.

Vico rarely left Naples. He endured extreme poverty and poor health. His work in philology and philosophy—and his ideas about metaphor—were largely ignored. That is, until 1825, when the Italian revolutionary Gioacchino de Prati introduced English poet Samuel Taylor Coleridge to Vico's *New Science*.

For a period of two years during the mid-1820s Prati, who was living in exile in England, visited Coleridge about once a week in Highgate in north London. Coleridge lived in the home of James Gilman, a surgeon, in part as a way to control his addiction to laudanum, a mixture of alcohol and opium derivatives.

Prati was a regular at the Gilmans' Thursday evening soirées, where Coleridge held forth on politics, religion, literature, and science. The two men also took long walks in the Gilmans' garden or sat in Coleridge's study to chat. Coleridge, famed for his verbosity, did most of the talking. Prati listened in rapt attention, comparing the poet's conversation to the dialogues of Plato.

"Coleridge expanded himself in a torrent of eloquence," Prati wrote in his autobiography. "All around him were so taken up with his speech, that seldom a word or a whisper was heard during the whole time he was addressing the company . . . The finest, loftiest ideas, pouring forth amidst the most blooming poetical phrases, allegories, and types, now spiced with Socratic irony, now strengthened by close and all-penetrating argumentation, afforded me an intellectual banquet, nowhere to be met either here or in any part of the continent."

During one of Prati and Coleridge's strolls, talk turned to the then obscure thinker Vico. Coleridge expressed an interest in Vico's work, so on his next visit Prati lent him a copy of *New Science*, wherein Coleridge was afforded an intellectual banquet of his own.

Coleridge immediately and enthusiastically embraced Vico as anticipating many of his own ideas about metaphor and the imagination. "I am more and more delighted with G. B. Vico," he wrote to Prati. "I should twenty times successively in the perusal of the first volume . . . have exclaimed: '*Pereant qui ante nos nostra dixere*'" (May they perish who have expressed our bright ideas before us). It was largely owing to Coleridge's enthusiasm that Vico's ideas became influential in England.

Vico believed that metaphorical thought was not only essential to philosophy but intensely enjoyable, too. In *The Art of Rhetoric*, he suggested that the pleasure of metaphor lies in the hidden link between the source and the target, a connection Vico called the *ligamen*, from the Latin word *ligare*, meaning "to bind." (*Ligare* is the etymological root of English words such as "ligament," "ligature," and even "religion.") The orator, Vico wrote,

> makes beauty which is left to the hearer to discover; for it is present by virtue of the rational connection [*ligamen*] which, when the hearer discovers it, unites the extremes to allow for the contemplation of similarity and thus reveals the beauty which the orator brought to pass. Thus the hearer seems ingenious to himself and the acute saying is delightful because it is more known by the hearer than presented by the speaker.

The *ligamen* links metaphors with jokes, both of which deliver the same kick of recognition. Both metaphors and jokes involve unexpected twists and violated expectations. There is an initial sense of surprise or consternation, followed by a burst of insight and closure. There is a moment when you "get" a metaphor just as you "get" a joke. And "get" is precisely the right verb, since deciphering a metaphor is no spectator sport. Readers actively retrieve a metaphor's meaning, just as a punch line requires listeners to resolve a joke's incongruencies for themselves.

Metaphors thus involve a "co-operative act of comprehension," according to philosopher Ted Cohen, an act that involves seeking the hidden connection, the *ligamen*, which makes sense of the metaphor. So, though the speaker may make the metaphor, the hearer makes its meaning. Hearer and speaker are accomplices; the one unpacks what the other presents. In terms of creativity, producing a metaphor and penetrating one are almost the same act.

Metaphors are so entertaining because of the pleasure we get from figuring them out, as in the following saying, a brilliantly condensed lesson in the uselessness of the wisdom that comes with age:

Experience is a comb that nature gives to bald men.

Or, take this description of the sound of a harpsichord by British conductor Thomas Beecham:

Like two skeletons copulating on a corrugated tin roof.

Or, how about this spectacular simile from *Cider with Rosie* by Laurie Lee, which describes the effects of a life-long snuff habit on Granny Trill's nasal passages:

She had nostrils like badger-holes.

Each of these metaphors requires us to find the thread, however tenuous, connecting experience to bald-headed men with combs, fornicating skeletons to harpsichords, and snuff-eroded nostrils to badger holes. Once we find that thread, we scurry across it, completing the connection between these utterly unlike things. The originator has already done this high-wire act in his or her own mind. Through the metaphor, we are forced to perform the same feat. And cognitive gymnastics like this are good for us since they boost mood and sharpen mental skills.

Researchers at Radboud University in the Netherlands showed a group of students different sets of images. One set depicted negative situations (scenes of violence, car accidents, and drug addiction) and the other depicted neutral situations (pictures of traffic, geometric shapes, and expressionless faces). After viewing the images, the students had to solve a math problem, either one that was relatively easy or one that was more difficult. Those who had seen the disturbing images and then solved the more difficult math problem reported feeling less troubled than those who had seen the same images but solved the less difficult problem.

The Radboud research group repeated the experiment, this time using a "humorous stimulus" (i.e., a joke or a cartoon) instead of a math problem. Once again, subjects looked at neutral or negative pictures. They then looked at a joke/cartoon or a non-humorous but positive stimulus, like a picture of a father holding a newborn baby. Those who had seen the disturbing images reported feeling less troubled after reading a joke or looking at a cartoon than those who had seen the same images but then saw the man and his child.

These studies do more than just state the obvious (jokes cheer you up) or prove the much less obvious (math cheers you up). What really cheers you up, the researchers concluded, is the effort to resolve the cognitive dissonance inherent in both jokes and math problems.

A lot of cognitive effort goes into understanding jokes and solving math problems. Incongruities must be worked out, variables evaluated, inconsistencies reconciled. What jokes and math problems have in common—with each other and with metaphor—is the need to resolve cognitively dissonant elements. The greater the cognitive exertion, the researchers found, the greater the subsequent positive feelings.

Brain scans of people laughing—as a result of watching television sitcoms, for example, or reading cartoons from the *New Yorker*—show that finding something funny activates the same primal pleasure centers as food and sex. Moreover, jokes also trigger the brain regions involved in language comprehension, incongruity resolution, and association formation, the same ones needed for metaphor processing.

Why should jokes and metaphors give such pleasure? Because

we can't stand very much ambiguity. Cognitive dissonance makes us uneasy, and for good reason—survival depends on making the world as predictable as possible. So when we figure something out, when we impose order on what seems chaotic, we heave a psychological sigh of relief. The reestablishment of coherence is largely achieved through good old pattern recognition or, as Vico would have described it, our instinctive *ligamen*-knitting abilities.

One type of brain cell in particular—Von Economo cells—seems especially skilled at detecting and resolving incongruities. Discovered by Constantin von Economo and Georg Koskinas in 1925, these cells reside primarily in the frontoinsula cortex (FI) and the anterior cingulate cortex (ACC). The latter brain region is found only in humans, the great apes, and some whale and elephant species. The FI and the ACC are active during the processing of humorous stimuli (i.e., when you get a joke), and the ACC has been associated with ambiguity and error detection (i.e., the resolution of cognitive dissonance).

Von Economo cells seem to be central to our ability to quickly resolve incongruities, and may thus be central to our metaphorical abilities, too. Individuals with Asperger's syndrome and other autism spectrum disorders (ASD) have fewer Von Economo cells than those without ASD, which might help explain why so many with ASD struggle with figurative language.

Von Economo cells could also be crucial to how we understand mixed metaphors, those delightfully discombobulated comparisons that switch metaphorical horses in midstream. The great Roman rhetorician Quintilian warned of the dangers of the mixed metaphor:

> Above all things, care is to be taken . . . that whatever kind of metaphor we begin with, we conclude with the same. But many speakers, after commencing with a tempest, end with a fire or the fall of a building, an incongruity which is most offensive.

Alas, we haven't paid much heed to Quintilian. The *New Yorker* has run "Block That Metaphor" as a recurring heading under its "Newsbreaks" rubric since 1959. Newsbreaks, often sent in by readers, are typically funny or erroneous excerpts from other publications that were originally used to fill up leftover column inches at the bottoms of stories. But they soon became popular features in their own right. This "Block That Metaphor" headline, from *Tulsa World*, shows why:

STEP UP TO THE PLATE AND FISH OR CUT BAIT

as does this sentence, from *Our Town, N.Y.*:

> The moment that you walk into the bowels of the armpit of the cesspool of crime, you immediately cringe.

Karyn Hollis, a professor in the English Department at Villanova University, has compiled a "Block That Metaphor" archive of her own, culled from high school English papers. While not exactly mixed, these metaphors have certainly been excessively shaken and stirred:

> She grew on him like she was a colony of E. coli and he was room-temperature Canadian beef.

> He was deeply in love. When she spoke, he thought he heard bells, as if she were a garbage truck backing up.

Mixed and meandering metaphors like these are so much fun because they put our Von Economo cells' noses to the cognitively dissonant grindstone and make them sweat blood. However outlandish the comparisons may seem, we can still locate the *ligamen*.

But because we have to look so much longer and work so much harder to find the link, these metaphors deliver even greater pleasure. To use Vico's terminology, the metaphor is delightful because "it is more known by the hearer than presented by the speaker."

Absurdist literature, which also contains high levels of cognitive dissonance, produces the same effect. Psychologists asked a panel of undergraduates to read a modified version of Franz Kafka's short story "The Country Doctor," a nightmarish tale of a physician who makes a bizarre house call on a sick boy and his family. One group read a version in which the narrative gradually broke down, ended abruptly with a series of non sequiturs, and was accompanied by bizarre and totally unrelated illustrations. Another group read a parallel tale that made conventional sense, contained no non sequiturs, and was accompanied by illustrations related to the story.

Researchers then gave both groups sixty different letter strings, each of which was made up of six to nine letters, and told them that half the strings contained a pattern. Their task: identify the pattern and all the letter strings containing it. Those who had read the more absurd version of "The Country Doctor" were almost twice as accurate in their answers as those who had read the conventional story.

The researchers concluded that the incongruities in illogical stories, like the incongruities in jokes, spur the brain to look for patterns it might not otherwise detect. The same thing happens with advertisements, which also often require us to figure them out. Presented with an absurd story, or an absurd metaphorical comparison, we want to quickly restore equilibrium, so we instinctively look for the *ligamen*.

But how do we know when we've got hold of a good *ligamen*? Philosopher and self-described "devotee of metaphor" Max Black suggested an answer.

According to Black, a metaphor activates two thoughts of two different things at the same time, similar to psychologist Alan Leslie's description of the way metarepresentations work. The metaphor's meaning results from the interaction of these two thoughts. Black used one of the oldest metaphors in the book to illustrate his "interaction theory":

Man is a wolf.

When we call man a wolf, Black argued, we activate complex networks of meanings related to the metaphor's source and target. For the metaphor to make sense, we must attend to both meanings at once. The source (wolf) is not a substitute for the target (man), nor is it a fanciful embellishment. Rather, in comprehending the "Man is a wolf" metaphor, what we know of wolves interacts with what we know of man. The result: a wolf-man.

"What is needed," Black wrote, "is not so much that the reader shall know the standard dictionary meaning of 'wolf'—or to be able to use that word in literal senses—as he shall know what I will call the system of associated commonplaces . . . The important thing for the metaphor's effectiveness is not that the commonplaces shall be true, but that they should be readily and freely evoked." Naturally, Black provided a metaphor for how associated commonplaces work:

Suppose I look at the night sky through a piece of heavily smoked glass on which certain lines have been left clear. Then I shall see only the stars that can be made to lie on the lines previously prepared upon the screen, and the stars I do see will be seen as organized by the screen's structure. We can think of a metaphor as such a screen and the system of "associated commonplaces" of the focal word as the network of lines upon the screen. We can say that the principal subject is "seen through" the metaphorical expression—

or, if we prefer, that the principal subject is "projected upon" the field of the subsidiary subject.

So, when we read "Man is a wolf," man is immediately seen through the prism of wolf-associated commonplaces. We zoom in on those aspects of wolves that apply to man—sly, predatory, hungry, vicious—while those aspects that do not apply—four-legged, furry, litter-bearing, living in the woods—fade into the background.

Metaphor is a lens that clarifies and distorts. It focuses our attention on a specific set of associated commonplaces, but in so doing also narrows our view. Experiments have provided a very clear demonstration of how Black's model of metaphor works. In one study conducted in the United Kingdom, researchers asked participants their opinions of a certain Donald Leavis, a resident of Northern Ireland. They were given no information whatsoever about Mr. Leavis, except the metaphorical description that he was "the George Wallace of Northern Ireland."

They then jotted down what they knew about George Wallace, the fiercely segregationist Alabama politician who was paralyzed from the waist down by an assassin's bullet in 1972. They correctly noted that he was a Southern conservative, was disabled, had been married numerous times, and was a staunch opponent of civil rights.

They then jotted down what they believed about Mr. Leavis. Eleven of the twenty-nine participants mentioned Wallace's complicated love life when asked about him, but only two mentioned Leavis's marital status. Similarly, twenty-four of the twenty-nine mentioned Wallace's disability but just seven mentioned this in relation to Leavis. Nearly everyone, however, concluded that Leavis was a conservative politician with bigoted views. What the participants did not know was that Donald Leavis did not exist; he was an entirely fictional character made up by the study's organizers. This experiment demonstrates how we use associated commonplaces to understand metaphors.

Wallace's conservatism and bigotry transfer well to Northern Irish politics; his antipathy toward African Americans is analogous to the antipathy of conservative Protestants toward Catholics. Wallace's other characteristics, such as his marital troubles and his disability, are not as relevant to Northern Ireland, so they are not carried over to Donald Leavis. Leavis is "seen through" the network of associated commonplaces characteristic of George Wallace—or, if we prefer, those commonplaces are "projected upon" him. Those associations that resonate with both Leavis and Wallace are highlighted; those that don't are blacked out.

Whether these associated commonplaces are actually true is, as Black pointed out, irrelevant. The effectiveness of a metaphor depends not on the truth of its associations but on their easy accessibility, as the experiment with the "nation = body" metaphor showed.

Once a metaphor aligns the stars in a specific constellation, we are primed to see things from exactly that point of view. And we seem ingenious to ourselves, and are therefore mightily pleased, when we unite the extremes that reveal the hidden similarities between source and target. Cicero identified this intellectual sleuthing as metaphor's essential pleasure principle:

Metaphorical terms give people much more pleasure, if the metaphor is a good one. I suppose that the cause of this is either that it is a mark of cleverness of a kind to jump over things that are obvious and choose other things that are far-fetched; or because the hearer's thoughts are led to something else and yet without going astray, which is a very great pleasure.

Of course, metaphors are not always good and we can go badly astray when looking for the *ligamen*. This is, in fact, what differentiates successful from unsuccessful metaphors.

The most successful metaphors are the least expected. "Metaphorical force requires a combination of novelty with fitness, of the odd with the obvious," as art historian Nelson Goodman put it. "The good metaphor satisfies while it startles." Metaphor is a bit like alchemy in this respect; it creates novelty by combining the already familiar, not by finding the utterly new. The more distant the source (badger holes, for instance) from the target (Granny Trill's nostrils), the more surprising and delightful the metaphor. But there has to be a conceptual tie that binds source to target. Otherwise, the result is mere surrealism.

It is difficult to think of two things more remote from one another than nostrils and badger holes. Yet this description immediately conveys a precise and vivid image. Both orifices are roughly oval in shape; the entrances to both are dark, permitting only limited visibility; and, depending on how far you want to burrow into this particular comparison, there is an analogy to be made between nose hairs and the tree roots dangling from the roofs of badger holes. All this makes Laurie Lee's line a successful metaphor.

The following line, by the poet Isidore Lucien Ducasse—Comte de Lautréamont, who was born in Uruguay and moved to Paris, where he wrote one startlingly beautiful book, *Les Chants de Maldoror*, before dying in 1870 at the age of twenty-four—is not a successful metaphor:

Beautiful like the accidental meeting of an umbrella and a sewing machine on a dissection table.

An umbrella, a sewing machine, and a dissection table are about as unlikely a combination as nostrils and badger holes. But the *liga-*

men connecting these three things is too threadbare to bear much weight. The image is vivid, but the *ligamen* doesn't lead anywhere.

Aristotle noted the need for connective tissue in his treatise on rhetoric. "In using metaphors to give names to nameless things, we must draw them not from remote but from kindred and similar things," he wrote, "so that the kinship is clearly perceived as soon as the words are said." For a good metaphor, juxtaposition is not enough; the things juxtaposed must ultimately gel. In *Biographia Literaria*, the rambling, rambunctious account of his literary beliefs, Coleridge described how this process of metaphorical fusion works.

Biographia Literaria was originally intended as the preface to a book of anecdotes about Coleridge's life and times. In typically prolix fashion, though, Coleridge inflated the preface into the book itself. He finished it in 1816 while residing in the Gilman household.

Coleridge, like Vico, believed the essence of thought was metaphor. He even coined a new adjective for this imaginative blending—esemplastic. "I constructed it myself," he wrote of the term, "from the Greek words [*esem*, meaning 'one,' and *plastic*, meaning 'to shape'], to shape into one."

In his notebooks, Coleridge provides an almost neuroscientific description of how esemplastic power works. It's almost as if he was thinking of Von Economo cells when he wrote:

I feel too intensely the omnipresence of all in each, platonically speaking; or, psychologically, my brain-fibers, or the spiritual light which abides in the brain-marrow, as visible light appears to do in sundry rotten mackerel and other smashy matters, is of too general an affinity with all things, and though it perceives the difference of things, yet is eternally pursuing the likenesses, or, rather, that which is common [among them].

In its eternal pursuit of likenesses, the brain spins out a clew of associated commonplaces, which it follows through the metaphorical labyrinth. It shuffles through all possible combinations, explores all possible routes, then brings together those strands that actually lead somewhere. Metaphor is the mind's great raveling.

Laudanum was Coleridge's drug of choice, but Polish science fiction author Stanislaw Lem discovered a far more addictive substance.

In *The Futurological Congress*, Lem describes an apocalyptic vision of the future in which all knowledge is derived from hallucinogens rather than direct experience. Persons of faith visit their local "psychedelicatessen" to purchase a dose of *genuflix* for those moments of spiritual awakening. *Algebrine* endows users with an encyclopedic knowledge of higher mathematics, while *amnesol* is just the thing for removing unwanted but persistent memories. *Authentium* creates instant memories of things that never happened: "A few grams of *dantine*, for instance, and a man goes around with the deep conviction that he has written *The Divine Comedy*."

The mother of all psychedelics, though, is surely *metamorphine*, which Lem praises for allowing partakers to "have an affair with a goat, thinking it's Venus de Milo herself."

In reality, we're all on metamorphine all the time—and we first get in the habit as children.

HOW SHOULD ONE REFER TO THE SKY?

The *Prose Edda*, the thirteenth-century Icelandic epic by Snorri Sturluson, is a handbook for aspiring poets wanting to master traditional forms of verse. It provides instruction in the linguistic conventions and poetic etiquette most likely to impress potential patrons. Sturluson, born in 1179 or thereabouts, was the undisputed master of this art.

Sturluson was descended from the Icelandic folk hero Egil Skallagrímsson. Another family raised him, however. Jon Loptsson, one of Iceland's most powerful and highly cultured leaders, adopted the young Snorri in order to settle a feud. Sturluson did well for himself, marrying one of the wealthiest women in Iceland and going on to become one of the kingdom's richest men.

But, during a stay in Norway, Sturluson became embroiled in political intrigue. He was branded a traitor back home and was assassinated, with an axe, in 1241 by two former sons-in-law.

The word "saga" is Old Norse for "tale," and most sagas—including those in the *Prose Edda*—are glamorized tales of Scandinavian folk history written between the eleventh and fourteenth centuries. The stories are based on an oral tradition dating back to the Viking Age, roughly between 800 and 1100.

The *Prose Edda* is different, though. In addition to the usual tales of derring-do, Sturluson offers tips for court poets, known as skalds, seeking royal patronage. By far the most important thing for skalds to know was how to make a proper kenning.

A kenning is a metaphorical circumlocution consisting of paired nouns or a noun phrase. For example, in ancient Icelandic verse, a sword is not a sword but an "icicle of blood"; a ship is not a ship but the "horse of the sea"; and eyes are not eyes but the "moons of the forehead." Similarly, the earth is "the floor of the hall of the winds" or "the sea trodden on by animals," while fire is "destroyer of timber" or "the sun of houses."

The *Prose Edda* contains lists of the most popular kennings for the characters populating various myths and legends. So it's also a kind of *Burke's Peerage and Gentry* for the gods and goddesses, heroes and villains of ancient Icelandic lore.

The word "kenning" comes from the Old Norse verb *kenna*, which is also a "seeing = knowing" metaphor, meaning "to know, recognize, or perceive." The etymology survives in words meaning "to know" in various Scandinavian languages as well as in German and Dutch. *Kenna* is also the source of the English "can" as well as the somewhat arcane "ken," as found in the expression "beyond my ken," meaning "beyond my knowledge."

Though invented by ancient Icelandic bards, kennings are still quite common. Simple phrases such as "house plant," "head ache," "brain storm" and "pay wall" are all basic kennings, however prosaic, as is "pain in the ass," as in you are not you but a "pain in the ass." My personal favorite is "prairie schooner," a kenning for the covered wagons in which nineteenth-century settlers sailed into the American West.

Kids are skilled skalds, too, and simple kenning-like re-namings are often among the first metaphors they produce. I remember standing at a window with my eldest son, Gilles, when he was about two. He pointed to the sun and blurted out "big sky lamp," a classic kenning if there ever was one.

My other son, Tristan, came up with a clever kenning after we got a kitten one Christmas. Inspired by the burrito-like sandwiches he liked for lunch, he christened the little plastic bags we used to remove the cat's droppings from the litter tray "crap wraps."

Further evidence for the primacy of kennings in the evolution of metaphor comes from bonobos, considered the closest living primate to humans. Bonobos communicate through hand gestures as well as vocalizations, and at least one bonobo, Kanzi, can make metaphors.

Primatologist Sue Savage-Rumbaugh taught Kanzi to communicate using a keyboard made up of geometric symbols. He can comprehend hundreds of spoken English words and, through the keyboard, can use hundreds of others. By combining the symbols on his keyboard, Kanzi can also make simple kennings. He produced a kenning for "duck," for example, by combining the symbols for "water" and "bird."

Children share with bonobos an instinctive metaphor-making ability. Every parent can recite the adorable metaphorical things their offspring say. Developmental research routinely finds that kids produce metaphors with alacrity and ease. In one study, a child described a flashlight battery as a "sleeping bag all rolled up and ready to go over to a friend's house"; another described a hairbrush as "a park with grass"; another described baldness as having a "barefoot head."

Most early childhood metaphors are simple noun-noun substitutions, or proto-kennings. These metaphors tend to emerge first during pretend play, when children are between the ages of twelve and twenty-four months. As psychologist Alan Leslie proposed in his theory of mind, children at this age start to create metarepresentations through which they imaginatively manipulate both the objects around them and their ideas about those objects. At this stage, metaphor is, literally, child's play. During pretend play, children effortlessly describe objects as other objects and then use them as such. A comb becomes a centipede; cornflakes become freckles; a crust of bread becomes a curb.

Metaphors like these are endearing but rudimentary, based exclusively on perceptual similarities among physical objects. Around the same time Gilles came up with his "big sky lamp" kenning, he paused during dinner one evening, lifted a sprig of broccoli from his plate, contemplated it for a minute, and exclaimed: "Tree!"—a classic Aristotelian case of giving the thing a name that belongs to something else.

Young children are such prolific metaphor producers because their pattern recognition circuits, not yet confined by conventional categorizations, are working full blast. So kids routinely come up with a profusion of metaphorical comparisons, but only a few of them are on target.

In one study, researchers told children ranging in age from preschoolers to college students a brief story—about someone who was very quiet, for example, or someone who was very sad. They then asked them to provide an appropriate simile to end the story. Preschoolers produced by far the most metaphors, but many of those metaphors—"quiet as a nose" or "sad as a shirt"—didn't make much sense. While young children are very good at giving things names that belong to other things, they are less adept with more complex forms of figurative language.

Children, like adults, are skilled in metaphors based on perceptual similarities. Psychologist Ellen Winner presented children between the ages of three and ten with a variety of objects—blocks of various shapes, odd kitchen gadgets, a clothespin, some crayons—and offered three possible names for each object: the literal name, an anomalous name (an upside-down mop was called "a toaster," for example), and a metaphorical name (the upside-down mop was called "a flower"). Even three-year-olds successfully selected the metaphorical names as more accurate than the anomalous ones.

But children can also be oblivious to the less obvious perceptual similarities contained in metaphors. I once observed my five-year-old daughter Hendrikje playing in the garden with one of her dolls. She laid the doll down among some plant stems and began covering it under a blanket of dried leaves and grass. When I asked Hendrikje what she was doing, she said, "It's time for my doll's nap in the flowerbed." Unaware of the metaphorical meaning of this kenning, Hendrikje interpreted "flowerbed" literally.

One study found that this literal streak is common when kids are confronted with more complex metaphors. Children listened to short stories that ended with either a literal or metaphorical sentence. In a story about a little girl on her way home, for example, the literal ending was "Sally was a girl running to her home," while the metaphoric ending was "Sally was a bird flying to her nest."

Researchers asked the children to act out the stories using a doll. Five- to six-year-olds tended to move the Sally doll through the air when the last sentence was "Sally was a bird flying to her nest," taking the phrase literally. Eight- to nine-year-olds, however, tended to move her quickly across the ground, taking the phrase metaphorically.

Children's understanding falters even more as metaphors become more conceptual. Researchers presented children between the ages of six and twelve with the metaphorical sentence "After many years of working at the jail, the prison guard had become a hard rock that could not be moved." They then asked them to paraphrase the sentence.

The youngest children said the guard had been physically transformed into a rock, or that the prison itself was somehow full of rocks. The eight-year-olds recognized that the guard himself was like a rock in some way. But they, too, focused on the physical, suggesting the guard had muscles that were as hard as rocks. Only those aged ten and above realized that the guard had become psychologically like a rock—insensitive and unfeeling.

In the 1960s, Solomon Asch and his collaborator Harriet Nerlove explored the evolution in children of what they called "double function terms," words like "warm" and "cold" and "bitter" and "sweet" that Asch had previously identified as describing the psychological characteristics of people as well as the physical properties of things. They theorized that we use physical terms to describe psychological states owing to a direct experience of similarity. The first person to describe someone as "cold," they suggested, sensed a resemblance between an object (a block of ice, perhaps) and a human being.

To trace the development of double function terms in children, Asch and Nerlove presented groups of kids with a collection of different objects—ice water, sugar cubes, powder puffs—and asked them to identify the ones that were cold, sweet, or soft. This, of course, they were easily able to do.

Asch and Nerlove then asked the children, Can a person be cold? Can a person be sweet? Can a person be soft? While preschoolers understood the literal physical references, they did not understand the metaphorical psychological references. They described cold people as those not dressed warmly; hard people were those with firm muscles. One preschooler described his mother as "sweet" but only because she cooked sweet things, not because she was nice.

Asch and Nerlove observed that only between the ages of seven and ten did children begin to understand the psychological meanings of these descriptions. Some seven- and eight-year-olds said that hard people are tough, bright people are cheerful, and crooked people do bad things. But only some of the eleven- and twelve-year-olds were able to actually describe the metaphorical link between the physical condition and the psychological state. Some nine- and ten-year-olds, for instance, were able to explain that both the sun and bright people "beamed." Children's metaphorical competence, it seems, is limited to basic perceptual metaphors, at least until early adolescence.

Max Black's theory of associated commonplaces suggests why children struggle with more complex metaphors. To understand how an upside-down mop is like a flower, a child has only to understand that the two things look alike. The metaphor is right there on the surface, easy to see. To understand how a prison guard is like a rock, however, involves understanding how a physical state resembles a psychological state, a much more difficult thing to see, especially when you have no experience of how harsh environments can make people emotionally callous.

Children have trouble understanding more sophisticated metaphors because they have not yet had the life experiences needed to acquire the relevant cache of associated commonplaces. They won't understand how a prison guard can become a hard rock until they have had a few run-ins with rock-hard people themselves.

In his studies of early childhood development, psychologist Jean Piaget found the same thing. He gave kids between the ages of nine and eleven a list of ten proverbs, such as "Little streams make mighty rivers" and "When the cat's away the mice will play." He also gave them a selection of sentences in random order, some of which expressed the meaning of the proverb in a different form. The children had to read the proverbs and find the most appropriate matches, which they consistently failed to do. The kids' performance improved, though, when they were provided with an appropriate context for the proverb. They did even better, a later study found, when shown pictures of possible proverb interpretations and asked to choose the right image.

I had firsthand experience of this childhood metaphor deficit with Tristan, that kenning connoisseur and budding skald, when he was eleven and had to write an essay about the poem "Nettles" by Vernon Scannell for a school entrance exam:

My son aged three fell in the nettle bed.
"Bed" seemed a curious name for those green spears,
That regiment of spite behind the shed:
It was no place for rest. With sobs and tears

The boy came seeking comfort and I saw
White blisters beaded on his tender skin.
We soothed him till his pain was not so raw.
At last he offered us a watery grin,
And then I took my billhook, honed the blade

And went outside and slashed in fury with it
Till not a nettle in that fierce parade
Stood upright any more. And then I lit
A funeral pyre to burn the fallen dead,
But in two weeks the busy sun and rain
Had called up tall recruits behind the shed:
My son would often feel sharp wounds again.

School entrance exams are, to use a kenning, the bane of eleven-year-olds. (The word "bane," incidentally, comes from the Icelandic *bani*, meaning "to slay or wound.") I had been working with

Tristan for almost a year to prepare for the tests. I doubt that I was much help with math, but I thought I could make a real contribution with literature. We went over dozens of poems and stories, and metaphor was one of the literary devices we discussed at some length.

The assignment for the essay was to explain what "Nettles" is about. Tristan answered that the poem is about a boy who is stung by nettles behind the shed and whose dad cuts down the nettles and burns them, but they grow back. So far, so good.

"Nettles" is indeed about a boy who is stung by nettles. But it's also about a father's desire to protect his son—from actual nettles and from all the metaphorical nettles that await the boy in later life. At the end of the poem, the father realizes he will never be able to do this. Tristan completely missed the poem's metaphorical significance. Those associated commonplaces were just not in place for him yet, and they may never be—unless he himself becomes a father one day. Needless to say, he didn't do so well on the test.

Cognitive scientist Dedre Gentner, who has done extensive research on metaphor and children, constructed a time line of metaphorical development in young people based on a sliding scale of increasingly complex similes. She presented three different age groups—five- to six-year-olds, nine- to ten-year-olds, and college students—with three different kinds of similes.

Attributional similes, such as "Pancakes are like nickels," were based on physical similarities; both are round and flat. Relational similes, such as "A roof is like a hat," were based on functional similarity; both sit on top of something to protect it. Double similes, such as "Plant stems are like drinking straws," were based on physical as well as functional similarities; both are long and cylindrical and both bring liquid from below to nourish a living thing.

Gentner found that youngsters in all age groups had no problem comprehending the attributional similes. But only the older kids understood the relational and double similes. In subsequent research, Gentner has found that giving young children additional context enhances their ability to pick up on the kind of relational comparisons characteristic of more complex metaphors.

Gentner and colleagues showed preschoolers a set of pictures, each of which depicted animals in distinct spatial configurations. Some pictures displayed physical similarities; the animals matched but the spatial configurations did not (a black cat above a white cat, for example, and a black cat next to a white cat). Other pictures displayed relational similarities; the spatial configurations matched but the animals did not (a black cat above a white cat and a black dog above a white dog). During the experiment, researchers showed a card depicting a relational similarity to the children while giving it a made-up name: "This is a zimbo." They then showed the children two other cards—one relational and one physical—and asked, "Which one of these is a zimbo?"

When children were given only one example of a zimbo—say, a black cat above a white cat—they tended to opt for a physical match, saying the picture of the black cat above the white cat was the same as the picture of the black cat next to the white cat. But when given two examples of a zimbo—a black cat above a white cat *and* a black dog above a white dog—they tended to opt for a relational match, selecting a picture of a black bird above a white bird rather than pictures of dogs or cats. Gentner and colleagues concluded that the extra context allowed children to make comparisons, which in turn enabled them to spot novel relational concepts.

Like the Asch and Nerlove experiments, Gentner's results suggest that though metaphor making starts early, metaphor comprehension develops in stages, beginning with basic physical comparisons before moving on to more conceptual and psychological domains. As children's knowledge of the world grows, so does their metaphorical range.

The same is true for adults. Any metaphor is comprehensible only to the extent that the domains from which it is drawn are familiar.

In the *Prose Edda*, for example, the answer, in kenning form, to the question "How should one refer to the sky?" is "Ymir's skull." That answer only makes sense if you happen to know that Ymir was a primeval giant whose body was believed to have formed the world, his skull becoming the dome of the sky and his blood becoming the ocean. Without a set of associated commonplaces that includes Old Norse myths and legends, anyone trying to understand this metaphor would be in the same position as Tristan trying to figure out the psychological significance of "Nettles."

This same lack of essential context is what perplexed the crew of the Starship *Enterprise* when they encountered the Tamarians in the "Darmok" episode of *Star Trek: The Next Generation*. The Tamarians speak a language no one has yet been able to fully decipher. The Tamarian tongue is so elusive because it is so allusive, consisting entirely of kennings from the alien race's mythology and history.

In Tamarian, for example, "cooperation" is expressed by the phrase "Darmok and Jalad at Tanagra" because Tamarian folklore includes the tale of Darmok and Jalad, two warriors who banded together to fight a common foe on the island of Tanagra. Other Tamarian kennings include "Darmok on the ocean" for loneliness, "Shaka, when the walls fell" for failure, "The river Temarc in winter" for silence, "Sokath, his eyes open" for understanding, and "Kiteo, his eyes closed" for refusal to understand. Snorri Sturluson could not have done better.

In comprehending metaphor, context is king. Behavioral economics pioneer Amos Tversky demonstrated how context influences our perception of similarities, and how our perception of similarities influences the way we—children and adults alike—interpret metaphors.

Tversky presented adults with the names of four different countries and asked them to sort the countries into the pairs that were most similar. Given the set Austria, Sweden, Poland, and Hungary, for example, subjects tended to group Austria with Sweden (two Western European countries) and Poland with Hungary (two Eastern European countries).

But when Tversky substituted "Norway" for "Poland," he got a different answer. Given the set Austria, Sweden, Norway and Hungary, subjects tended to group Sweden with Norway (two Nordic countries) and Austria with Hungary (two Central European countries). In psychology, this shift in context is known as framing, a process analogous to the clearing of lines on Max Black's piece of heavily smoked glass. The context of a comparison determines which lines we focus on, and those lines in turn demarcate the boundaries of what we see.

So the way a question is framed—which alternatives are offered, which words are chosen to describe those alternatives, and which associated commonplaces those alternatives evoke—has a powerful effect on which answers people give. Imagine the responses, for example, if Donald Leavis had been described as "the Nelson Mandela of Northern Ireland."

The correspondences conjured by metaphor are not fixed. They advance and recede based on context. When the frame changes, so do the associated commonplaces. Tversky therefore concluded that assessments of similarity are made on the fly, in the same way as interpretations of metaphors, an observation he demonstrated using a simile:

A good metaphor is like a good detective story. The solution should not be apparent in advance to maintain the reader's interest, yet it should seem plausible after the fact to maintain coherence of the story. Consider the simile "An essay is like a fish." At first, the statement is puzzling. An essay is not expected to be fishy, slippery, or wet. The puzzle is resolved when we recall that (like a fish) an essay has a head and a body, and it occasionally ends with a flip of the tail.

Psychologist Sam Glucksberg carried out a variation on Tversky's experiment, in which frame flipping is clearly evident. He presented adults with a set of four objects—paintings, billboards, pimples, and warts—and asked them to pair off those that were most similar. Most people grouped paintings with billboards and pimples with warts, an obvious enough choice. After all, paintings and billboards are both visual displays, while pimples and warts are both dermatological blemishes.

But then Glucksberg tilted the frame, substituting "statues" for "pimples." Given this new set—paintings, billboards, statues, and warts—most people grouped paintings with statues and billboards with warts. Paintings and statues are both forms of visual art, while warts and billboards are both blemishes—the former on a person's body, the latter on the landscape. As a result of the substitution, a fresh network of associated commonplaces emerged. The new frame produced a new metaphorical meaning. "The same pair of objects can be viewed as similar or different depending on the choice of a frame of reference," Tversky observed.

In metaphor, framing is the name of the game and our ability to swiftly swap frames increases with age. Take John Donne's famous line:

No man is an island.

This statement is one of those surprisingly common metaphors that are also literally true. It is, of course, blindingly obvious that no individual human being is a land mass surrounded on all sides by water. But seen through a different frame, these words take on an entirely different set of associated commonplaces. Like the "prison guard = rock" comparison, however, you have to have the relevant emotional experience and psychological knowledge before those associations fall into place.

This is one of the marvels of metaphor. Fresh, successful metaphors do not depend on conventional pre-existing associations. Instead, they highlight novel, unexpected similarities not particularly characteristic of either the source or the target—at least until the metaphor itself points them out.

Cognitive psychologists Roger Tourangeau and Lance Rips cite a beautiful example from the poem "90 North" by Randall Jarrell:

Like a bear to its floe, / I clambered to bed.

On the surface, a bed and an ice floe don't share many common features. One is cold, the other warm; one is hard, the other soft; one is typically found floating in the Arctic, the other is not. Yet, consider the simile for a moment and hidden similarities emerge.

The act of a bear climbing onto an ice floe is similar to the act of a person climbing into a bed. Both ice floes and beds are pale, flat, smooth, and white. The novelty of these associations—the fact that two such unlike things nevertheless share such striking similarities—makes this simile startling and beautiful. The best metaphors transform as they transfer.

In quizzing study participants about their favorite metaphors, Tourangeau and Rips found that people overwhelmingly prefer metaphors based on these kinds of emergent rather than obvious associations. Tourangeau and Rips asked a group of adults to rate a collection of metaphors on their aptness and comprehensibility. All the metaphors were simple X = Y statements involving animals.

In this particular collection, "The eagle is a lion among birds" was rated as the best and most comprehensible metaphor, while "The gorilla is a troop transport among land mammals" was rated as the worst and least comprehensible.

For "The eagle is a lion among birds" metaphor, the researchers also asked participants to list the properties they associated with the source (lion) and the target (eagle), just as in the Donald Leavis experiment. For lions, the most popular associations were: they live in Africa; they are cats; they are gold in color, large and strong; and they are predators. For eagles, the most popular associations were: they are endangered; they have feathers; they fly; and they are large and predatory.

The aptness of this metaphor, like the aptness of the ice floe–bed simile, depends on a small number of shared associations, and these associations are typically not the first things that spring to mind when considering either the source or the target in isolation. As Max Black put it, "It would be more illuminating . . . to say that the metaphor creates the similarity than to say that it formulates some similarity antecedently existing."

So the next time you admonish a rambunctious seven-year-old with the wise words "Look before you leap," don't be surprised if all that greets you is a blank stare. The wisdom of those words won't sink in until she has taken a few falls for herself. Similarly, a despondent teenager recovering from his first unrequited love affair won't find "There are plenty of fish in the sea" very helpful, at least not until he hooks up with someone else he likes even better. We see the world darkly, through Black's piece of heavily smoked glass. It takes time and lots of real-life encounters before children are able to clear new lines of sight.

The world is full of stinging nettles that grow back as fast as we can cut them down. "Experience is a good school," the German poet Heinrich Heine once quipped. "But the fees are high."

THE EARTH IS LIKE A
RICE PUDDING

C. S. Lewis—scholar, critic, Christian apologist—was an astute student of metaphor. In his 1939 essay "Bluspels and Flalansferes," he described a thought experiment in which the world had four dimensions instead of the three we can perceive. A four-dimensional world seems inconceivable, but he likened the task of imagining it to explaining to Flatlanders—a race of people who only know two dimensions: back and front, and left and right—that the world is round.

The Flatlanders think they live on an edgeless plane extending infinitely in all directions. They have no concept of, much less words for, height and depth. So how can anyone get across to them the idea of up and down? "As these Flatlanders are to you, so you might be to a creature who intuited four dimensions," Lewis wrote. Thanks to this analogy, what before was impossible to conceive—a four-dimensional world—acquires some semblance of meaning.

Over time, Lewis suggested, the analogy of "the Flatlanders' sphere" would become part of the culture, a kind of intellectual shorthand for the idea of a four-dimensional world. As time went on, "the Flatlanders' sphere" would be abbreviated to, say, Flalansfere and the term's connection to the original analogy would gradually be forgotten. The word "Flalansfere" would then become an extinct metaphor, the etymology of which was irretrievably lost.

Flalansfere "had an air of mystery from the first," Lewis mused. "Before the end I shall probably be building temples to it, and exhorting my countrymen to fight and die for the Flalansfere. But the Flalansfere, when once we have forgotten the metaphor, is only a noise."

Lewis's brief history of the Flalansfere is more or less how metaphors actually evolve, as evidenced through etymology itself and as demonstrated by Sam Glucksberg, the psychologist who performed the metaphorical Stroop test and adapted Amos Tversky's frame-flipping experiment.

Glucksberg put groups of people in a room and asked them to talk to one another about a collection of novel geometric shapes that did not have conventional names. Participants were free to describe the forms in any way they wished. They overwhelmingly chose to describe the shapes through analogies, and they very quickly compressed their analogies into metaphors.

One shape, for instance, consisted of two triangles placed one above the other. The triangle on top was inverted, with an arc curving down from it on both sides. This form was often described along the lines of "an hourglass with legs on each side." Once the form had been several times thus described, participants progressively shortened the description to the fewest possible words— from "hourglass with the legs" to "hourglass-shaped thing" to simply "hourglass." Thus was a metaphor born.

Name that shape: "hourglass" or "two triangles placed one above the other with the top one inverted, with an arc curving down on both sides"? *Courtesy of Sam Glucksberg.*

The point of Lewis's thought experiment, and of Glucksberg's actual experiment, is that the unknown can only be made known through metaphor and analogy. "When we pass beyond pointing to individual sensible objects, when we begin to think of causes, relations, of mental states or acts, we become incurably metaphorical," Lewis wrote. "We apprehend none of these things except through metaphor."

The analogical form of metaphor is especially useful when scientists communicate new discoveries. The history of science is, in fact, the history of good analogies. In 1665, Robert Hooke published *Micrographia*, his observations through a primitive microscope of everything from fly's eyes to pieces of cork. He was the first to observe that plants consisted of formations of small compartments, which Hooke called "cells" because of their resemblance to the rooms in which monks lived in monasteries.

French mathematician Jean-Baptiste-Joseph Fourier expressed his discovery of the "greenhouse effect" by comparing the atmosphere to a huge glass dome that trapped heat, thereby increasing the surface temperature of the earth, a metaphor that has lost much of its explanatory power, as the research of Cultural Logic has shown. German physicist Max Planck, a gifted pianist and cellist, conceived quantum theory in part by imagining electron orbits as the vibrating strings of a musical instrument.

Even string theory, which attempts to encompass matter and the fundamental forces of gravity, electromagnetism, and weak and strong interactions into a single framework, likens the universe to a lattice of eleven-dimensional oscillating strings. Try explaining *that* to the Flatlanders.

In response to a questionnaire about his working methods, Albert Einstein described the nature of analogical thinking with an analogy of his own:

> The words or the language, as they are written or spoken, do not seem to play any role in my mechanism of thought. The physical entities which seem to serve as elements in thought are certain signs and more or less clear images which can be "voluntarily" reproduced and combined . . . this combinatory play seems to be the essential feature in productive thought.

For Einstein, "combinatory play" was the essence of creative thought. It is also the essence of analogy, the process whereby a network of known relations is playfully combined with a network of postulated or newly discovered relations so that the former informs the latter. Analogical thinking makes unmapped terrain a little less wild by comparing it to what has already been tamed.

What philosopher Suzanne K. Langer wrote of metaphor is true of analogy, too: "Language, in its literal capacity, is a stiff and conventional medium, unadapted to the expression of genuinely new ideas, which usually have to break in upon the mind through some great and bewildering metaphor."

The analogical imperative is captured nicely in one of the tales of Hui Tzu, a philosopher who lived in China during the fourth century B.C.E. Hui Tzu was a kind of Chinese Zeno, famous for philosophical non sequiturs and paradoxes, such as "I set off for Yueh [a state in southern China] today and came there yesterday" and "The sun at noon is the sun setting; the thing born is the thing dying."

Hui Tzu was famous for his eloquence. When people asked for explanations of natural phenomena like wind, rain, and thunder, Hui Tzu is said to have "responded without hesitation, answered without thinking, and explained all the myriad things . . . without rest, going on without stopping, still thought it too little, and then added some marvel to it."

One story about Hui Tzu in particular, related by the ancient Chinese sage Mencius, suggests he would have felt right at home in C. S. Lewis's Flalansfere:

An advisor to the King of Liang warned the monarch of Hui Tzu's use of analogical reasoning. "Hui Tzu is very good at using analogies when putting forth his views," the advisor said. "If your Majesty would stop him from using analogies, he will be at a loss what to say."

"Very well, I will do that," the King said.

When he received Hui Tzu the following day, the King said to him: "If you have anything to say, I wish you would say it plainly and not resort to analogies."

Hui Tzu said, "Suppose there is a man here who does not know what a *tan* is, and you say to him, 'A *tan* is like a *tan*.' Would he understand?"

"No," the King said.

"Then were you to say to him, 'A *tan* is like a bow, but has a strip of bamboo in place of the string.' Would he understand?"

"Yes, he would," the King replied.

"A man who explains necessarily makes intelligible that which is not known by comparing it with what is known," Hui Tzu said.

Lewis called this type of analogy—the type that compares the unknown with the known—a "master's metaphor," or metaphor as teaching tool. Like Langer, Lewis argued that master metaphors are essential to communicate any kind of innovative, original thinking.

In the case of the Flalansfere, Lewis argued, we could dispense with the analogy only if we could directly study or even imagine a four-dimensional world. But we can't. For those of us not conversant with the highly specialized vocabulary of theoretical physics, analogy is our only access to the Flalansfere. "Our thought is independent of the metaphors we employ, in so far as these metaphors are optional," Lewis wrote, "that is, in so far as we are able to have the same idea without them." But when it comes to understanding and communicating the great, bewildering truths of science, there are no ideas but in analogies.

Our analogical abilities start early. To pinpoint the onset of analogical reasoning, researchers told children a story about a genie who moved precious jewels from one bottle to another by rolling up his magic carpet into a tube and bowling the jewels through it. They then presented the children with two bowls (one containing some balls and the other empty), an aluminum walking cane, a large sheet of heavy paper, scissors, tape, paper clips, and rubber bands. The children had to use these tools to come up with as many ways as possible to get the balls into the empty bowl.

Only about 10 percent of the children between the ages of four and six thought of rolling up the paper and using it as the genie used his magic carpet, even after researchers suggested to them that something in the story might help. All the children aged ten to twelve came up with this solution, though some needed a helpful nudge. The study suggests that analogical reasoning takes hold in early adolescence, around the same time kids become able to understand more complex conceptual metaphors.

The timing may be more than coincidence since analogies, like complex conceptual metaphors, typically involve sources and targets drawn from very distant domains. And, just as the appropriate set of associated commonplaces must be in place in order to understand a complex conceptual metaphor, you must know something of an analogy's source if you are to understand how it informs, or misinforms, the target.

The theoretical physicist Richard Feynman was such a lauded lecturer in large part because, like Hui Tzu, he was skilled in finding the right analogies to illustrate his explanations of extremely abstract—and extremely difficult—concepts. He once compared a drop of water magnified 2,000 times to "a kind of teeming . . . like a crowd at a football game as seen from a very great distance." That description has all the precision of good physics and good poetry.

To convey the operation of electromagnetic fields, Feynman used the master metaphor of two corks floating in a pool of water. If you move one cork around in the water, you immediately notice that the other one moves, too. Looking only at the two corks, Feynman explained, a naïve physicist might be forgiven for thinking there was some kind of interaction between the corks that caused the one to move in response to the other.

The second cork, however, is not moved directly by the first cork but by the movement of the water. "If we jiggle the cork . . . *waves* travel away," Feynman explained, "so that by jiggling, there is an influence *very much farther out*, an oscillatory influence. That cannot be understood by the direct interaction. Therefore the idea of direct interaction must be replaced with the existence of the water, or in the electrical case, with what we call the *electromagnetic field*."

Note, though, that in science as in every area where the combinatory play of metaphor applies, analogy comes only after the

facts. To know that the tale of two corks is an accurate comparison, Feynman must already have known how electromagnetic
fields operate, just as in order to know the meaning of "Man is
a wolf" you must already be familiar with that lean and hungry
look. As Hungarian-born mathematician George Pólya put it,
"When you have satisfied yourself that the theorem is true, you
start proving it."

This is exactly how discovery works, according to David
Deutsch, a theoretical physicist at Oxford University. The process
starts with a problem, a conflict between two ideas or theories, he
says. The first step in solving the problem is to tweak the existing
theories so they fit. Failing that, you introduce another theory that
resolves the incompatibility.

Assuming you do this successfully, Deutsch says, the outcome
is, "You don't understand the resulting theory. It solves the theoretical problems, but you can't see what it means. You don't understand how that could be a description of the actual world, or what
the world would have to be like for that to be true. Then you think
of an analogy."

Deutsch cites the theory of continental drift as an example. As
early as the sixteenth century, natural philosophers had observed
that the shapes of the continents, particularly Africa and South
America, seemed as if they would fit snugly together. But until
the early twentieth century, no one had come up with a plausible
mechanism by which a single land mass could have fragmented
and drifted apart. Finally, in the 1960s, the theory of plate tectonics
provided the answer.

But, Deutsch points out, having the correct theory is not the
full story. We still need to know what the theory says about reality,
what plate tectonics means for the actual history of Earth. This is
where analogy comes in handy.

"Maybe the Earth is like a rice pudding," Deutsch says of the analogical reasoning that followed the plate tectonics theory, "hard and brittle on top but pliable and liquid underneath. Sometimes, the surface skin ruptures and pulls apart. The metaphor is useful because it answers the question of how something can be. It makes the theory easier to understand because it is similar to something else."

If analogies are useful in understanding what the world is like according to plate tectonics theory, they are essential in understanding the most abstract, least directly observable sciences, such as Deutsch's specialty, quantum physics.

In the quantum world, Feynman observed, things "do not behave like waves, they do not behave like particles, they do not behave like clouds, or billiard balls, or weights on springs, or like anything that you have ever seen . . . So we have to learn about them in a sort of abstract or imaginative fashion." This abstract, imaginative fashion is analogy, the only way we learn about anything of which we can have no direct experience, whether it's the behavior of subatomic particles or the content of other people's experience.

The philosopher Thomas Nagel posed the curious question, What is it like to be a bat? To the extent that an organism has conscious mental states, he argued, "there is something it is *like* to be that organism." Every conscious organism must have private, directly apprehended mental states that define "what it is like" to be that organism. Known as "qualia," these subjective characteristics of experience include qualities like the pain of a stubbed toe or the redness of a red, red rose.

Nagel wanted to know what it is like to be a bat because bats are so different from us. They perceive the world primarily through echolocation, bouncing sound waves off objects in the environment to determine their size, shape, and motion. This is nothing like how we perceive the world, so there is little in our direct experience to suggest what it must be like to be a bat. A bat's qualia are inaccessible to us.

Nagel concluded from this thought experiment that we can never know what it is like to be a bat and, therefore, that there are facts we can neither comprehend nor express in language. "I want to know what it is like for a bat to be a bat," he wrote. "Yet if I try to imagine this, I am restricted to the resources of my own mind, and those resources are inadequate to the task."

Our resources are indeed inadequate to the task of directly knowing the quality of a bat's experience, just as they are inadequate to the task of directly knowing the dimensions of the Flalansfere or the quality of the pain someone else feels when he stubs his toe. We can never know what it *is* to be a bat.

But metaphor can always tell us what it is *like*, by providing the right analogy from our own experience. Indeed, the fact that we cannot pose such questions—What is it *like* to be a bat? What is a four-dimensional universe *like*? What must the earth be *like* if the plate tectonics theory is true?—without using the word "like" suggests analogy's central role in understanding these most recalcitrant, recondite aspects of the world.

So, what is it like to be a bat? It is like pinpointing the location of a fluttering scarf while walking blindfolded through the Grand Canyon using as a guide only the echo of your own voice reverberating from the canyon walls.

What is it like for two particles to be in a state of quantum entanglement, in which a change to one particle effects an immediate and corresponding change to the other particle even though a vast physical distance separates both? It is like one person, in Peoria, instantly catching cold when another person, on Pluto, sneezes.

In a speech about the role of analogy in science, another physicist, J. Robert Oppenheimer, said this:

We cannot, coming into something new, deal with it except on the basis of the familiar and the old-fashioned . . . We cannot learn to be surprised or astonished at something unless we have a view of how it ought to be; and that view is almost certainly an analogy. We cannot learn that we have made a mistake unless we can make a mistake; and our mistake is almost always in the form of an analogy to some other piece of experience.

Scientific analogies must be empirically verifiable to be of use. It is possible to test whether the earth is like a rice pudding, for instance, in ways that it is not possible to test whether my love is like a red, red rose. Experiment leads to more and better information, which leads to more and better analogies. Finally, after sufficient testing and modification, the new and improved analogy becomes a scientific model, a useful conceptual description of a concrete physical reality.

But Deutsch warns against prematurely invoking metaphor. As Oppenheimer pointed out, analogies are always flawed because one thing is never *exactly like* some other thing. Analogy can never be accepted as proof, because one theory is never correct merely because it's *like* some other theory that happens to be correct. "Metaphor is useful to understand deep meaning, but only after the theory," Deutsch says. "Before the theory, metaphor is misleading and can be a powerful source of error because we can't know which aspects of the analogy are right or wrong."

In science, metaphor tells you what things are *like*, not what they *are*. After analogy, Deutsch says, the final step in the discovery process is "to understand the thing in its own right, not metaphorically. Once you do this, you can dispense with the metaphor and understand the world as it actually is."

In *The Structure of Scientific Revolutions*, Thomas Kuhn noted that metaphor "plays an essential role in establishing a link between scientific language and the world." He noted, too, that those links are not set in stone: "Theory change, in particular, is accompanied by a change in some of the relevant metaphors and in the corresponding parts of the network of similarities through which terms attach to nature." Thus, the danger of an analogy like the Flalansfere, according to C. S. Lewis, is not that it may be incorrect but that people may forget it is an analogy.

"I too play with symbols," the mathematician and astronomer Johannes Kepler wrote, anticipating Einstein's analogy of scientific creativity, "but I play in such a way that I do not forget that I am playing. For nothing is proved by symbols . . . unless by sure reasons it can be demonstrated that they are not merely symbolic but are descriptions of the ways in which the two things are connected and of the causes of this connexion."

Metaphors, once forgotten or ignored, are easily mistaken for objective facts. If that happens in science, analogies congeal into dogmas, losing the elasticity that made them useful in the first place. Science is like a rice pudding: firm and fully formed on top but pliable and in constant motion underneath.

John Stuart Mill, one of the nineteenth century's few philosophical fans of metaphorical thinking, said that a metaphor "is not to be considered as an argument, but as an assertion that an argument exists." Lewis would surely have agreed. Metaphor and analogy prove nothing, but they are the only ways we have of showing what the world must be *like* when scientific proofs are true. For Lewis, that meant we must never lose sight of the fact that metaphors are metaphors, models of things rather than the things themselves.

"We are never less the slaves of metaphor than when we are making metaphor, or hearing it new made," Lewis wrote in "Bluspels and Flalansferes." "When we are thinking hard of Flatlanders, and at the same time fully aware that they *are* a metaphor, we are in a situation almost infinitely superior to that of the man who talks of the Flalansferes and thinks that he is being literal and straightforward . . . If our thinking is ever true, then the metaphors by which we think must have been good metaphors."

MIGHTY DARN GOOD LIES

A few years ago, a Spanish artist gave my wife and me one of his prints, a thank-you gift for putting him up at our house for a couple of nights. We really liked the vivacity and cheerfulness of the work, which we hung in the living room in a spot previously occupied by a clutch of black-and-white drawings. The print brightened up that whole corner of the room. But even as our new acquisition cast the living room in an entirely new light, it occasioned other, somewhat darker thoughts.

The black outlines of dust on the wall where the old frames hung were now clearly visible, like the chalk lines around the corpse at a murder scene. We would have to paint over those, I thought.

And that section of plaster near the corner of the ceiling—where the damage occurred the night our daughter Hendrikje was sick and the humidifier water spilled across the floor of her room upstairs, trickling down along this wall—we would have to do something about that, too. It looked too much as if that part of the room had some kind of strange dermatological condition.

And that gash in the ceiling where a chunk of plaster collapsed years ago: Why the hell haven't we fixed that?

And, while we're at it, I'm sick and tired of constantly stumbling over the lip of the stairs where the carpet is worn away. Let's get new carpets for the whole stairway.

With our recent acquisition barely in place, the list of essential home improvements suddenly seemed endless. Yes, before our enthusiasm for the print had even cooled, we had succumbed to the dreaded "Diderot effect."

The Diderot effect is named after eighteenth-century French philosopher Denis Diderot, who spent twenty-five years editing the massive *Encyclopaedia*, one of the founding documents of the Enlightenment. Diderot is also the author of a charming essay called "Regrets on Parting with My Old Dressing Gown," in which he describes how the gift of a beautiful scarlet dressing gown plunges him into debt and turns his life upside down.

Initially pleased with the unexpected gift, Diderot describes how he soon came to rue the day he received his new garment. Compared to his elegant new dressing gown, the rest of his possessions seemed tawdry. His old straw chair, for example, just wouldn't do. So he replaced it with an armchair covered in Moroccan leather. And the rickety old desk that groaned under his papers? That was out, too, and in came an expensive new writing table. Even the beloved prints that hung on his walls had to make way for newer, more costly works.

Diderot spent far more than he could afford on upgrading his accommodations, realizing too late that his opulent robe was actually a poisoned chalice. "I was absolute master of my old dressing gown," Diderot wrote in his essay, the subtitle of which is "A Warning to Those with More Taste than Money," "but I have become a slave to my new one . . . Beware of the contamination of sudden wealth. Let my example be a lesson to you. The poor man may take his ease without thinking of appearances, but the rich man is always under a strain."

"Regrets on Parting with My Old Dressing Gown" is a delightful essay. It is also an excellent example of parable, or metaphor in story form.

Like metaphors, parables have double meanings. Diderot's essay is about the financial catastrophe occasioned by his receipt of a beautiful scarlet dressing gown. But it is also about how any of life's little upgrades—new cars, new dresses, new lovers—can initiate a dizzying and potentially ruinous spiral of desire for more and better acquisitions.

Parables come in a variety of forms. An allegory, like Bunyan's *Pilgrim's Progress* or Dante's *Divine Comedy*, is a theatrical parable with lots of different characters. A fable is simply a parable starring animals. A myth is nothing more than an epic parable. Edwin Paxton Hood, a late nineteenth-century English preacher popular on both sides of the Atlantic despite what the *New York Times* described as "an unpleasant peculiarity in his voice and a somewhat eccentric mannerism," provided the best definition:

> Etymologically, [parable] signifies simply to place side by side; and it is, in fact, fancy by the side of fact; it is spiritual truth side by side with natural truth; it is truth at once fruitful and floral.

Parables are narrated metaphors; they place a fictional story by the side of a fact of life. Just as grandmother cells, neurons that fire in response to images of specific people or objects, encode both the actual image and the abstract concept of the person or object, parables encode both an actual experience and an abstract category of experiences. Thus, "Regrets on Parting with My Old Dressing Gown" is the sad tale of Diderot in debt as well as an object lesson in what happens when acquisitiveness exceeds assets.

Parables are teaching tales. Through them, we are given that greatest of all opportunities—the chance to learn from someone else's mistakes. And this education consists of more than mere sentimental words of wisdom like "Always live within your means," a warning Diderot clearly didn't heed. Neuroimaging studies show that practical learning, too, takes place whenever we read stories.

When we read a story, our brains plot everything that's going on, from the characters' physical locations in space to their interactions with objects in the environment to their pursuit of various psychological and emotional goals. Many of the brain areas active while reading are also active when we actually take part in or observe similar situations in real life. The regions involved in processing goal-directed activity and the manipulation of objects, for example, are at work during both fictional and factual encounters. Just as we understand metaphors by mentally simulating what they describe, we understand stories by imaginatively acting them out in our minds. Stories are rehearsals for real life.

This merger of fact with fiction may have evolved as an efficient and vivid means of communicating essential information. As Denis Dutton argues in *The Art Instinct: Beauty, Pleasure and Human Evolution*, the evolutionary advantage of stories, metaphorical or otherwise, is that they provide an understanding of the inner lives of others, the complexities of social relations, and our own hidden motivations.

Parables are the most compressed and concentrated form of story. They are compact metaphorical thought experiments that help us solve essential psychological and social problems in the real world.

Parables are common to every country and culture, but few have taken the practice to such extremes as the Managalese, a people inhabiting the mountainous regions of the Oro Province in Papua New Guinea.

The Managalese live in villages of anywhere between 50 and 250 people. The extended family, or kin group, serves as the basic unit of social, political, and economic organization. To preserve amity, the Managalese use circumlocutions to conduct negotiations or resolve contentious disputes. When confronting the trickiest issues—arranging marriages, reproving kinsfolk, informing relatives of the deaths of loved ones—they prefer indirection. So they tell parables. Indeed, parabolic activity is so highly prized that the Managalese often compete to see who can come up with the best ones.

After her son eloped with a widow, one Managalese woman related the following parable, as recorded by anthropologist and Managalese parable expert William H. McKellin:

> When I was a young woman and visited people's houses, people gave me fresh juicy young betel nuts to chew. Now I am older. When I visit I am given old, hard betel nut. When I chew it, my teeth and gums hurt and bleed. This makes me unhappy and upset.

Betel nuts symbolize marriage among the Managalese. This mother clearly disapproves of her son's decision, comparing the widow with whom he eloped to an old, hard betel nut. But she is expressing her disapproval in a non-confrontational way, through parable.

The Managalese opt for a metaphorical mode of discourse to defuse the tension in emotionally charged situations. We do the same whenever we choose a euphemism instead of more direct speech. When we speak of "collateral damage" instead of "dead civilians" or "right-sizing" instead of "mandatory job losses," we are seeking to cushion the blow of bad news by couching the information in a kinder, gentler metaphor. Parables and allegories are, according to McKellin, "the trial balloons or political Rorschach tests of social relations."

Parables can make bitter pills easier to swallow, but they can also make difficult concepts easier to grasp, as exemplified in the moral and spiritual tales of everyone from Buddha, Jesus, and Muhammad to Søren Kierkegaard and Franz Kafka. The educational and existential aspects of parables also account for their perennial popularity. Probably no collection of parables is more popular than *Aesop's Fables*:

> A boy was gathering berries from a hedge when a nettle stung his hand. Smarting with the pain, he ran to tell his mother, and said to her between his sobs, "I only touched it ever so slightly, mother." "That's just why you got stung, my son," said she; "if you had grasped it firmly, it wouldn't have hurt you in the least."

Aesop's fables are usually about animals, like the tortoise and the hare or the ant and the grasshopper. But a few, like this one, feature human beings. Either way, the stories describe some concrete scene—what Hood called a "natural truth"—from which readers must deduce an abstract message, or "spiritual truth." In this parable, the natural truth is the boy's encounter with the stinging nettles and the spiritual truth is, to put it proverbially, "Grab the bull by the horns." I wonder what my son Tristan would make of this lesson.

Proverbs were often appended to Aesop's fables as a way to sum up and re-enforce the story's import. In fact, if parables are metaphors in story form, then proverbs are parables in miniature.

Like parables, proverbs often feature animals ("You can lead a horse to water but you can't make it drink") and always contain hidden moral lessons ("A nod is as good as a wink to a blind man"). They are, in essence, one-sentence stories, which John Russell, twice British prime minister in the nineteenth century, succinctly defined as "The wit of one, the wisdom of many."

Proverbs, again like parables, are found in every country and culture, like this one from China

It is hard to dismount from a tiger

and this one from Korea

Chase two hares, both get away.

The proverb and its close relation, the aphorism, are the world's oldest written art forms. They are also the oldest written examples of metaphor.

In ancient Sumer, where writing itself was invented around 3500 B.C.E., proverb collections were used as textbooks. A handful of museums hold small oblong clay tablets, thousands of years old, on which ancient Sumerian students have copied out proverbs as both school spelling assignments and exercises in moral education. Some of the tablets still bear the scratch marks where a student made a mistake, crossed it out, and started over again.

Despite their antiquity, these proverbs still ring true, instantly calling to mind contemporary echoes. The Sumerian saying

Wealth is hard to come by, but poverty is always at hand

anticipates

The poor are always with us.

The ancient admonishment

Possessions are sparrows in flight that can find no place to alight reminds us that

A bird in the hand is worth two in the bush.

The Sumerians used proverbs as moral instruction manuals; we use them in the same way today. Proverbs are trotted out whenever someone (usually an older person) decides that someone else (usually a younger person) needs to be taught a lesson. Lectures on frugality invariably include the catchphrase "A penny saved is a penny earned" and monologues about the birds and the bees inevitably feature the warning "Better safe than sorry." In this way, proverbs remain one of the few forms of oral literature still actively practiced around the world.

Practice perfected the proverb in many African cultures, where these metaphorical words of wisdom are invoked for everything from resolving arguments to socializing children to settling legal disputes.

Among the Igbo, an ethnic group of about 9 million people who live in the rain forests of southeastern Nigeria, proverbs are a highly esteemed form of communication. Adults, especially men, establish their authority and maintain their status in large part through the deft deployment of proverbs. "Knowing proverbs and using them appropriately means that you are intelligent," according to one Igbo man, "because it's just like being able to find out something in a textbook or dictionary."

The Igbo and other African ethnic groups consult their proverb dictionaries daily. Proverbs feature prominently in court cases, with both the prosecution and the defense enlisting them to bolster their arguments. Judges will often cite a proverb at the end of a case much as Western judges cite legal precedents. One judge, a member of the Anang, another Nigerian ethnic group, regularly deployed the saying

If you visit the home of the toads, stoop

to emphasize that litigants must conform to the law.

The Igbo, Anang, and other African ethnic groups place so much faith in the problem-solving power of proverbs that they even have a proverb for it:

If something that demands a proverb happens, a proverb will be cited.

Africans are not alone in using proverbs for moral instruction and, perhaps just as often, moral justification. Psychologist Daniel Stalder asked university students to read stories in which they took part in behavior—engaging in unsafe sex, wasting hundreds of gallons of water during a drought, or joyriding in a stolen car—that contradicted their personal values. After reading the story, some participants then read a short list of irrelevant proverbs (e.g., "An apple a day keeps the doctor away"), some read relevant proverbs (e.g., "Everybody makes mistakes"), some read a mix of relevant and irrelevant proverbs, and the rest didn't read any proverbs at all. Those who had read relevant proverbs expressed fewer feelings of regret and guilt than those who had read only irrelevant proverbs or no proverbs at all. But, Stalder found, this effect was evident only in men. He concluded that men were quicker to use proverbs to excuse their behavior because the sayings placed their actions in the context of a social norm—After all, everybody makes mistakes now and then. What's the big deal? Women, in contrast, did not accept that the proverbial social norm, however reassuring, offered justification for their actions.

Giambattista Vico, always ahead of the pack in spotting metaphor's formative role in thought, also noted the cross-cultural importance of proverbs. "The nature of human institutions presupposes a conceptual language which is common to all nations," he wrote in *New Science*. "This language uniformly grasps the substance of all the elements of human society, but expresses them differently according to their different aspects. We witness the truth of this in proverbs, which are maxims of popular wisdom. For their meanings, while substantially the same, are expressed under as many different aspects as there are ancient and modern nations."

Though proverbs are universal, the metaphorical menageries through which they tell their stories vary. One survey of economics texts from the United Kingdom and France, for example, found that the British used gardening proverbs more than three times as often as the French, while the French used food proverbs nearly five times as often as the British. National stereotypes, it seems, contain more than just a proverbial grain of truth.

There are also cultural nuances in the way proverbs are visualized. Asked to provide imagery for the idiom "spill the beans," a phrase used metaphorically more than 99 percent of the time, Americans reported that the beans are uncooked and in a container about the size of a human head. Brits, on the other hand, preferred baked beans in a tin can. There is no accounting for taste, not even proverbially.

Both nature and nurture are at work in the choice of proverbial metaphors. Cultural preferences, such as the British passion for gardening and the French love of food, play a role, but so does the physical environment. This is especially evident in Afrikaans, a form of Dutch spoken by the descendants of Dutch settlers in South Africa.

In 1652, some intrepid Dutch farmers and their families settled along the coast of what is now South Africa. The settlement was initially intended only as a supply station for the ships of the East India Company, but it eventually grew into a thriving colony in its own right. As time passed, the form of Dutch spoken there veered from the mother tongue as spoken in the Netherlands to become the Afrikaans vernacular. Comparing proverbs from the two languages illustrates how the metaphorical landscape of a proverb may change while the meaning remains the same.

The Dutch language possesses an embarrassment of proverbial riches. Proverbs are present in all forms of communication, from political discourse and journalism to ordinary conversation and even painting, which is in itself a rich source of visual metaphors. Pieter Bruegel the Elder's *Netherlandish Proverbs*, painted in 1559, includes lurid, lavish, and often ludic depictions of more than one hundred sayings from the Low Countries, including perennial favorites like

No one looks for others in an oven unless he's been in there himself.
(It takes one to know one.)

Fill the well after the calf has drowned.
(Shut the barn door after the horses have bolted.)

He who eats fire shits sparks.
(Play with fire and you'll get burned.)

Bruegel was someone who clearly took Addison's test of a true metaphor—"whether or not there is sufficient detail for it to be painted"—literally.

Many Dutch proverbial expressions are nautical in nature, because of Holland's seafaring past and the fact that more than half the country lies below sea level. "To carry water to the sea," for example, is the Dutch equivalent of the British expression "to carry coals to Newcastle"; both phrases mean "to perform a superfluous task by adding more of something that is already in abundance."

The Dutch saying "That doesn't add any sod to the dike" has a related significance, meaning "to perform a task that does not have the desired effect." In English, this might be rendered by the equally delightful, "It butters no parsnips."

And then there is the evocative "to jab someone under water," which means "to surreptitiously undermine someone's position." The saying is derived from what happens when a ship's hull is breeched below the waterline; the damage is invisible and therefore all the more dangerous.

The Dutch landscape is, of course, dotted with windmills, and windmills, too, turn up in dozens of Dutch proverbs, such as:

Turn the mill to the wind.
(Equivalent to the English proverb, Trim your sails to the wind.)

That's grist for his mill.
(It's in the works. Literally, in Dutch, "It's in the mill.")

She got hit by the windmill.
(She has a screw loose.)

Unlike the Netherlands, however, South Africa has no windmills, so windmills are conspicuously absent from South African proverbs.

South Africa and the Netherlands have different animal populations as well as different landscapes, so the proverbs from each country also feature different non-human casts of characters. The Dutch expression

The fox may lose its fur, but not its tricks

is replaced in Afrikaans by

Jackals may change their fur, but never their tricks

because there are few foxes in South Africa but plenty of jackals. Afrikaners carried over the original proverb from Dutch but endowed the native jackal with the fox's proverbial reputation for slyness and cunning.

To be effective, though, proverbs and parables must not be too culturally specific. The scene must be detailed enough to be credible but general enough to be universally applicable. Otherwise, minutiae outweigh metaphor and parable degenerates into anecdote.

As G. K. Chesterton wrote in his introduction to *Aesop's Fables*, "For a fable, all the persons must be impersonal. They must be like abstractions in algebra, or like pieces in chess." The parable of the farmer and his chickens is a case in point:

A farmer was proud of his prize chickens. But he started to lose some of them to raids by skunks on the henhouse. One night he heard a loud cackling from the chickens and crept out with his shotgun to find a half-dozen of the black-and-white critters running in and out of the shed. Thinking to clean out the whole tribe, he put a double charge in the gun and fired away. Somehow he hit only one, and the rest scampered off. The neighbors asked why the farmer didn't follow up the skunks and kill the rest. "Blast it," the farmer said. "It was eleven weeks before I got over killin' one."

This fable is not by Aesop but by Abraham Lincoln. Lincoln told this story after he dismissed his Secretary of War Simon Cameron for incompetence and corruption during the Civil War. At the time, Lincoln's advisors urged him to carry out a much wider shake-up of the underperformers in his administration. He explained his reluctance to do so not with a detailed exposition of the political chaos that would result from a more comprehensive purge but with this folksy, homespun tale.

Lincoln was a great lover of all forms of parable. His favorite books were the King James Bible, *Pilgrim's Progress*, Shakespeare, and *Aesop's Fables*. He carried Shakespeare, along with Burns and Byron, in his saddlebags while riding across Illinois making court appearances during his years as a lawyer. As a boy, he spent a lot of time poring over Aesop in particular. Lincoln occasionally cited one of Aesop's sayings in political tracts to bolster his arguments, just as Anang judges cite proverbs as precedents. His cousin, Dennis Hanks, used to tease Lincoln about his preoccupation with Aesop: "Abe, them yarns is all lies." Lincoln glanced up from his book and replied: "Mighty darn good lies."

Lincoln was such an effective orator because he could tell such mighty darn good lies himself. "No man could tell a story as well as he could," one friend recalled. "He could convey his ideas on any subject through the form of a simple story or homely illustration with better effect than any man I knew." The paradox of parable and proverb is that issues as complex as governing unruly Cabinet members can be compressed into such simple stories.

As a child, Lincoln became irritated whenever he couldn't understand an adult conversation. After listening to his father chatting with neighbors one evening, Lincoln lay awake until he had figured out what they were saying. "I was not satisfied," he recalled, "until I had put it in language plain enough, as I thought, for any boy I knew to comprehend. This was a kind of passion with me, and it has stuck by me."

The plain language of parable and proverb makes these metaphorical forms so potent and so entertaining. It also enables them to deliver powerful, provocative messages with unparalleled zest. Nothing else gives a bigger bang for the buck, as in this Zen koan:

> Whenever Gutei Osho was asked about Zen, he simply raised a finger. Once a visitor asked Gutei's boy attendant, "What does your master teach?" The boy too raised his finger. Hearing of this, Gutei cut off the boy's finger with a knife. The boy, screaming with pain, began to run away. Gutei called to him, and when he turned around, Gutei raised his finger. The boy suddenly became enlightened.

Mullah Nasrudin, a medieval folk hero claimed by many countries, including Afghanistan, Iran, and Turkey, was a master of the parabolic zinger:

> Nasrudin sometimes took people for trips in his boat. One day a fussy pedagogue hired him to ferry him across a very wide river. As soon as they were afloat, the scholar asked whether it was going to be rough.
> "Don't ask me nothing about it," said Nasrudin.
> "Have you never studied grammar?" the pedant remarked.
> "No," said the Mullah.
> "In that case, half your life has been wasted," was the pompous pedagogue's reply.
> The Mullah said nothing. Soon a terrible storm blew up. The Mullah's crazy cockleshell was filling with water. He leaned over to his companion and asked: "Have you ever learned to swim?"
> "No," said the terrified pedant.
> "In that case, schoolmaster, all your life has been wasted, for we are sinking."

Mullah Nasrudin is part court jester, part Socratic philosopher.

His adventures are still widely quoted throughout the Middle East and parts of Asia. He is, for example, one of the early sources for the old joke about the drunk looking for his car keys under a lamp-post, though in Nasrudin's time, of course, the drunk would have lost something other than car keys. "Where did you lose them?" his friend asks. "At home," the drunk says. "Then why are you looking here?" "Because the light is better."

Nasrudin was a Sufi, and these followers of the mystical strand of Islam still use his exploits much as Zen Buddhists use koans— to break down conventional thinking to achieve a breakthrough into wisdom. Nasrudin's shenanigans have the double meanings characteristic of all metaphors. The crazy cockleshell story is an amusing tale of how a fussy pedagogue gets his comeuppance as well as a moral reminder that "book learning" alone won't get you far in life.

Yet there is something puzzling about parables and proverbs. Indeed, the Igbo call proverbs "riddles," a word that literally trans-lates as "making a comparison"—in other words, metaphor. In a conventional metaphor, such as "Juliet is the sun," the source and the target are obvious. The metaphor makes perfectly clear that aspects of the sun are meant to apply to Juliet.

But parables and proverbs are all source and no target. There is no explicit link between the events described and the meaning as-cribed. There is not the slightest clue in either parables or proverbs as to their ultimate significance, yet we immediately understand what they mean.

Why, for example, are we sure that Mullah Nasrudin is telling more than just another funny story? How do we extract the em-ployee management tips from Lincoln's tale of the farmer and his prize chickens? What convinces us that the Chinese tiger proverb is anything other than a bizarre non sequitur? After all, most of us have never dismounted a tiger—or mounted one, for that matter—and it is more than a little odd to be informed that this is likely to be a difficult task. In short, how do we decide which spiritual truth to set side by side with which natural truth?

Max Black's associated commonplaces are decisive in deciphering parables and proverbs, though the places associated with these forms of figurative language are anything but common. The source of a proverb or parable may be the animal kingdom, but the target is always the kingdom of our psychological and spiritual lives. "Metaphors only seem to describe the outer world of time and place," scholar of world mythology Joseph Campbell wrote. "Their real universe is the spiritual realm of the inner life."

This marriage of the physical and the metaphysical is celebrated in extraordinary fashion in the Chhandogya Upanishad, part of the collection of Indian sacred literature compiled between 1500 and 500 B.C.E. This text describes a conversation between Svetaketu, a conceited twenty-four-year-old, and his father, Uddilaka. Sent away to study when he was twelve years old, Svetaketu has recently returned home, with a rather high opinion of himself and his spiritual learning.

Uddilaka questions his son about the Brahman, the Hindu concept of the Self as the ultimate reality and the source of all Being. When Svetaketu confesses his ignorance and asks his father to explain, Uddilaka delivers a series of lovely parables comparing the spiritual truth of Brahman to a variety of natural truths. At the end of each parable, Uddilaka repeats the mantra-like phrase *Tat tvam asi*, which translates roughly as "Thou art that."

"Bees make honey by collecting juices from different trees and reducing them into one essence," Uddilaka explains. "These juices have no discrimination such as 'I am the juice of this tree, I am the juice of that tree.' Even so, dear boy, all these creatures hav-

ing merged into Being do not know 'We have merged into Being.'
Thou art that."

"These eastern rivers flow along to the east and the western ones
to the west," Uddilaka continues. "They rise from the ocean and
merge in the ocean and become that ocean itself. These rivers do
not know themselves as 'I am this river, I am that river.' Even so,
dear boy, all these creatures, having come from Being, do not know
'We have come from Being.' Thou art that."

Uddilaka tells Svetaketu to put some salt into water before going
to bed and then bring the salt to him again in the morning. When
Svetaketu is unable to find the salt, Uddilaka says, "Take a sip from
the top of this water. How is it?"

"It is salt," Svetaketu says.

"Take a sip from the middle. How is it?"

"It is salt."

"Take a sip from the bottom. How is it?"

"It is salt."

"Dear boy, as you do not see what is present in this water though
indeed it exists in it, similarly Being exists indeed in this body.
Thou art that, O Svetaketu."

Parables and proverbs feature so prominently in folk wisdom
and religious scripture because there is no way to convey spiritual
truths other than to set them side by side with natural truths. The
numinous is the nitty-gritty. Thou art that. I is an other.

MAKE IT STRANGE

arriet Monroe, the founding editor of *Poetry* magazine, described Wallace Stevens as "supersensitive to beauty but encased in the protective armor of the business attorney." Stevens joined the Hartford Accident and Indemnity Company in 1916, became a vice president in 1934, and remained with the firm for nearly forty years, until his death at the age of seventy in 1955.

Stevens was a respected and successful businessman. He also happened to be one of the greatest American poets of the twentieth century. Supersensitive to metaphor as well as to beauty, Stevens believed, like his fellow poets Robert Frost and C. S. Lewis, that metaphor was far too important to be confined to verse.

In the essay "Three Academic Pieces," Stevens described metaphor as "the creation of resemblance by the imagination." Metaphor is the imagination at work and "its singularity," he wrote, "is that in the act of satisfying the desire for resemblance it touches the sense of reality, it enhances the sense of reality, heightens it, intensifies it." Elsewhere, Stevens expressed the same thought more concisely:

> Metaphor creates a new reality from which the original
> appears to be unreal.

Around the time of Wallace Stevens's death, corporate executives William J. J. Gordon and George Prince discovered that metaphors could create new realities for businesses, too. Gordon, an executive with the industrial research firm Arthur D. Little, and his colleague Prince invented "Synectics," a method for stimulating innovation through the systematic application of metaphor.

At Arthur D. Little, Gordon was in the habit of tape-recording "brainstorming sessions," a term popularized by Alex Osborn, another great believer in the creative power of metaphor for business. Listening to the tapes, Gordon heard participants use crazy analogies and far-fetched comparisons to generate new ideas. He realized that these outlandish links among unrelated things changed the way people thought about a problem and that, if used correctly, they could spark practical solutions.

In his book *Synectics: The Development of Creative Capacity,* published in 1961, Gordon describes the process like this:

> We noticed that, in launching a series of sessions which culminated
> in the successful solution of a given problem, we were constantly
> attempting to "make the familiar strange." Faced with the all too
> familiar, without understanding entirely what we were doing, we
> would attempt at first radically to shift our vision so that the famil-
> iar (the codified, the set world of the usual) was made strange and
> new, and therefore subject to new patterns and new laws of opera-
> tion—subject to invention.

Gordon made up the term "synectics" just as Coleridge made up the term "esemplastic," deriving it from the Greek *synektiktein*, which translates somewhat awkwardly as "joining together different and apparently unrelated elements."

Gordon chose participants in Synectics sessions on the basis of their metaphoric abilities. He and his team listened to candidates talk; the ones displaying the most inventive use of language and analogy were invited to join the group. Synectics members had to have a high tolerance for the irrelevant, a childlike willingness to engage in combinatory play, and an advanced ability to suspend criticism and disbelief. They also had to perform extended role-playing. If a team was tasked with developing a new kind of unbreakable glass, for example, they were asked to imagine and articulate what it would be like to be a piece of glass, in much the same way that Iowa Writers' Workshop participants were asked to imagine what kind of smoke Marlon Brando might be.

Personal analogy, Gordon and Prince believed, solved problems. "One identifies oneself with a purely non-human entity which figures in the problem . . . speculating on how that thing would 'feel' and act in the problem situation," Prince said. "Personal identification with the elements of a problem releases the individual from viewing the problem in terms of its previously analyzed elements."

According to Gordon, the Synectics process involves two things: making the strange familiar and making the familiar strange. Playing with metaphor, he believed, is the best way to do that: "Ultimate solutions to problems are rational, the process of finding them is not." Aristotle was on to a similar idea when he wrote: "Strange words simply puzzle us; ordinary words convey only what we know already. It is from metaphor that we can best get hold of something fresh."

Gordon and Prince probably weren't familiar with the work of Russian literary critic Victor Shklovsky, but they would have certainly found him very congenial reading. Shklovsky was one of the Russian formalists, a group of theorists active in Russia in the early part of the twentieth century who believed the purpose of art was to estrange us from conventional perceptions. Shklovsky coined the term "defamiliarization"—in Russian, *ostranenie*, or "to make strange"—for this effect, arguing, "Art removes objects from the automatism of perception . . . The technique of art is to make objects 'unfamiliar.'" As art estranges us from the convention, Shklovsky suggested, it reaquaints us with the vividness and originality of life, thus letting us get hold of something fresh.

Gordon and Prince founded a company called Synectics to develop defamiliarization as a tool for developing new products and devising more efficient manufacturing processes. Synectics still exists. Now known as Synecticsworld and headquartered in Cambridge, Massachusetts, the company helps corporations invent and innovate through metaphor—new products and services, new strategies, new business models, new ways to gain insight into what consumers and customers want and need.

Connie Williams, Synecticsworld's general managing partner and chief knowledge officer, used Gordon and Prince's techniques to help one client, a health insurance company, create new products for the deliberately uninsured, those consumers who could afford to purchase health insurance but consciously decided not to.

The client identified the deliberately uninsured as an untapped market since they were largely part-time workers, self-employed, or sole proprietors of their own businesses, earning roughly $50,000 a year. Most had previously held health insurance coverage, until a job change or the launch of their own business altered their benefits status. They paid out of pocket, convinced that they obtained care more cheaply by avoiding insurance and paying cash. In the post-healthcare reform market, this demographic is even more attractive, since most will soon be required to have insurance.

Previous efforts to reach the deliberately uninsured, through premium reductions and benefit restructuring, achieved only incremental success. So the client came to Synecticsworld with two objectives: to better understand this group's perspective on health insurance and to develop new product concepts that might induce them to buy coverage.

Over a period of about six months, Williams convened Synectics sessions involving a core team of representatives from across the client's business. She assembled a consumer panel of the uninsured and sent the client team on little ethnographic field trips to observe and interact with them. They conducted in-home interviews with members of the target group and lived their lives for a day, accompanying them to work and on shopping errands. The goal: to understand their values and their reasons for making the choices they made.

"The client team had a negative impression of the group going in," Williams says, "thinking they didn't understand how catastrophic a serious illness could be to their personal and financial well-being if they didn't have insurance." By the time the Synectics exercise was finished, that attitude had been dramatically transformed.

Williams instructed the client team in how to recognize and solicit metaphors while working with consumers in the field. They used the tried and tested personification method, for instance, asking the panel: "If insurance companies were animals, what kind of animals would they be?"

The resulting metaphors were not very flattering to the health insurance industry. One member of the panel said, "Hyenas, out for what they can get, won't cover anything, preys on others." Another said, "Leeches, suck the blood, take your money."

Williams taught them how to fish for analogies through which they might catch crucial market insights. The client team regularly asked seemingly off-the-wall questions, like "What was your favorite toy growing up?" and then encouraged members of the consumer panel to think about how health insurance could be *like* that toy.

One person's favorite childhood toy was model trains. This person made the link with health insurance via the idea of universal affordability. Model trains are "sold for everyone," this person said. "You can be a super-high-end hobbyist and spend $400, $500, or $600 a piece for it, or you can be an everyday kid who's six years old and get a whole thing for $50. It's geared for everyone, not just a certain group."

The client team also asked the uninsured panel members to make visual collages of the health insurance industry, a longtime Synectics technique similar to that used in a ZMET study. One person chose frigid images—two people in a cold, wild place wrapped in fur coats and a polar bear on an ice floe in the middle of the Arctic—complemented by a picture of a man sitting outside a big house smoking a cigar. "Me and mine have to take care of ourselves," this person explained. "No one is rushing out to help us. [The polar bear] has walked to the farthest point that he has and can't find the path that he wants, like me trying to find the right insurance." The cigar-smoking man represented "the industry living a lifestyle off of us."

In working with this material, Williams encouraged the client team to practice "metaphor mining: Find out what's below the surface. Pull out things that are surprising, paradoxical, or don't make sense, things that might reveal what the consumer intended without knowing he intended it." Or, as Gordon and Prince would say, look for things that make it strange.

One former executive who took part in the Synectics sessions hit pay dirt when a member of the consumer panel described health insurance as "like paying a cover charge at a bar but paying for every drink as well." This person expected some benefit up front as part of the premium. "That really opened my eyes," the former executive says. "We realized that though this group could afford to pay the premiums, they could not afford to actually use their health insurance because of high deductibles, co-pays, and out-of-pocket costs."

Another metaphor that yielded valuable product development nuggets was one retiree's description of healthcare costs as "the bogeyman in the closet that could jump out at any moment." Budgeting is essential if retirees' money is to last as long as they do. But the bogeyman in the closet highlighted how healthcare is the one cost that cannot be adequately budgeted in retirement.

"The metaphors made us stop in our tracks and think of products in a whole new way," says the former exec. The metaphors even became marketing mantras for the group. Whenever new product concepts were discussed, members asked themselves: Who's paying for the first few drinks? Does this let the bogeyman out of the closet without undue fear or alarm?

The metaphors led to specific product innovations as well. To address the "cover charge" concerns, the company came up with plans that built in more coverage up front. The premium was a bit more expensive but it also included more, like paying a slightly higher cover charge at the bar but getting two free drinks. To prevent the healthcare bogeyman from scaring retirees to death, the company devised a scheme that standardized costs over a set number of years, thereby allowing better budgeting.

Having gone into the Synectics process thinking the uninsured were making a strategic and possibly costly mistake, the client team came out thinking they were smart, generally well-informed people who felt they were making an intelligent, cost-effective choice. The Synectics work helped them to understand this target group's perspective on the industry and to develop new product ideas that met their needs while also addressing their worries.

For the former executive, the experience left a lasting impression: "Metaphors are so powerful in helping people see things in a new light. My aperture of sensitivity to metaphor is so much higher now."

While Synecticsworld's client made the familiar world of health insurance strange by exploring the metaphors of the uninsured, practitioners of the emerging field of biomimicry make the strange world of nature familiar by emulating the survival strategies of living things to solve human problems.

Biomimicry is yet another term imported from the Greek, drawn from the prefix *bio* (life) and the noun *mimesis* (imitation). Biomimicry is, literally, the imitation of life. Janine Benyus, the field's most prominent theorist, calls biomimicry "innovation inspired by nature." Faced with a human problem—say, how to prevent hospital-acquired infections, like the "super-bug" methicillin-resistant *Staphylococcus aureus* (MRSA)—biomimics look for natural models in which the same or a similar problem has already been solved. Once a suitable model is found, inventors, designers, and scientists copy it, adapting nature's solution to fit the human need.

"Animals, plants, and microbes are the consummate engineers," Benyus has said. "They have found what works, what is appropriate, and most important, what lasts here on Earth . . . After 3.8 billion years of research and development, failures are fossils, and what surrounds us is the secret to survival."

Nature's R&D department may have already solved one of the biggest problems buffeting the shipping industry: fouling, the accretion of marine organisms on hulls. Coincidentally, this innovation could also help prevent hospital-acquired infections.

As sticky marine critters accumulate on a hull, they act as a drag on the ship, decreasing efficiency and increasing fuel consumption. In pondering this problem, Anthony Brennan, founder of Sharklet Technologies, made it strange by thinking about sharks. It occurred to him that, unlike other slow-moving sea creatures, such as whales, sharks aren't bothered much by barnacles. Why not?

To find out, Brennan and a University of Florida research team took impressions of shark skin and noticed that it featured a distinctive diamond pattern on its surface, kind of like the raised lozenges on manhole covers. They mimicked that pattern on a microscopic scale—millions of miniature raised bars arranged in diamond-like arrays—and found that it inhibited the adhesion of microorganisms. Applied to the hull of a ship, the pattern could help discourage fouling. Applied to hospital surfaces—such as nurse call buttons, bed rails, and bathroom doors—it could help deter the growth of the bacteria that cause MRSA.

Sharklet Technologies has developed an adhesive film imprinted with the shark skin topography that can be applied to surfaces to inhibit germ growth. The company is also experimenting with ways to print the pattern directly onto objects, including everything from ship hulls to medical devices. The technology can be used in addition to—or better yet, instead of—marine paints, which can contaminate water, and antibiotics, which can encourage bacterial resistance.

Biomimicry is a more practically minded variation on the *objets trouvés* movement in art. Artists working with *objets trouvés*, "found objects" or "readymades," look to the environment for inspiration and innovation. Instead of creating a work from scratch, the artist identifies a pre-existing natural or man-made object and adapts it to serve his or her artistic purpose.

Pablo Picasso made *objets trouvés*. After World War II, he had a studio in the French town of Vallauris next to a vacant lot used by local artisans as a junkyard. To create his 1950 sculpture *She-Goat*, Picasso scavenged the yard for discarded ceramic fragments and metal shards. Two jugs became the goat's udders and an old wicker basket became its rib cage. Describing his working method for this piece, Picasso said: "I follow the way back from the basket to the rib cage: from the metaphor to reality. I make reality visible, because I use the metaphor."

Biomimics and Synectics practitioners also use metaphor to make reality visible. Biomimics "biologize" their questions, identifying themselves with a purely non-human entity and speculating about how that entity would solve the problem in question, just as Gordon and Prince suggested. Ask not how I can solve that problem but how nature has already solved it, is the biomimic's motto.

Biomimics interrogate flora and fauna to find models that can be carried over into the human environment, just as Synectics practitioners question consumers and apply their metaphors to new product development. Both biomimicry and Synectics find patterns in the data that lead to new perspectives and new possibilities, just as Picasso found a she-goat in a heap of rubbish.

Biomimics and Synectics practitioners, like found artists, are metaphorical handymen, creating new and useful things by recycling bits and pieces already made by nature or by others. This is an odd job but not an uncommon one. Innovation and invention have always progressed by looking for correlations and connections in nature. Biomimicry and Synectics are just the latest names for an age-old practice by which we apply metaphorical thinking to transform what we have at hand into what we have in mind.

Alexander Graham Bell invented the telephone after studying the operation of the bones inside the human ear. Isambard Kingdom Brunel, engineer of Britain's Industrial Revolution, realized how to dig tunnels under the Thames for the London Underground by watching a worm burrow into a piece of timber. The distinctive design of Pringles resulted from a Synectics session in which participants thought about how compaction was accomplished in nature; an analogy with the way fallen leaves stack together led to the innovative shape of the potato chip and its vertical packaging.

Benjamin Franklin made many of his discoveries about electricity by looking to nature for analogies. Franklin observed that electricity behaved a lot like lightning, a resemblance he described in detail in a journal entry on November 7, 1749:

Electrical fluid agrees with lightning in these particulars: 1. Giving light. 2. Color of the light. 3. Crooked direction. 4. Swift motion. 5. Being conducted by metals. 6. Crack or noise in exploding. 7. Subsisting in water or ice. 8. Rending bodies as it passes through. 9. Destroying animals. 10. Melting metals. 11. Firing inflammable substances. 12. Sulphurous smell. The electric fluid is attracted by points. We do not know whether this property is in lightning. But since they agree in all the particulars wherein we can already compare them, is it not probable they agree likewise in this? Let the experiment be made.

A good metaphor, like a bolt of lightning, provides a sudden flash of insight, a glimpse of illuminated ground on which experiments can be made. Things look strange when lit by lightning, but it is that very strangeness that enables us to see them differently.

Freud described "the uncanny" as "that class of the frightening which leads back to what is known of old and long familiar . . . An uncanny effect is often and easily produced when the distinction between imagination and reality is effaced." There is something of the uncanny about metaphor. Metaphors do not efface the distinction between imagination and reality but they do, to use Wallace Stevens's language, enhance and intensify it. In the act of satisfying the desire for innovation—in design, in business, or in the arts— metaphor has an uncanny knack for bringing imagination to life.

A LITTLE SPLASH OF COLOR
FROM MY MOTHER

Synectics consultants use metaphor to spur business innovation; psychotherapists James Lawley and Penny Tompkins use it to inspire psychological insight. Through a process called symbolic modeling, they help clients create and explore metaphors around crucial emotions or personal dilemmas. To learn more about the technique, I booked a session with Lawley and Tompkins. A few weeks before our appointment, my mother died and I decided that my mother's death would be the starting point for our conversation.

By the time I met with Lawley and Tompkins, my mother's funeral was over. The initial shock had passed. I had spent a week cleaning out her house, the house in which I grew up. Now things were getting back to normal. The routine business of living had resumed. As I struggled to identify exactly how I felt, to reconcile the contrast between the intensity of my mother's death and the abrupt return to normalcy, the best I could come up with was, "No different."

"Anything else about that 'No different'?" Lawley asked.

"The feeling is everywhere, diffuse," I said, "like a light blanket, not noticeable because it's so light. The most remarkable thing about it is that it has so few characteristics. It's almost nothing, like wallpaper."

"Anything else about that 'wallpaper'?"

"You ignore it, especially if it's drab."

"Anything else about that 'drab wallpaper'?"

"I don't like it, its drabness. It reminds me of the house I grew up in."

My family moved to the house I grew up in when it was brand new, in the early 1970s. As a teenager, I loathed that house. It symbolized to me everything that was flimsy and oppressive about growing up in the suburbs.

The hollow plywood door to my bedroom still had the deep gash cut into it when my brother threw his shoe at me and missed. The plastic towel rack in the bathroom still fell off the wall every time I tried to hang a wet towel on it. The lawn and the driveway were still impeccably maintained, just like every other lawn and driveway on this impeccably maintained street.

In going through my mother's things, I was struck by how few personal possessions she had. She had lots of bric-a-brac— Norman Rockwell commemorative plates, several plaques with "An Irish Blessing" printed on them, some mildly patriotic trinkets—but little else.

The trinkets kept turning up everywhere, not just on the walls but also in drawers, under beds, in closets, many of them sealed in plastic bags. My mother also had an astonishing array of Christmas and Halloween decorations, which she carefully packed up and stored after displaying for the holidays. This stuff had always made me inexpressibly depressed, something about the impersonal sameness of it all, like wallpaper.

Then, in the powder room closet under some old packets of aspirin, bottles of foot spray, and a variety of stray Christmas tree ornaments (all sealed in individual plastic bags), I found my mom's 1944 high school yearbook. In its warped and moldy pages was a pile of old photographs along with the drawings I had made as a kid for Mother's Day, Christmas, and my parents' wedding anniversaries.

The photographs showed my mom in all her glory—dressed as Mother Earth, wrapped in a bed sheet with a plastic Christmas wreath on her head, during one of the many parties my parents threw in the basement; at the front door during her surprise fiftieth birthday bash, gasping in delight and disbelief as she watched Aunt Peggy outfitted as a drum majorette leading a parade of friends and relatives down the middle of our street; tanning in a lawn chair in the backyard with slices of cucumber strategically placed over her eyes.

Among my colorful crayon drawings—full of balloons, exploding fireworks, and huge red hearts—was an apologetic note in which my mother explained that the drawings of my sister and brothers were missing because they had been ruined in one of the frequent post-rainstorm floods in our basement.

"My mom was fun and funny," I said. "The drab wallpaper blotted out the colorful patches."

"Anything else about that 'blotted out'?" Lawley asked.

"That's what blots out feelings. Memories of my mother can be splashes of color."

"When you think about those 'splashes of color,' then what happens?"

"It's not so drab anymore. It comes alive."

The drab wallpaper concealed a lot of feelings—about my mother, my childhood, the house I grew up in. By following the metaphor, aided by Lawley's gentle promptings, I uncovered memories and emotions that had been papered over long ago.

Lawley and Tompkins are practitioners of "clean language," a form of talk therapy developed by New Zealand psychotherapist David Grove. Grove, who died in 2008 at the age of fifty-seven, worked with people suffering from post-traumatic stress disorder (PTSD)—war veterans and victims of violent crime or psychological or sexual abuse. In the 1980s, he began noticing that when clients described their most troubling emotions and most traumatic memories, they always spoke in metaphors.

It is easy enough to label a specific emotion, such as grief, fear, pride, or happiness. It is much harder to convey the actual qualitative experience of that emotion. But metaphorical language can describe the indescribable. Saying that grief is like "having your heart ripped out" or that joy is "popping out of your body like a champagne cork" is not just the most vivid way to express the experience of these feelings, it is the *only* way to express the experience of these feelings.

"We can so seldom declare what a thing is, except by saying it is something else," George Eliot wrote in *The Mill on the Floss*. In saying that my feelings about my mother's death were like drab wallpaper, I discovered what my feelings really were.

Lawley and Tompkins, who are based in the United Kingdom, spent five years studying with Grove to produce a systematic account of his approach to metaphor in their book *Metaphors in Mind: Transformation through Symbolic Modelling*. "I noticed, if I didn't force people when they were talking they would naturally start using metaphor to describe their experience," Grove told them. "So I realized here was another way to structure experience. I decided that metaphor was a whole language worthy of study."

Grove paid careful attention to clients' metaphors, observing that they gradually took on a highly personalized significance. If a client stayed with a metaphor long enough, it became increasingly elaborate, often evolving into a kind of parable that contained an important lesson. The metaphors had a consistent structure and a direct relevance to the client's experience. And when the metaphors changed, Grove noticed, the people changed, too. Grove devised clean language as a technique to help clients, those with PTSD and those without, develop their own metaphors—and use those metaphors to achieve emotional insight and psychological change.

Grove's clean language is in many ways a dialect of Jung's active imagination. Both practices rely on client-generated imagery and metaphors to facilitate the process of change. But clean language is not the only psychological discipline to tap into the transformative power of metaphor.

The practice of "guided imagery" is a kind of active imagination employed to help people resolve and recover from illness. Metaphors alone don't cure physical afflictions, of course, just as they don't on their own resolve political disputes. But as research reveals more and more links between physical and mental health, metaphor is increasingly recognized as a method by which the mind can boost the body's healing processes.

A study of fifty-six patients scheduled for elective cardiac surgery, for instance, found that individuals' beliefs about their conditions before their operations correlated with their quality of life, feelings of depression, and levels of disability three months after the operations. Those patients who believed that their illness would be short, that it would not result in serious complications, and that their recovery depended to some extent on themselves recuperated faster than those who believed the opposite. The researchers concluded that patients' beliefs about their illness strongly influenced their recovery, and they recommended counseling sessions to help put people in a more healing frame of mind.

That is not to say patients should be given overly optimistic—or overly pessimistic—expectations about their prognoses. This is what Susan Sontag rightly decried about the commonly used metaphors for cancer and HIV/AIDS. But the way a condition is described primes patients' beliefs about and attitudes toward that condition. Medical metaphors are therefore more than just a matter of a pleasant bedside manner.

Indeed, nurses trained in clean language reported that patients felt better understood when they articulated their own metaphors for their symptoms than when they accepted pre-existing metaphors. Empowering patients through metaphor can be particularly helpful for stress-related illnesses, such as heart conditions, in which a patient's state of mind has a clear impact on his or her state of health.

What makes Grove's work, and Lawley and Tompkins's systematization of it, different from techniques like guided imagery is the relentless pursuit of the unexpected and idiosyncratic in client metaphors and the commitment to hold fast to the client's own words and imagery. What Jung wrote about images Grove believed of metaphors: "Images have a life of their own. When you concentrate on a mental picture, it begins to stir, the image becomes enriched by details, it moves and develops."

Jung described the active imagination technique in a letter to a certain Mr. O., who had written to Jung asking for advice about dream interpretation. The description applies equally well to clean language:

> Start with any image . . . Contemplate it and carefully observe how the picture begins to unfold or to change. Don't try to make it into something, just do nothing but observe what its spontaneous changes are. Any mental picture you contemplate in this way will sooner or later change through a spontaneous association that

causes a slight alteration of the picture. You must carefully avoid impatient jumping from one subject to another. Hold fast to the one image you have chosen and wait until it changes by itself. Note all these changes and eventually step into the picture yourself, and if it is a speaking figure at all then say what you have to say to that figure and listen to what he or she has to say. Thus you cannot only analyze your unconscious but you also give your unconscious a chance to analyze yourself.

Allowing the client's unconscious to analyze and learn from itself is key to how Grovian therapy works. But the clean language process is not like Jungian dream interpretation. Grove believed that client metaphors were unique to individuals rather than being of universal significance like Jungian archetypes. He also went out of his way to avoid interpreting client metaphors, a practice he believed only interfered with the therapeutic process.

Grove called his language "clean" precisely because it pared away the therapist's own assumptions, ideas, and biases. Clean language is meant to be a blank slate on which the client paints a metaphorical landscape. The technique, he once told Lawley, is for the client to "interrogate the metaphor until it confesses its strengths."

To facilitate these interrogations, Grove devised questions to elicit and enhance client metaphors. After studying transcripts of Grove's client work over about a decade, Lawley and Tompkins picked out a dozen key queries and organized them into three main categories.

Grove's questions address the metaphor itself, not what the client or the therapist happens to think about the metaphor. The therapist's role is "to pay unbelievable attention to the client's exact words," according to Tompkins. "You have to walk side by side with the person through their metaphor landscape. You have to keep the attention on their experience in the moment. The power of directing attention where people don't normally go is astronomical. When you notice the uncanny in a metaphor, when you hear the shock in the client's voice, you know you've hit pay dirt."

So, when a client uses a metaphor in a clean session, the therapist treats the phrase literally and begins asking questions of it. "When someone says, 'I'm a ticking bomb,' normal logic says, 'That's not real,'" Lawley explains. "Clean language asks, 'What kind of bomb? Is there anything else about that ticking?'"

The first six clean questions, known as "developing" questions, are signposts to direct clients deeper into their metaphor landscapes. Each question begins with "and" to emphasize the sense of a continuing narrative and the expectation that the metaphor, if followed, will actually lead somewhere. The therapist also repeats the client's exact words when posing questions, thus keeping the landscape clear of everything but the client's own metaphors.

The six developing questions are as follows (X and Y represent verbatim quotations of what the client has previously said):

And is there anything else about X?
And what kind of X is that X?
And where/whereabouts is X?
And that X is like what?
And is there a relationship between X and Y?
And when X, what happens to Y?

The second set of questions, known as "moving time" questions, create the metaphor's backstory, sketching in the context against which the metaphor plays out. The three moving time questions are:

And then what happens?/And what happens next?
And what happens just before X?
And where could/does X come from?

The final set of basic questions, known as "intention" questions, nudge the metaphor toward the client's actual experience, connecting the metaphor landscape with the changes the client would like to see in his or her actual life. The three intention questions are as follows (the material in brackets represents the exact words the client has previously used):

And what would you/X like to have happen?
And what needs to happen for X to [achieve what X would like to have happen]?
And can X [achieve what X would like to have happen]?

For Grove, the therapist has a vital but limited role in a clean session. Metaphors carry information, he believed, and that information can only be accessed through the metaphors themselves, not through a therapist's or a client's clever explications of them. Explication is not only unnecessary but also unhelpful. "Questions couched in 'normal' language ask the client to *comment* on his experience," Grove wrote in *Resolving Traumatic Memories: Metaphors and Symbols in Psychotherapy*. "Every time he does that he comes out of a state of self-absorption to perform an intellectual task which interrupts the process we are working to encourage and to facilitate." That process—the process of personal transformation—is about experience rather than interpretation.

Tompkins and Lawley describe a client who came to them wanting to break what he felt was a destructive pattern of relationships. Over the past two decades or so, he had fathered five children with three different women. In each case, he remained with his partner for about seven years, or until the eldest child born from the relationship was about four. Then he would fall in love with another woman and leave his partner. When he came to see Tompkins and Lawley, he was just embarking on a new relationship and did not want the same thing to happen again.

The man's metaphor for his pattern of behavior was an apple that he kept throwing away but which always ended up back in his hand.

He worked with Tompkins and Lawley for several months. During that time, they noticed that when he wasn't using his right hand to enact the movement of throwing away an apple, he often sat with that hand cupped around his eye, as if blocking something from view.

During one session, Tompkins asked: "And what happens just before you throw away the apple?"

The man momentarily dropped his right hand from around his eye, turned his head to look down to his right, and fought back a deep sob.

Tompkins responded with "And where did that come from?"

The man began to weep. He described a memory of playing at the top of a hill as a small child. It was foggy. As the fog gradually cleared, he saw his village below. He saw the front door of his house. He saw his father leave the house, close the front door, and walk away down the street.

He never saw his father again; he abandoned his family without any explanation. The client was four years old at the time.

The client's metaphor metamorphosed into the memory of being abandoned by his father. For the first time, he saw the connection between his own behavior and that of his father. Today, he remains happily married to his partner and they have two teenage children.

Why did he cup his right hand around his eye? Because it blocked the line of sight from which he had seen his father leave, a metaphorical gesture that shielded him from real emotional pain.

Metaphor has a paradoxical power. It distances an experience by equating it with something else, but in so doing actually brings that experience closer. "By talking about what something is not, you understand what it is," as Lawley puts it.

For Grove, clean language created an objective correlative for the client's experience. "Our questions will have given a form, made manifest some particular aspect of the client's internal experience in [a] way that he has not experienced before," Grove wrote. "The experience is alive and real; not just contained in words or dissipated in answers. We structure an environment internally: the client is going to *experience* rather than *describe* what the experience is like."

Clean language is not limited to therapeutic encounters. The practice has been used by the British police force to help officers with their interviewing techniques; by the British National Health Service to improve patient-doctor communication; in Northern Ireland and Bosnia as part of the post-conflict reconciliation process; and by major consultancy firms as an aspect of their management training schemes.

Lawley recalls one session with a senior manager in a multinational firm who wanted advice on dealing with difficult colleagues. During their initial meeting, the manager described what was going on in the office. Lawley jotted down some of the man's metaphors. The manager said he wanted "to be able to *hold the line*" against aggressive senior colleagues. "I have to *defend* my people," "The *troops* are falling by the wayside," and "I can lose it in *the heat of battle*" were some of his other remarks.

It didn't take long for Lawley to identify the manager's main metaphor: WORK IS WAR. When Lawley repeated aloud the roll call of military metaphors, the manager said he was *"shell-shocked."* Lawley then deployed his secret weapon—the clean language questions.

"And where does being 'in the heat of battle' come from?"

"You must defend your territory to be on the winning side," the manager snapped back.

"And when 'you must defend your territory to be on the winning side,' what would you like to have happen?"

This question breached the manager's defenses. He hesitated, real emotion appearing for the first time on his face and in his voice. The man shook his head and, taking a first step toward retreat, said: "Not to have to defend myself."

Lawley spent the rest of the session developing the manager's alternative metaphor: WORK IS PLAYING IN AN ORCHESTRA. The man understood that soldiering on with his martial metaphors would only escalate hostilities. So he made a conscious decision to change his tune, seeking harmony where previously there had been discord.

Caitlin Walker, a consultant who designs learning and development programs that address diversity, conflict, and leadership issues, has used clean language with unruly British adolescents in the context of anger management sessions. Working with one teenage boy who had a long history of getting into fistfights, she asked: "What happens just before you hit someone?"

"I just switch, Miss," he replied, snapping his fingers. "I go red. Everything just goes quiet."

"You 'go red.' You 'switch,'" Walker repeated, snapping her fingers. "'Everything just goes quiet.' And when it 'goes quiet,' what kind of quiet?"

"Like shutters, Miss," the boy said, cupping his hands around his eyes like horse blinkers. "I can't hear anything in my head and it's like I can only see the one in front of me. The next thing I know is people are shouting, someone's lying on the ground, and I'm in trouble."

Walker then asked the boy some "moving time" questions to find out what happened just before he hit someone.

"You 'go red,' and when you 'go red,' what kind of red is it?"

"Blood red. It just gets red and I get angry, like my blood's boiling." (For this boy, anger is a heated fluid in a container.)

"And when 'my blood's boiling,' what happens just before it's 'blood red' and 'boiling'?"

"It's cooler!"

"And when 'it's cooler,' 'it's cooler' like what?"

"It's cool blue, like the sky, like my Mum," he replied, looking upward and—uncharacteristically—smiling.

"And 'cool blue, like the sky, like your Mum,' then 'blood red' like your 'blood's boiling,' and then what happens after 'blood's boiling'?"

"I get raj [enraged] and attack. Then it's out of me and I run and look at the sky and think of my Mum and breathe in blue until the red's gone."

Through this clean interrogation, Walker helped the boy see the full spectrum of thoughts and feelings preceding a violent encounter. She asked the boy to think of his color metaphors the next time he felt himself losing his temper, and to use the metaphors to get himself out of the situation before fists started flying.

When they next met, he reported back: "You know I go red? Well, yesterday I felt it happening. I get up in the morning, blue and relaxed. Then I see Dad's drunk—red! Then I have to put dirty clothes back on cause he hasn't done laundry—red! No money for the bus—red! I'm cold and I'm late for school—red! I get to school and get detention and I'm red and anyone says anything it boils! So, I thought, what if I walk to school past the duck pond and I stop and look in the water, cause that makes me blue and if I breathe in blue and think of my Mum then I won't boil so fast."

Now, every time this boy feels himself going red, he breathes in blue by the duck pond near his school. With his anger under better control, he has been able for the first time to start building friendships with his classmates.

This translation from metaphor to real life is a central tenet of Grovian therapy. To encourage that transition, Grove often asked clients to actually do something related to their metaphor, a technique he picked up from Milton H. Erickson, a psychiatrist who specialized in clinical hypnosis.

Erickson often used parables in his therapeutic work, coupling these with specific tasks for clients to perform. One of Erickson's clients was an alcoholic. Erickson told this man a bit about the humble cactus, how the plant conserves water and can survive for up to three years in the desert without rainfall. He then told the man to go to the local botanical gardens to observe cacti.

Erickson never heard from the man again. Many years later, after this client had died, the man's daughter visited Erickson to tell him that her father had been sober since the day he went to the botanical gardens.

Erickson called these tasks "ambiguous-function assignments," but their role in furthering psychological change has become far less ambiguous since he began experimenting with them. In describing difficult emotions, we often use metaphors of containment: we keep our feelings *bottled up,* our bad memories *sealed off,* and our resentments *buried.* To test whether the physical acting out of these metaphors had a psychological impact on the experience of these emotions, researchers in Singapore and Canada devised an ambiguous-function assignment of their own. They first asked participants to write down their recollections of a recent decision they regretted. Half the group then sealed their texts in an envelope before handing it in; the other half did not. When subsequently asked how they felt about the regrettable decision, those who had sealed their recollections in an envelope reported significantly fewer negative emotions.

In a related experiment, the same research team asked subjects to write down two things: their account of a news report about an infant's accidental death and their plans for the weekend. Half the group sealed their account of the infant's death in an envelope; the other half sealed their plans for the weekend. The researchers found that those who had sealed up the story of the infant's death recalled fewer details of the event than those who had sealed up their plans for the weekend. Their conclusion: physical closure helps achieve psychological closure.

Grove used ambiguous-function assignments with his clients, too. If, for example, a client had said "I'm in a brick tunnel and I can't see either end," Grove might have sent the client to a transport museum to find out about tunnels, to a bricklayer to learn how tunnels are built, or to a DIY store to buy material to construct a replica tunnel. The goal: to translate insight into action.

After I finished cleaning out my mother's house, there was only one place left to look: the attic. The entrance to the attic was through the top of my bedroom closet. I knew we never kept much of anything up there, because that was where I hid things—my teenage diaries, in particular—that I didn't want my mother to discover. Still, I thought I would check the attic just to make sure nothing was left behind.

When I popped my head into the attic, I discovered three dilapidated hatboxes. In each of the three boxes was one of my mother's hats from the 1960s. One hat in particular I recognized: a pillbox hat made of bright pink feathers. Black-and-white shots of my mother wearing this hat were among the cache of photos I had found in her high school yearbook.

The hat was covered in fine black dust and a few of the feathers had fallen out. But, despite nearly forty years in the attic, it was still intact.

I took the hat home. I had it cleaned and repaired. It now occupies pride of place on our mantelpiece, a little splash of color from my mother.

THE LOGIC OF METAPHOR

Hart Crane briefly tried his hand as an advertising copy-writer, a shipyard laborer, and a worker in his father's candy manufacturing business. But, as a teenager and as an adult, all he ever wanted to be was a poet. In the summer of 1926, the twenty-seven-year-old Crane wrote a letter to Harriet Monroe, the founding editor of *Poetry*. Crane had submitted some poems to the venerable journal, to which Monroe had replied with consternation.

She was puzzled by Crane's use of imagery and asked him for clarification, in particular with regard to some lines from the poem "At Melville's Tomb": "The dice of drowned men's bones he saw bequeath / An embassy" and "Frosted eyes there were that lifted altars." Monroe failed to see how "drowned men's bones" could be "dice" or how "frosted eyes" could lift anything, let alone "altars."

Crane wrote two books of poetry before committing suicide in 1932 by leaping into the Gulf of Mexico from the deck of the *Ori-*

zaba, the ship that was sailing him back from Mexico to New York City. Crane took a Rimbaudian approach to life and to literature. He applied, pretty much literally, Rimbaud's call for a systematized disorganization of the senses, through alcohol abuse and a volatile and sometimes violent emotional life.

Like Rimbaud, Crane regarded the poet as a professional visionary, and his poems are filled with intense, vivid, and startling images. Crane's response to Monroe is his own version of Rimbaud's Seer Letters.

Before going on to clarify his poem, Crane cited two other poets, William Blake and T. S. Eliot, in his defense. He asked how Blake could possibly say, "a sigh is a sword of an Angel King" or how Eliot could believe "Every street lamp that I pass beats like a fatalistic drum," both images from famous poems of which Monroe presumably approved. Crane believed that associative leaps like these—from sighs to swords, from street lamps to drums, from frosted eyes to lifted altars—were essential to poetry and, indeed, to all creative thought. He wrote to Monroe:

> As a poet I may very possibly be more interested in the so-called illogical impingements of the connotations of words on the consciousness (and their combinations and interplay in metaphor on this basis) than I am interested in the preservation of their logically rigid significations . . . [A metaphor's] apparent illogic operates so logically in conjunction with its context in the poem as to establish its claim to another logic.

Crane called this other logic the "logic of metaphor."

The logic of metaphor is the logic of our lives. Metaphor impinges on everything, allowing us—poets and non-poets alike— to experience and think about the world in fluid, unusual ways. Metaphor is the bridge we fling between the utterly strange and the utterly familiar, between dice and drowned men's bones, between I and an other.

People have lived along the banks of the Thames for tens of thousands of years, more or less as long as there have been people. The place where they settled in the greatest numbers, though, has only been known as London for a couple thousand years.

The Thames is a blunt, muscular river that meanders through the city in wide leisurely arcs before merging with the North Sea. Like all rivers, it is both a lifeline and a timeline. For millennia, the Thames has afforded Londoners a living and preserved a record of their lives. Prehistoric stone tools, Bronze and Iron Age metalwork, old boots and discarded bicycles, human and animal bones—all the treasure and debris of human life—have been fished from its waters, forming its bequest to us. The Thames is, as British politician John Burns described it, "liquid history."

But London is actually riddled with rivers; the Thames is just the biggest. There are about a dozen others running through the city, smaller streams that have long been forgotten as London has grown from a parcel of separate villages into a major metropolis. In his *Survey of London*, published in 1598, historian John Stow wrote of the Walbrooke, which still flows secretly under The City, London's financial district:

> This water-course, having divers bridges, was afterwards vaulted over with brick, and paved level with the streets and lanes where through it passed; and since that, also houses have been built thereon, so that the course of the Walbrooke is now hidden underground, and thereby hardly known.

A tributary of one of London's lost rivers flows under my street. Several hundred years ago, the river darted along the place where I live now, then an open field dotted with ponds. Up until the early nineteenth century, people fished in it, a pastime commemorated in the etymology of a nearby street name: Anglers Lane. Then, somewhere along the line, the river started to sink. People built next to, on top of, and over it. They diverted it into gullies and ditches.

But however people tried to deflect it, the river just kept coming. So, rather than fight it, they funneled it into pipes laid along its natural course and submerged those beneath new roads and homes. The river retreated underground. People lost track of it.

Now it only surfaces during heavy rains, when it percolates into people's basements or bursts its buried banks and streams into the street, turning it once more into a river.

This is how the river, like a long-forgotten metaphor, reminds us that it's still there, even though we can't see it; that it's still fleet, still flowing, and knows exactly where it's going.

Acknowledgments

"What resembles nothing does not exist," the French poet Paul Valéry wrote in one of his many encomiums to metaphor. This book would not exist without the insights and assistance of Simon Baron-Cohen, who helped me make the right connections among autism, synesthesia, and metaphor; Max Brockbank, master weaver of my many-stranded Web site; Michael Brunton, for whom no research request was too bizarre and no academic paper too obscure; David Deutsch, for his tasty analogical rice puddings; James Lawley and Penny Tompkins, who, in addition to taking me on a guided tour of clean language, read the entire penultimate version of this book and made comments that opened up new vistas in my metaphor landscape; Sara Levine, for sharing with me her spotty metaphor bibliography, which turned out to hit exactly the right spot; Rebecca Mead, who suggested the eye test chart idea used on the paperback edition of this book; the literary estate of Vernon Scannell for permission to reproduce the poem "Nettles"; ZMETicians Richard Smith and Noleen Robinson of Business Development Research Consultants in London (and Olson Zaltman Associates, which licenses ZMET to BDRC), for my ZMET consultation and collage; Adam Somlai-Fischer of Prezi.com, who gave my metaphor talk its Prezi panache; Connie Williams of Synecticsworld, for making the strange world of synectics familiar; Jason Zweig, whose comments on the "How High Can a Dead Cat Bounce?" chapter were right on the money and whose own book, *Your Money and Your Brain*, informed much of my thinking about behavioral economics; those individuals who agreed to be interviewed for this book but did not want their identities revealed; Gillian Blake, Katinka Matson, and Jeanette Perez, for—literally—making this book happen; and Linda, Gilles, Tristan, and Hendrikje: apples of my eye and icing on my cake.

Notes

Foreword Why I Is an Other

1 "A Poet makes himself a visionary . . ." Rimbaud, Arthur. *Complete Works.* Translated by Paul Schmidt. New York: Harper Colophon Books, 1976, p. 102.

1 A language that "will include everything . . ." Ibid., p. 103.

2 "I got used to elementary hallucination . . ." Ibid., p. 205.

2 "I is an other." Ibid., p. 100.

2–3 "A round goblet never lacking mixed wine." Hunt, Patrick. *Poetry in the Song of Songs: A Literary Analysis.* Frankfurt: Peter Lang, 2008, p. 327.

3 "The gazelle has stolen its eyes from my beloved." Al-Jurjani, Abdalqahir. *The Mysteries of Eloquence.* Ritter, Hellmut, ed. Istanbul: Government Press, 1954, p. 20.

Metaphor and Thought All Shook Up

5 One metaphor for every ten to twenty-five words. Cameron, Lynne. "Metaphor and Talk." In: *The Cambridge Handbook of Metaphor and Thought.* Gibbs, Raymond W., Jr., ed. Cambridge: Cambridge University Press, 2008, p. 199. This figure comes from an analysis of different types of talk, including ordinary discourse, college lectures, and doctor–patient interviews. An analysis of TV shows found speakers used approximately one metaphor for every twenty-five words. See: Bowdle, Brian F., and Gentner, Dedre. "The Career of Metaphor." *Psychological Review* 112, 1, 2005, p. 193.

5 Six metaphors a minute. Gibbs, Raymond W., Jr. *The Poetics of Mind: Figurative Thought, Language, and Understanding.* Cambridge: Cambridge University Press, 1994, pp. 123–124. Gibbs based this statistic on analyses of psychotherapeutic interviews, essays, the 1960 Kennedy–Nixon presidential debates, and episodes of the MacNeil/Lehrer news program on PBS.

5 The Australian weather forecast. From the Weather page of the BBC Web site on March 15, 2010.

6 "Risks to U.K. Recovery *Lurk* behind *Cloudy Outlook*." From a Reuters article on March 15, 2010. Available at uk.reuters.com/article/idUKLNE62903A20100310.

6 Abraham Lincoln's Gettysburg Address. Available at http://www.visit-gettysburg.com/the-gettysburg-address-text.html.

6 The fourth paragraph of Barack Obama's inaugural address. Available at http://www.nytimes.com/2009/01/20/us/politics/20text-obama.html.

7 "She touched my hand . . ." "All Shook Up." Music and lyrics by Otis Blackwell/Elvis Presley.

8 "Giving the thing a name . . ." Aristotle. *The Rhetoric and the Poetics of Aristotle.* Introduction by Edward P. J. Corbett. New York: Modern Library, 1984, p. 251.

8 "Juliet is the sun." *Romeo and Juliet,* Act II, Scene ii, Line 3.

9 "When something that can scarcely be conveyed by the proper term . . ." Cicero. *De Oratore* Volume 2. Translated by H. Rackham. London: William Heinemann, 1942, p. 123.

9 The Arabic word for metaphor is *isti'ara,* or "loan." Al-Jurjani, Abdalqahir. *The Mysteries of Eloquence.* Ritter, Hellmut, ed. Istanbul: Government Press, 1954, p. 9.

10 The variety of metaphorical meanings for the word "shoulder." Deignan, Alice. "Corpus-based Research into Metaphor." In: *Researching and Applying Metaphor.* Cameron, Lynne, and Low, Graham, eds. Cambridge: Cambridge University Press, 1999, pp. 185–189.

11 Participants exposed to a bare illuminated lightbulb performed better at solving spatial, verbal, and mathematical problems. Slepian, M. L., Weisbuch, M., Rutchick, A. M., Newman, L. S., and Ambady, N. "Shedding Light on Insight: Priming Bright Ideas." *Journal of Experimental Social Psychology* 46, 2010, pp. 696–700.

11 "Metaphor permeates all discourse . . ." Goodman, Nelson. *Languages of Art.* Indianapolis: Hackett, 1976, p. 80.

12 "My love is like a red, red rose." This is the first line of Burns's lyric "A Red, Red Rose."

13 "A sign of genius . . ." Aristotle. *The Rhetoric and the Poetics of Aristotle,* p. 255.

13 "Atoms are unlimited in size and number . . ." Cited in: Jones, W. T. *A History of Western Philosophy: The Classical Mind.* New York: Harcourt Brace Jovanovich, 1970, p. 76.

14 "No collision would take place . . ." Lucretius. *On the Nature of the Universe.* Book II, 220–225. Available at http://classics.mit.edu/Carus/nature _things.html.

14 Poincaré was "short and plump . . ." In: Newman, James R. *The World of Mathematics.* Volume 2. Mineola, NY: Dover, 2000, p. 1374.

15 "During the complete repose of the mind . . ." Poincaré, Henri. *The Foundations of Science.* Lancaster, PA: Science Press, 1946, pp. 393–394.

Metaphor and Etymology Language Is Fossil Poetry

17 Elvis the Pelvis. "Elvis the Pelvis" is an example of synecdoche, a type of metaphor in which one distinctive part of a thing is used to represent the whole. Another example of synecdoche is "Old Blue Eyes" as a reference to Frank Sinatra. Metonymy is closely related to synecdoche but substitutes an attribute for the thing itself, as in the use of "crown" to signify a monarchy or "Washington" to refer to the U.S. government.

18 "Abuses of speech." Hobbes, Thomas. *Leviathan.* Oxford: Oxford University Press, 1998, p. 21.

18 "Use words metaphorically . . ." Ibid., p. 21.

18 "Reasoning upon [metaphor] . . ." Ibid., p. 32.

18 "A philosopher should abstain . . ." Cited in: Gentner, Dedre, and Jeziorski, Michael. "The Shift from Metaphor to Analogy in Western Science." In: *Metaphor and Thought.* Ortony, Andrew, ed. Cambridge: Cambridge University Press, 1993, p. 448.

18 "If we would speak of things as they are . . ." Locke, John. *An Essay Concerning Human Understanding.* Book 3, Chapter 10. Available at http://oregonstate .edu/instruct/phl302/texts/locke/locke1/Essay_contents.html.

20 "When a new thing . . ." Barfield, Owen. *History in English Words.* London: Faber and Faber, 1962, p. 20.

22 The first use of "hot" as a metaphor. Williams, J. "Synaesthetic Adjectives: A Possible Law of Semantic Change." *Language* 52, 2, 1976, p. 475.

22 The first use of "bridge" as a metaphor. Zharikov, S., and Gentner, D. "Why Do Metaphors Seem Deeper than Similes?" In: *Proceedings of the Twenty-Fourth Annual Conference of the Cognitive Science Society.* Gray, W. D., and Schunn, C. D., eds. Fairfax, VA: George Mason University, 2002, pp. 980–981.

22 Common phrases with intricate metaphorical etymologies. See: E. Cobham Brewer's *The Dictionary of Phrase & Fable,* William and Mary Morris's *Dictionary of Word and Phrase Origins,* James Rogers's *The Dictionary of Clichés,* and Walter W. Skeat's *Concise Dictionary of English Etymology.*

22 Deadline. Gentner, Dedre, and Bowdle, Brian. "The Psychology of Metaphor Processing." In: *Encyclopedia of Cognitive Science.* London: Nature Publishing Group, 2002, p. 21.

23 "Our knowledge grows . . ." Cited in: Wheelwright, Philip. *The Burning*

Fountain: A Study in the Language of Symbolism. Bloomington and London: Indiana University Press, 1968, p. 181.

23 "Three-fourths of our language . . ." Ibid., p. 120.

23 The etymological roots of "seeing is knowing." Sweetser, Eve. *From Etymology to Pragmatics: Metaphorical and Cultural Aspects of Semantic Structure.* Cambridge: Cambridge University Press, 1990, p. 9. See also: Kovecses, Zoltan. *Metaphor: A Practical Introduction.* Oxford: Oxford University Press, 2002, pp. 218–219.

23 The verb "grasp" means "to understand." Kleparski, Grzegorz A. "Hot Pants, Cold Fish and Cool Customers: The Search for Historical Metaphorical Extensions in the Realm of Temperature Terms." *Studia Anglica Resoviensia* 4, 2007, p. 115.

24 Tunisian Arabic speakers say their *brains are boiling.* Wilkowski, Benjamin M., et al. "Hot-Headed Is More Than an Expression: The Embodied Representation of Anger in Terms of Heat." *Emotion* 9, 4, 2009, p. 464.

24 In the Sotho languages, angry people are described as *hot-blooded.* Kleparski, Grzegorz A. "Hot Pants, Cold Fish and Cool Customers: The Search for Historical Metaphorical Extensions in the Realm of Temperature Terms," pp. 100–118.

24 Japanese metaphors for anger. Matsuki, Keiko. "Metaphors of Anger in Japanese." In: *Language and the Cognitive Construal of the World.* Taylor, John R., and MacLaury, Robert E., eds. Berlin: de Gruyter, 1995, pp. 137–151.

24 Anger in American Sign Language. Taub, Sarah F. *Language from the Body: Iconicity and Metaphor in American Sign Language.* Cambridge: Cambridge University Press, 2004, p. 3.

24 Chinese metaphors. Yu, Ning. "Metaphorical Expressions of Anger and Happiness in English and Chinese." *Metaphor and Symbolic Activity* 10, 1995, pp. 59–92.

24 Hungarian metaphors. Kovecses, Zoltan. *Metaphor: A Practical Introduction,* p. 168.

24 The equation of bigness with significance. Grady, Joseph E. "A Typology of Motivation for Conceptual Metaphor: Correlation vs. Resemblance." In: *Metaphor in Cognitive Linguistics.* Selected Papers from the Fifth International Cognitive Linguistics Conference, Amsterdam, July 1997. Gibbs, Raymond W., Jr., and Steen, Gerard J., eds. Amsterdam: John Benjamins, 1999, p. 80.

24 The use of the sense of smell to indicate suspicion. Ibarretxe-Antuñano, Iraide. "Metaphorical Mappings in the Sense of Smell." In: *Metaphor in Cognitive Linguistics,* p. 32.

24 "Low-level metaphorical associations between concepts, based directly on experiential correlation." Grady, Joseph. "Cross-linguistic Regularities in Metaphorical Extension." A talk delivered at the Linguistic Society of America Annual Meeting, Los Angeles, January 9, 1999.

25 "With progressive loss of its virility . . ." Goodman, Nelson. *Languages of Art*. Indianapolis: Hackett, 1976, p. 68.

26 "Every modern language . . ." Barfield, Owen. *Poetic Diction: A Study in Meaning*. Middletown, CT: Wesleyan University Press, 1973, p. 63.

26 "A man cannot utter a dozen words . . ." Ibid., p. 69.

26 Louis de Broglie and the theory of electron *waves*. Gamow, George. *Thirty Years That Shook Physics: The Story of Quantum Theory*. New York: Dover, 1966, pp. 80–81.

27 The word "broker." My thanks to Jason Zweig for his insights into the etymology of the words "broker" and "stock."

27 "The width of a swollen barleycorn." Cited in: "Thirteenth-century Tally Sticks." The U.K. National Archive Web site, http://www.nationalarchives .gov.uk/museum/item.asp?item_id=6. See also: Dyson, George. "Economic Dis-Equilibrium: Can You Have Your House and Spend It Too?" The Edge Web site, http://edge.org/3rd_culture/dysong08.1/dysong08.1 _index.html.

28 Language as "fossil poetry." Emerson, Ralph Waldo. *Selected Prose and Poetry*. New York: Holt, Rinehart and Winston, 1969, p. 130.

28 "The poets made all the words . . ." Ibid., p. 130.

Metaphor and Money How High Can a Dead Cat Bounce?

29 Commentators from Helsinki to Hong Kong. Smith, G. P. "How High Can a Dead Cat Bounce?: Metaphor and the Hong Kong Stock Market." *Organizational Behavior and Human Decision Processes* 18, 1995, pp. 43–57. See also: Schmidt, Christopher M. "Metaphor and Cognition: A Cross-Cultural Study of Indigenous and Universal Constructs in Stock Exchange Reports." *Intercultural Communication* 5, 2002, http://www.immi.se/ intercultural.

30 "Stock prices took a rollercoaster ride . . ." Cited in: Smith, G. P. "How High Can a Dead Cat Bounce?: Metaphor and the Hong Kong Stock Market," pp. 43–57.

30 "The most important example of economic rhetoric . . ." McCloskey, Deirdre N. *The Rhetoric of Economics*. Second edition. Madison: University of Wisconsin Press, 1998, p. 40.

31 "Agent metaphors tend to be evoked . . ." Morris, Michael W., Sheldon, Oliver J., Ames, Daniel R., and Young, Maia J. "Metaphors and the Market: Consequences and Preconditions of Agent and Object Metaphors in Stock Market Commentary." *Organizational Behavior and Human Decision Processes* 102, 2, 2007, p. 178.

31 "Agent metaphors imply . . ." Ibid., p. 177.

31 The rush to assumption in financial decision-making. Bechara, Antoine, and Damasio, Antonio R. "The Somatic Marker Hypothesis: A Neural

Theory of Economic Decision." *Games and Economic Behavior* 52, 2005, p. 359. See also: Zweig, Jason. *Your Money and Your Brain*. London: Souvenir Press, 2007, p. 60 and p. 69.

32 Our brains are always prospecting for pattern. Huettel, Scott A., et al. "Perceiving Patterns in Random Series: Dynamic Processing of Sequence in the Prefrontal Cortex." *Nature Neuroscience* 5, 5, 2002, pp. 485–490. See also: Gibbs, Raymond W., Jr. *The Poetics of Mind: Figurative Thought, Language, and Understanding*. Cambridge: Cambridge University Press, 1994, p. 412.

33 The "interpreter." Wolford, George, et al. "The Left Hemisphere's Role in Hypothesis Formation." *The Journal of Neuroscience* 20, 2000, pp. 1–4.

34 A fleck of brain tissue roughly the size of a large match head. Edelman, Gerald M. *Bright Air, Brilliant Fire: On the Matter of the Mind*. London: Penguin Books, 1994, p. 17.

34 "Brains operate . . . not by logic . . ." Edelman, Gerald M. *Second Nature: Brain Science and Human Knowledge*. New Haven and London: Yale University Press, 2006, p. 58.

35 "Education by Poetry" delivered at Amherst College in 1930. Parini, Jay. *Robert Frost: A Life*. London: Pimlico, 2001, p. 265.

35 "I have wanted in late years . . ." Frost's essay "Education by Poetry" is available at http://www.en.utexas.edu/amlit/amlitprivate/scans/edbypo.html.

37 "Bug perceivers." Lettvin, J. Y., Maturana, H. R., McCulloch, W. S., and Pitts, W. H. "What the Frog's Eye Tells the Frog's Brain." *Proceedings of the IRE* 47, 11, 1959, pp. 1940–1959. Reprinted in: McCulloch, Warren S. *Embodiments of Mind*. Cambridge, MA: MIT Press, 1965, p. 254.

37 "Not only spots of light . . ." *Embodiments of Mind*, p. 237.

38 "The frog does not seem to see . . ." Ibid., p. 231.

38 "That the eye speaks to the brain . . ." Ibid., p. 251.

39 "A better chance of making a shot . . ." Gilovich, T., Vallone, R., and Tversky, A. "The Hot Hand in Basketball: On the Misperception of Random Sequences." *Cognitive Psychology* 17, 1985, p. 296.

39 "A general misconception of chance . . ." Ibid., p. 296.

39 "If random sequences are perceived as streak shooting . . ." Ibid., p. 312.

40 Heider and Simmel's animated film. Heider, F., and Simmel, M. "An Experimental Study of Apparent Behavior." *American Journal of Psychology* 57, 1944, pp. 243–259. You can watch Heider and Simmel's film on YouTube, at http://www.youtube.com/watch?v=sZBKer6PMtM.

40 Physiognomic perception. Marks, Lawrence E. "On Perceptual Metaphors." *Metaphor and Symbolic Activity* 11, 1, 1996, pp. 44–45.

41 "You see A *cause* the motion of B." Scholl, B. J., and Tremoulet, P. D. "Perceptual Causality and Animacy." *Trends in Cognitive Sciences* 4, 8, 2000,

p. 299. This and other classic Scholl shorts can be seen at http://www.yale
.edu/perception/Brian/demos/causality-Basics.html. Scholl has updated
the Heider and Simmel film, too, in color. You can see it at http://research
.yale.edu/perception/animacy/HS-Blocks-QT.mov.

41 Living things are special. Frith, Chris. *Making Up the Mind: How the Brain
Creates Our Mental World*. Oxford: Blackwell, 2007, p. 148.

41 Sarah, the chimpanzee. Premack, D., and Woodruff, G. "Does the Chimpanzee Have a Theory of Mind?" *Behavioral and Brain Sciences* 4, 1978,
pp. 515–526.

42 Sarah's analogical abilities. Gillan, D. J., Premack, D., and Woodruff, G.
"Reasoning in the Chimpanzee 1: Analogical Reasoning." *Journal of Experi-
mental Psychology–Animal Behavior Processes* 7, 1, 1981, pp. 1–17. See also:
Holyoak, Keith J., and Thagard, Paul. *Mental Leaps: Analogy in Creative
Thought*. Cambridge, MA: MIT Press, 1995, pp. 47–48.

42 "Uptrend stimulus trajectories . . ." Morris, Michael W., et al. "Metaphors
and the Market: Consequences and Preconditions of Agent and Object
Metaphors in Stock Market Commentary," p. 179.

42 Dragging bulls and bears into it. Jason Zweig observes that our contemporary market menagerie really consists only of bulls and bears, but dozens of
animal metaphors—lambs and rams, pointers, setters, wolves, foxes, and
on and on—populated the early English stock exchange.

42 "People making sense of stock charts . . ." Morris, Michael W., et al. "Metaphors and the Market: Consequences and Preconditions of Agent and Object Metaphors in Stock Market Commentary," p. 178.

43 "Unexamined metaphor . . ." McCloskey, Deirdre N. *The Rhetoric of Economics*, p. 46.

Metaphor and the Mind   Imagining an Apple in Someone's Eye

46 They do not attribute intentions or emotions . . . Heberlein, Andrea S., and
Adolphs, Ralph. "Impaired Spontaneous Anthropomorphizing Despite
Intact Perception and Social Knowledge." *Proceedings of the National Acad-
emy of Sciences* 101, 19, 2004, pp. 7487–7491.

46 "I laughed my socks off." Haddon, Mark. *The Curious Incident of the Dog in
the Night-time*. London: Vintage, 2004, p. 19.

46 "When you describe something . . ." Ibid., p. 20.

47 "I think it should be called a lie . . ." Ibid., p. 20.

48 "The test of a true metaphor . . ." Addison, Joseph. "Pleasures of the Imagination." *Spectator* 411, 1712, p. 21. My thanks to Alberto Manguel for alert-
ing me to Addison's observation.

48 People consistently rate metaphors with vivid, concrete imagery as most
memorable . . . *Metaphor and Thought*. Ortony, Andrew, ed. Cambridge:
Cambridge University Press, 1993, p. 326.

49 "Every metaphor, provided it be a good one . . ." Cicero. *De Oratore*, Volume 2, pp. 125–127.

49 The policeman, the burglar, and ASD. Happé, Francesca, et al. " 'Theory of Mind' in the Brain: Evidence from a PET Scan Study of Asperger Syndrome." *NeuroReport* 8, 1996, p. 198.

50 Participants in the study did not get the irony of the story . . . Irony is another form of metaphorical thinking, since it involves saying one thing but meaning another. If you mutter "Another lovely day" as you step from your front door into a violent thunderstorm, you are using metaphor by giving your actual opinion an expression that belongs to something else.

50 Social language "is riddled with figurative phrases . . ." Baron-Cohen, Simon. *Mindblindness: An Essay on Autism and Theory of Mind.* Cambridge, MA: MIT Press, 1997, p. 142.

50 "In decoding figurative speech . . ." Ibid., p. 27.

51 "How is it possible . . ." Leslie, A. M. "Pretense and Representation: The Origins of 'Theory of Mind.' " *Psychological Review* 94, 1987, p. 412.

51 Functional and perceptual similarity. McCune-Nicolich, Lorraine. "Toward Symbolic Functioning: Structure of Early Pretend Games and Potential Parallels with Language." *Child Development* 52, 3, 1981, pp. 785–797.

51 "It's like a machine for putting in petrol." Gibbs, Raymond W., Jr. *The Poetics of Mind: Figurative Thought, Language, and Understanding,* p. 399.

51 The definition of syncretism. Piaget, Jean. *The Language and Thought of the Child.* London: Routledge & Kegan Paul, 1960, p. 158.

52 The truth is "quarantined." Leslie, A. M. "Pretense and Representation: The Origins of 'Theory of Mind,' " p. 415.

52 "Not representations of the world . . ." Ibid., p. 417.

52 "Pretence is . . ." Ibid., p. 416.

53 Mirror neurons. Rizzolatti, G., and Craighero, L. "The Mirror-Neuron System." *Annual Review of Neuroscience* 27, 2004, pp. 169–192.

53 Mirror neurons, disgust, and pain. Rizzolatti, G., Fogassi, L., and Gallese, V. "Mirror Neurons in the Mind." *Scientific American*, November 2006, pp. 54–69.

53 Malfunctioning mirror neuron system and ASD. Dapretto, Mirella, et al. "Understanding Emotions in Others: Mirror Neuron Dysfunction in Children with Autism Spectrum Disorders." *Nature Neuroscience* 9, 2006, pp. 28–30.

54 The correlation between mirror system dysfunction, ASD, and theory of mind. Frith, Uta. "Mindblindness and the Brain in Autism." *Neuron* 32, 2001, pp. 969–979.

54 "To mind-read . . ." Baron-Cohen, Simon. "The Biology of the Imagination." *Entelechy Journal* 9, Summer/Fall 2007, http://www.entelechyjournal .com/simonbaroncohen.htm.

54 "A chance word or name . . ." Tammet, Daniel. *Born on a Blue Day: A Memoir of Asperger's and an Extraordinary Mind.* London: Hodder & Stoughton, 2007, p. 96.

54 "Complexity" and "fragile peace." Ibid., p. 207.

55 *Kellokült.* Ibid., p. 218.

55 *Pullo.* Tammet, Daniel. *Embracing the Wide Sky: A Tour Across the Horizons of the Mind.* London: Hodder & Stoughton, 2009, p. 222.

56 *Devil's advocate.* Stuart-Hamilton, Ian. *An Asperger Dictionary of Everyday Expressions.* London and Philadelphia: Jessica Kingsley, 2007, p. 181.

56 *Cold shoulder.* Ibid., p. 98.

Metaphor and Advertising
Imaginary Gardens with Real Toads in Them

58 How to play Smoke. Gardner, John. *On Moral Fiction.* New York: Basic Books, 2000, p. 118.

59 "No one can achieve profound characterization . . ." Ibid., p. 119.

60 Personifications of Absolut and Stolichnaya vodkas and the five core elements of "brand personality." Aaker, J. L. "Dimensions of Brand Personality." *Journal of Marketing Research* 34, 3, 1997, p. 347.

60 Personifications of cars. Piller, Ingrid. "Extended Metaphor in Automobile Fan Discourse." *Poetics Today* 20, 3, 1999, pp. 483–498.

60 Asking consumers about their buying intentions. Levav, Jonathan, and Fitzsimons, Gavan J. "When Questions Change Behavior: The Role of Ease of Representation." *Psychological Science* 17, 3, 2006, pp. 207–213.

60 "Limit 12 per customer." Chapman, Gretchen B., and Johnson, Eric J. "Incorporating the Irrelevant: Anchors in Judgments of Belief and Value." In: *Heuristics and Biases: The Psychology of Intuitive Judgment.* Gilovich, Thomas, Griffin, Dale, and Kahneman, Daniel, eds. Cambridge: Cambridge University Press, 2002, p. 120.

61 Groups with the coolest, most alluring affective profiles. MacGregor, D. G., Slovic, P., Dreman, D., and Berry, M. "Imagery, Affect, and Financial Judgment." *The Journal of Psychology and Financial Markets* 1, 2, 2000, p. 104–110.

62 "Representations of objects and events . . ." Finucane, M. L., Alhakami, A., Slovic, P., and Johnson, S. M. "The Affect Heuristic in Judgments of Risks and Benefits." *Journal of Behavioral Decision Making* 13, 2000, p. 3.

62 "Deep metaphors." Zaltman, Gerald, and Zaltman, Lindsay. *Marketing Metaphoria: What Deep Metaphors Reveal About the Minds of Consumers.* Boston: Harvard Business Press, 2008, p. xv.

63 Presented with images with few or no recognizable features . . . The technical term for seeing the Virgin Mary in a grilled cheese sandwich and other

feats of physiognomic perception is "pareidolia," a word derived from the Greek *para*, meaning "beside," and *eidolon*, meaning "image."

63–64 "When we concentrate on an inner picture . . ." Jung, Carl Gustav. *Jung on Active Imagination*. Key Readings Selected and Introduced by Joan Chodorow. London: Routledge, 1997, p. 145.

65 Seven deep metaphors. Zaltman, Gerald, and Zaltman, Lindsay. *Marketing Metaphoria: What Deep Metaphors Reveal about the Minds of Consumers*, p. 17.

65 "Those people who are least aware of their unconscious side . . ." Jung, Carl Gustav. "The Transcendent Function." In: Miller, Jeffrey C. *The Transcendent Function: Jung's Model of Psychological Growth through Dialogue with the Unconscious*. Albany: State University of New York Press, 2004, p. 159.

66 Life is a journey. The StrategyOne results can be found at http://www.poll ster.com/blogs/life_metaphors.php.

66 "Deep metaphors are . . ." Zaltman, Gerald, and Zaltman, Lindsay. *Marketing Metaphoria: What Deep Metaphors Reveal About the Minds of Consumers*, p. xv.

69 Everything from chocolates to automobiles to beer . . . These examples come from "Visual Metaphor and Conventionality," a talk given by Didier Hodiamont at the Eighth International Conference on Researching and Applying Metaphor, July 2010, Amsterdam.

69 One study even found that people are more likely to respond to symbols that have once been widely known . . . Schorn, Robert, Tappeiner, Gottfried, and Walde, Janette. "Analyzing 'Spooky Action at a Distance' Concerning Brand Logos." *Innovative Marketing* 2, 1, 2006, pp. 45–60.

70 "Because they contain an essential truth . . ." Thompson, Philip, and Davenport, Peter. *The Dictionary of Visual Language*. London: Penguin, 1982, p. vii.

70 A ZMET study conducted for a major agricultural corporation. Olson, J., Waltersdorff, K., and Forr, J. "Incorporating Deep Customer Insights in the Innovation Process." Available at http:// www.olsonzaltman.com/down loads/2008%20Insights%20in%20the%20Innovation%20Process.pdf.

71 The Senseo and Hourglass coffeemakers. These examples come from "Understanding Product Metaphors," a talk given by Nazil Cila at the Eighth International Conference on Researching and Applying Metaphor, July 2010, Amsterdam.

71–72 Advertisements "provide a structure . . ." Williamson, Judith. *Decoding Advertisements: Ideology and Meaning in Advertising*. London and New York: Marion Boyars, 1985, p. 12.

72 The objective correlative. Eliot, T. S. *Selected Essays*. London: Faber and Faber, 1972, p. 145.

72 "'Objective correlatives' end up by *being* . . ." Williamson, Judith. *Decoding Advertisements: Ideology and Meaning in Advertising*, p. 37.

73 Children consumed 45 percent more snacks when exposed to food ads. Harris, J. L., Bargh, J. A., and Brownell, K. D. "Priming Effects of Television Food Advertising on Eating Behavior." *Health Psychology* 28, 2009, pp. 404–413.

73 Exposure to the logos of major fast-food chains increased people's feelings of impatience and reduced their willingness to save money. Zhong, Chen-Bo, and DeVoe, Sanford E. "You Are How You Eat: Fast Food and Impatience." *Psychological Science* 21, 3, 2010, pp. 1–4.

74 "Poetry." Marianne Moore's poem is available at http://www.poemhunter .com/poem/poetry/.

Metaphor and the Brain Bright Sneezes and Loud Sunlight

76 Equating brightness with loudness and high-pitched sounds. Marks, Lawrence E., et al. "Perceiving Similarity and Comprehending Metaphor." *Monographs of the Society for Research in Child Development* 52, 1, 1987, pp. 1–100. See also: Cacciari, Cristina. "Crossing the Senses in Metaphorical Language." In: *The Cambridge Handbook of Metaphor and Thought.* Gibbs, Raymond W., Jr., ed., p. 429.

76 Even children as young as four . . . Marks, Lawrence E., et al. "Perceiving Similarity and Comprehending Metaphor," pp. 32–33.

77 Synesthetic metaphors follow a remarkably consistent pattern. Shen, Yeshayahu, and Eisenamn, Ravid. "Heard Melodies Are Sweet, but Those Unheard Are Sweeter: Synaesthesia and Cognition." *Language and Literature* 17, 2, 2008, pp. 101–121.

78 Some researchers suggest this movement from less to more immediate parallels the physiological development of the senses themselves. Williams, J. "Synaesthetic Adjectives: A Possible Law of Semantic Change." *Language* 52, 2, 1976, pp. 461–478.

78 "Sweet silence" versus "silent sweetness" and studies of nineteenth-century English, French, and Hungarian verse and twentieth-century poetry in Hebrew. Cited in: Shen, Yeshayahu, and Cohen, Michal. "How Come Silence Is Sweet but Sweetness Is Not Silent: A Cognitive Account of Directionality in Poetic Synesthesia." *Language and Literature* 7, 2, 1998, pp. 123–140.

79 "Love Is Like a Bottle of Gin." I first heard about this Stephin Merritt song in a talk by Dedre Gentner.

79 "Wednesdays are always blue . . ." Tammet, Daniel. *Born on a Blue Day: A Memoir of Asperger's and an Extraordinary Mind,* p. 1.

79 "Five is a clap of thunder . . ." Ibid., p. 3.

79 Metaphor may have evolved from early synesthetic abilities. Ramachandran, Vilayanur S., and Hubbard, Edward M. "Neural Cross Wiring and Synesthesia." *Journal of Vision* 1, 3, 2001, http://www.journalofvision.org/ content/1/3/67.

80 "Can it be a coincidence . . ." Ramachandran, Vilayanur S., and Hubbard, Edward M. "Synesthesia: A Window into Perception, Thought, and Language." *Journal of Consciousness Studies* 8, 12, 2001, p. 9.

80 The bouba-kiki effect. Ramachandran, Vilayanur S. "Broken Mirrors: A Theory of Autism." *Scientific American*, November 2006, pp. 62–69.

81 "This result suggests . . ." Ibid., p. 69.

81 Even very young children associate visual and auditory stimuli. Winner, Ellen. *The Point of Words: Children's Understanding of Metaphor and Irony.* Cambridge, MA: Harvard University Press, 1988, pp. 69–70. See also: Wagner, Sheldon, et al. " 'Metaphorical' Mapping in Human Infants." *Child Development* 52, 2, 1981, pp. 728–731.

82 Young macaque monkeys preferred a cloth surrogate mother (warmed by a 100-watt lightbulb). Harlow, Harry. "The Nature of Love." *American Psychologist* 13, 1958, pp. 673–685.

83 Those whose list included the word "warm" formed far more positive impressions of the person than those whose list included the word "cold." Asch, S. E. "Forming Impressions of Personality." *Journal of Abnormal and Social Psychology* 41, 1946, pp. 258–290.

83 "When we describe the workings of emotions, ideas, or trends of character . . ." Asch, S. E. "The Metaphor: A Psychological Inquiry." In: *Person Perception and Interpersonal Behavior.* Taguiri, R., and Petrullo, L., eds. Stanford, CA: Stanford University Press, 1955, pp. 86–87.

83 Hot coffee–holders versus cold coffee–holders. Williams, Lawrence E., and Bargh, John A. "Experiencing Physical Warmth Promotes Interpersonal Warmth." *Science* 322, 5901, 2008, pp. 606–607.

83 Social exclusion, reductions in room temperature, and a virtual game of "catch." Zhong, Chen-Bo, and Leonardelli, Geoffrey J. "Cold and Lonely: Does Social Exclusion Literally Feel Cold?" *Psychological Science* 19, 9, 2008, pp. 838–842.

84 Conquest asks consumer panels to use online avatars . . . Penn, David. "Getting Animated About Emotion." A talk delivered at the European Society for Opinion and Marketing Research Congress 2008, Montreal, September 22, 2008.

85 Clipboards and weighty subjects. Jostmann, Nils B., Lakens, Daniel, and Schubert, Thomas W. "Weight as an Embodiment of Importance." *Psychological Science* 20, 9, 2009, pp. 1169–1174.

85 Similar studies have shown that people interviewing job applicants while holding a heavy rather than a light clipboard . . . Ackerman, Joshua M., Nocera, Christopher C., and Bargh, John A. "Incidental Haptic Sensations Influence Social Judgments and Decisions." *Science* 328, 5986, 25 June, 2010, pp. 1712–1715.

85 The angular gyrus and metaphor. Ramachandran, Vilayanur S., and Hubbard, Edward M. "Synesthesia: A Window into Perception, Thought, and Language." *Journal of Consciousness Studies* 8, 12, 2001, pp. 3–34.

86 "There lies, in our most basic apprehension of music . . ." Scruton, Roger. *The Aesthetics of Music*. Oxford: Oxford University Press, 1999, p. 92.

86 Mathematical thought may be tethered to the body. Loetscher, T., et al. "Eye Position Predicts What Number You Have in Mind." *Current Biology* 20, 6, 2010, pp. 264–265.

87 The synesthetic link between music and space. Marks, Lawrence E., et al. "Perceiving Similarity and Comprehending Metaphor." *Monographs of the Society for Research in Child Development* 52, 1, 1987, p. 54.

87 Scaffolding. Williams, Lawrence E., Huang, Julie Y., and Bargh, John A. "The Scaffolded Mind: Higher Mental Processes Are Grounded in Early Experience of the Physical World." *European Journal of Social Psychology* 39, 2009, pp. 1257–1267.

88 "If all abstract thought is metaphorical . . ." Pinker, Steven. *The Stuff of Thought*. London: Allen Lane, 2007, p. 242–243.

89 People recognize negative words faster in a low versus a high vertical position. Meier, Brian P., and Robinson, Michael D. "Why the Sunny Side Is Up: Associations Between Affect and Vertical Position." *Psychological Science* 15, 2004, pp. 243–247.

89 The taller the vertical lines on a company's organizational chart, the more powerful people judge that company's executives to be. Giessner, Steven R., and Schubert, Thomas W. "High in the Hierarchy: How Vertical Location and Judgments of Leaders' Power Are Interrelated." *Organizational Behavior and Human Decision Processes* 100, 2006, pp. 160–176.

89 People reporting symptoms of depression respond faster to objects in the lower portions of their fields of vision. Meier, Brian P., and Robinson, Michael D. "Does 'Feeling Down' Mean Seeing Down? Depressive Symptoms and Vertical Selective Attention." *Journal of Research in Personality* 40, 2006, pp. 451–461.

89 Moving marbles from a lower to a higher position causes people to recall positive memories more quickly. Casasanto, Daniel, and Dijkstra, Katinka. "Motor Action and Emotional Memory." *Cognition* 115, 2010, pp. 179–185.

89 Study participants evaluate positive words more quickly when they are presented in larger font sizes . . . Meier, Brian P., Robinson, Michael D., and Caven, Andrew J. "Why a Big Mac Is a Good Mac: Associations Between Affect and Size." *Basic and Applied Social Psychology* 30, 2008, pp. 46–55.

90 "Taste played as important a part in their imagery . . ." Stapledon, Olaf. *Star Maker*. London: Victor Gollancz, 2001, p. 29.

90 Common conceptual metaphors. Kovecses, Zoltan. *Metaphor: A Practical Introduction*. Oxford: Oxford University Press, 2002, p. 5.

91 "Basic conceptual metaphors . . ." Lakoff, George, and Turner, Mark. *More than Cool Reason: A Field Guide to Poetic Metaphor*. Chicago: University of Chicago Press, 1989, p. 51.

92 The "Halle Berry neuron." Quian Quiroga, R., et al. "Invariant Visual Representation by Single Neurons in the Human Brain." *Nature* 435, 2005, pp. 1102–1107.

92 Experiments with monkeys show that certain neurons respond to correlations among objects. Cited in: Dehaene, Stanislas. *Reading in the Brain: The Science of Evolution of a Human Invention.* New York: Viking, 2009, p. 143.

92 "The 'dead metaphor' account . . ." Kovecses, Zoltan. *Metaphor: A Practical Introduction,* p. ix.

Metaphor and the Body Anger Is a Heated Fluid in a Container

94 When we think about time, the regions devoted to motion and spatial relations are active as well. Pinker, Steven. *The Stuff of Thought.* London: Allen Lane, 2007, p. 238.

95 "Next Wednesday's meeting has been *moved forward* two days." Boroditsky, L., and Ramscar, M. "The Roles of Body and Mind in Abstract Thought." *Psychological Science* 13, 2, 2002, pp. 185–188. See also: Gibbs, Raymond W., Jr., and Matlock, Teenie. "Metaphor, Imagination, and Simulation: Psycholinguistic Evidence." In: *The Cambridge Handbook of Metaphor and Thought.* Gibbs, Raymond W., Jr., ed., p. 168.

95 Students waiting in line at a café and people on a moving train. Boroditsky, L., and Ramscar, M. "The Roles of Body and Mind in Abstract Thought," pp. 185–188.

97 People asked to plot points on a line relatively far apart. Williams, Lawrence E., and Bargh, J. A. "Experiencing Physical Warmth Promotes Interpersonal Warmth." *Science* 322, 2008, pp. 606–607.

97 People seated in an upright position. Stepper, S., and Strack, F. "Proprioceptive Determinants of Emotional and Nonemotional Feelings." *Journal of Personality and Social Psychology* 64, 1993, pp. 211–220. Also cited in: Williams, Lawrence E., Huang, Julie Y., and Bargh, John A. "The Scaffolded Mind: Higher Mental Processes Are Grounded in Early Experience of the Physical World." *European Journal of Social Psychology* 39, 2009, p. 1261.

97 People shown texts containing metaphors for speed . . . Described in "Iconicity in Metaphorical Storytelling," a talk given by Marlene Johansson Falck at the Eighth International Conference on Researching and Applying Metaphor, July 2010, Amsterdam.

97 Solomon Asch researched other, very different languages. Asch, S. E. "The Metaphor: A Psychological Inquiry." In: *Person Perception and Interpersonal Behavior.* Taguiri, R., and Petrullo, L., eds. Stanford, CA: Stanford University Press, 1955, pp. 88–89.

98 Words like these "do not denote exclusively the 'raw materials' of experience." Ibid., p. 93.

98 Participants contemplating the future even tended to lean forward while people recalling the past tended to lean backward. Miles, Lynden K., Nind, Louise K., and Macrae, C. Neil. "Moving through Time." *Psychological Science* 21, 1, 2010, pp. 1–2.

98 Speakers of Aymara gesture behind themselves when talking about the future. Cienki, Alan, and Muller, Cornelia. "Metaphor, Gesture, and

Thought." In: *The Cambridge Handbook of Metaphor and Thought.* Gibbs, Raymond W., Jr., ed. Cambridge: Cambridge University Press, 2008, p. 492.

98   The different space-related metaphors that English and Mandarin speakers use to think and talk about time. Boroditsky, Lera. "Does Language Shape Thought? English and Mandarin Speakers' Conceptions of Time." *Cognitive Psychology* 43, 1, 2001, pp. 1–22.

99   "Differences in talking do indeed lead to differences in thinking." Ibid., p. 18.

99–100   People "use spatial knowledge to think about time . . ." Ibid., p. 6.

101   Those primed by pictures of business-related objects consistently interpreted the situation as more competitive . . . Kay, Aaron C., et al. "Material Priming: The Influence of Mundane Physical Objects on Situational Construal and Competitive Behavior Choice." *Organizational Behavior and Human Decision Processes* 95, 2004, pp. 83–96.

101   Anger and heat. Wilkowski, Benjamin M., et al. "Hot-Headed Is More than an Expression: The Embodied Representation of Anger in Terms of Heat." *Emotion* 9, 4, 2009, pp. 464–477.

102   Subjects are quicker to identify anger-related words after being primed with heat imagery. Valenzuela, Javier, and Soriano, Cristina. "Looking at Metaphors: A Picture-Word Priming Task as a Test for the Existence of Conceptual Metaphor." Fifth Annual AELCO/SCOLA Conference, University of Zaragoza, Spain, 2004.

103   How color affects behavior. Elkan, Daniel. "Winners Wear Red: How Colour Twists Your Mind." *New Scientist* 2723, 26, 2009.

103   Participants rated teams in darker professional football and hockey uniforms as more malevolent than teams in lighter uniforms. Frank, M. G., and Gilovich, T. "The Dark Side of Self and Social Perception: Black Uniforms and Aggression in Professional Sports." *Journal of Personality and Social Psychology* 54, 1988, pp. 74–85. Cited in: Meier, Brian P., and Robinson, Michael D. "The Metaphorical Representation of Affect." *Metaphor and Symbol* 20, 4, 2005, pp. 239–257.

104   *In the red.* My thanks to Jason Zweig for these musings on the economic impact of the color red.

104   People using red rather than blue pens . . . Rutchick, Abraham M., Slepian, Michael L., and Ferris, Bennett D. "The Pen Is Mightier than the Word: Object Priming of Evaluative Standards." *European Journal of Social Psychology* 40, 5, 2010, pp. 704–708.

105   The neural systems responsible for physical disgust. Moll, J., et al. "The Moral Affiliations of Disgust: A Functional MRI Study." *Cognitive and Behavioral Neurology* 18, 1, 2005, pp. 68–78. Cited in: Williams, Lawrence E., and Bargh, J. A. "Experiencing Physical Warmth Promotes Interpersonal Warmth." *Science* 322, 2008, pp. 606–607.

105   Heart and breathing rates accelerate when we see pictures of threatening objects. Cited in: Kosslyn, Stephen M., Ganis, G., and Thompson, W. L.

"Neural Foundations of Imagery." *Nature Reviews Neuroscience* 2, 2001, pp. 635–642.

105 The brain's visual circuits respond when we see something and when we see it only in our mind. Kosslyn, Stephen M., and Thompson, William L. "Shared Mechanisms in Visual Imagery and Visual Perception: Insights from Cognitive Neuroscience." In: *The New Cognitive Neurosciences.* Gazzaniga, Michael S., editor in chief. Cambridge, MA: MIT Press, 2000, pp. 975–985.

105 Mental simulation was as effective as physical practice in walking the simplest routes. Vieilledent, Stephane, Kosslyn, Stephen M., Berthoz, Alain, and Giraudo, Marie Dominique. "Does Mental Simulation of Following a Path Improve Navigation Performance Without Vision?" *Cognitive Brain Research* 16, 2003, pp. 238–249.

105 When test subjects are asked to imagine walking specific distances . . . Feldman, Jerome A. *From Molecule to Metaphor: A Neural Theory of Language.* Cambridge, MA: MIT Press, 2006, p. 215.

105 Thinking is a kind of simulated interaction with the world. Decety, Jean, and Grezes, Julie. "The Power of Simulation: Imagining One's Own and Other's Behavior." *Brain Research* 1079, 2006, pp. 4–14. See also Coulson, Seana. "Metaphor Comprehension and the Brain." In: *The Cambridge Handbook of Metaphor and Thought.* Gibbs, Raymond W., Jr., ed. Cambridge: Cambridge University Press, 2008, p. 189.

106 Physical actions related to specific metaphors. Gibbs, Raymond W., Jr., and Matlock, Teenie. "Metaphor, Imagination, and Simulation: Psycholinguistic Evidence." In: *The Cambridge Handbook of Metaphor and Thought.* Gibbs, Raymond W., Jr., ed. Cambridge: Cambridge University Press, 2008, p. 167. See also: Gibbs, Raymond W., Jr. *Embodiment and Cognitive Science.* Cambridge: Cambridge University Press, 2006, pp. 183–184.

106 "Performing an action facilitates understanding . . ." Gibbs, Raymond W., Jr., and Matlock, Teenie. "Metaphor, Imagination, and Simulation: Psycholinguistic Evidence," p. 167.

106 The literal meanings of verbs like "kick" and "walk" activate neurons in the brain regions involved in the physical actions of kicking and walking. Cited in: Dehaene, Stanislas. *Reading in the Brain: The Science of Evolution of a Human Invention.* New York: Viking, 2009, p. 113.

106 Making a fist and the accessibility of the concept of power. Schubert, Thomas W. "The Power in Your Hand: Gender Differences in Bodily Feedback from Making a Fist." *Personality and Social Psychology Bulletin* 30, 6, 2004, pp. 757–769 and Schubert, Thomas W., and Kooleb, Sander L. "The Embodied Self: Making a Fist Enhances Men's Power-related Self-conceptions." *Journal of Experimental Social Psychology* 45, 2009, pp. 828–834.

107 "If language was given to men to conceal their thoughts . . ." Napier, John. *Hands.* Revised by Russell H. Tuttle. Princeton, NJ: Princeton University Press, 1993, p. 157.

107 The "nose thumb," "fingers crossed," and "OK sign." McNeill, David. *Hand and Mind: What Gestures Reveal about Thought.* Chicago and London: University of Chicago Press, 1992, pp. 57–59.

108 The anatomical term for the middle finger. Napier, John. *Hands*, pp. 22–23.

108 "Language is inseparable from imagery . . ." McNeill, David. *Gesture and Thought.* Chicago and London: University of Chicago Press, 2005, p. 4.

108 Mirror neurons, gesture, and the origins of language. Rizzolatti, Giacomo, and Arbib, Michael A. "Language within Our Grasp." *Trends in Neuroscience* 21, 1998, pp. 188–194.

109 "What made us human crucially depended at one point on gestures." Arbib, Michael A. "From Monkey-like Action Recognition to Human Language: An Evolutionary Framework for Neurolinguistics." *Behavioral and Brain Sciences* 28, 2005, pp. 105–167.

109 As much as 90 percent of spoken descriptions is accompanied by gestures of some sort. McNeill, David. *Gesture and Thought*, p. 4.

109 The blind gesture during speech with the same frequency as the sighted. Goldin-Meadow, Susan. *Hearing Gesture: How Our Hands Help Us Think.* Cambridge, MA: Harvard University Press, 2003, pp. 141–144.

109 Metaphors in American Sign Language. Taub, Sarah F. *Language from the Body: Iconicity and Metaphor in American Sign Language.* Cambridge: Cambridge University Press, 2004, pp. 3–4.

109 When adults have their limbs restrained during speech, they produce less vivid imagery. Goldin-Meadow, Susan. *Hearing Gesture: How Our Hands Help Us Think*, p. 165.

110 "In a metaphoric gesture . . ." McNeill, David. *Gesture and Thought*, p. 39.

110 "The gestures provide imagery for the non-imageable." Ibid., p. 45.

110 The woman described her former boyfriend as depressive. Müller, Cornelia. *Metaphors Dead and Alive, Sleeping and Waking: A Dynamic View.* Chicago: University of Chicago Press, 2008, pp. 77–79.

110 The phrase "It sparked" is a colloquialism for falling in love. Ibid., pp. 32–34.

110 Speakers of Turkana use a similar gesture to convey the concept of knowledge. McNeill, David. *Gesture and Thought*, pp. 46–47.

Metaphor and Politics Freedom Fries and Liberty Cabbage

113 Lhermitte casually mentioned the word "museum" and the rude/polite university students. Bargh, John A. "Bypassing the Will: Towards Demystifying the Nonconscious Control of Social Behavior." In: *The New Unconscious.* Uleman, James S., and Bargh, John A., eds. New York: Oxford University Press, pp. 37–58.

113 Subjects presented with primes relating to the elderly. Cited in: Holland, Rob W., Hendriks, Merel, and Aarts, Henk. "Smells Like Clean Spirit:

Nonconscious Effects of Scent on Cognition and Behavior." *Psychological Science* 16, 9, 2005, pp. 689–693.

113 Subjects presented with primes relating to cooperation and achievement. Bargh, John A. "Bypassing the Will: Toward Demystifying the Nonconscious Control of Social Behavior." In: *The New Unconscious*, p. 39.

114 German trial judges read the details of a criminal case. Mussweiler, T., and Strack, F. "Comparing Is Believing: A Selective Accessibility Model of Judgmental Anchoring." In: *European Review of Social Psychology* 10, 1999, pp. 135–136.

114 "Poets are the unacknowledged legislators of the world." From Shelley's "A Defence of Poetry." Available at http://www.bartleby.com/27/23.html.

115 "Language is vitally metaphorical . . ." Cited in: Richards, I. A. *The Philosophy of Rhetoric*. Oxford: Oxford University Press, 1965, pp. 90–91.

115 "Arbitrary coherence." Ariely, Dan. *Predictably Irrational: The Hidden Forces That Shape Our Decisions*. London: HarperCollins, 2008, p. 26.

116 "The people who get to impose their metaphors on the culture get to define what we consider to be true." Lakoff, George, and Johnson, Mark. *Metaphors We Live By*. Chicago: University of Chicago Press, 2003, p. 160.

116 "What therefore is truth?" Nietzsche, Friedrich. "On Truth and Falsity in Their Ultramoral Sense." In: *The Complete Works of Friedrich Nietzsche*. Levy, Oscar, ed. New York: MacMillan, 1911, pp. 183–184.

116 A small democratic country of no vital interest to U.S. national security. Gilovich, T. "Seeing the Past in the Present: The Effect of Associations to Familiar Events on Judgments and Decisions." *Journal of Personality and Social Psychology* 40, 7, 1981, pp. 797–808.

117 "When one must make a decision . . ." Ibid., p. 807.

117 The Stroop effect. Stroop, J. Ridley. "Studies of Interference in Serial Verbal Reactions." *Journal of Experimental Psychology* 18, 1935, pp. 643–662. See also: Glucksberg, Sam, et al. "On Understanding Non-literal Speech: Can People Ignore Metaphors?" *Journal of Verbal Learning and Verbal Behavior* 21, 1, 1982, pp. 85–98.

119 "Metaphorical meanings are apprehended . . ." and "We can no more shut off . . ." Glucksberg, Sam. *Understanding Figurative Language: From Metaphors to Idioms*. New York: Oxford University Press, 2001, p. 21 and p. 28.

119 "A small but symbolic effort . . ." See: "US Congress opts for 'freedom fries'," BBC News, March 12, 2003, http://news.bbc.co.uk/1/hi/world/americas/2842493.stm.

120 Alternatives to "global warming." See: "Seeking to Save the Planet, with a Thesaurus," *New York Times*, May 1, 2009, http://www.nytimes.com/2009/05/02/us/politics/02enviro.html?th&emc=th.

122 "Public structures." Aubrun, Axel, and Grady, Joseph. " 'Public Structures' as a Simplifying Model for Government." A report commissioned by the FrameWorks Institute on behalf of the Council for Excellence in Government and Demos, October 2005.

124 Participants read a short passage about the economy, either one that explicitly compared economic development to auto racing or one that did not. Krennmayr, Tina. "When Do People Think Metaphorically?" The Eighth International Conference on Researching and Applying Metaphor, July 2010, Amsterdam.

125 Surrendering the phrase "war on drugs." See: "White House Czar Calls for End to 'War on Drugs'," *Wall Street Journal*, May 14, 2009, http://online .wsj.com/article/SB124225891527617397.html.

125 There are around 1,700 sports metaphors in common use and fifty-nine football metaphors deployed during the Gulf War. Herbeck, Dale A. "Sports Metaphors and Public Policy: The Football Theme in Desert Storm Discourse." In: *Metaphorical World Politics*. Beer, Francis A., and De Landtsheer, Christ'l, eds. East Lansing: Michigan State University Press, 2004, p. 123.

126 George Carlin on football versus baseball metaphors. Carlin's clip can be viewed at http://learning.writing101.net/com102/blog/2010/02/08/lesson -4-more-on-metaphor/.

128 "Give America a chance to digest . . ." Cited in: O'Brien, Gerald V. "Indigestible Food, Conquering Hordes, and Waste Materials: Metaphors of Immigrants and the Early Immigration Restriction Debate in the United States." *Metaphor and Symbol* 18, 1, 2003, pp. 36–37.

128 One experiment specifically designed to explore the priming effects of the "nation = body" metaphor. Landau, Mark J., et al. "Evidence that Self-Relevant Motives and Metaphoric Framing Interact to Influence Political and Social Attitudes." *Psychological Science* 20, 11, 2009, pp. 1421–1427.

130 "When fertilization fails to occur . . ." Martin, Emily. *The Woman in the Body: A Cultural Analysis of Reproduction*. Boston: Beacon Press, 1992, p. 45.

130 "At every point in the system, functions 'fail' and falter." Ibid., p. 42.

130 "Illness is not a metaphor . . ." Sontag, Susan. *Illness as Metaphor*. New York: Random House, 1983, p. 7.

130 The moral Stroop test. Sherman, Gary D., and Clore, Gerald L. "The Color of Sin: White and Black Are Perceptual Symbols of Moral Purity and Pollution." *Psychological Science* 20, 8, 2009, pp. 1019–1025.

131 A study involving participants from twenty different countries. Meier, Brian P., and Robinson, Michael D. "The Metaphorical Representation of Affect." *Metaphor and Symbol* 20, 4, 2005, pp. 239–257.

131 "Just as the word 'lemon' activates 'yellow' . . ." Sherman, Gary D., and Clore, Gerald L. "The Color of Sin: White and Black Are Perceptual Symbols of Moral Purity and Pollution," p. 1021.

132 People automatically assume that bright objects are good and dark objects are bad. Meier, Brian P., Robinson, Michael D., and Clore, Gerald L. "Why Good Guys Wear White: Automatic Inferences about Stimulus Valence Based on Brightness." *Psychological Science* 15, 2, 2004, pp. 82–87.

132 Children even tend to assume that black boxes contain negative objects. Sherman, Gary D., and Clore, Gerald L. "The Color of Sin: White and Black Are Perceptual Symbols of Moral Purity and Pollution," p. 1019.

132 People subliminally primed with black faces were more hostile. Kay, Aaron C., et al. "Material Priming: The Influence of Mundane Physical Objects on Situational Construal and Competitive Behavior Choice." *Organizational Behavior and Human Decision Processes* 95, 2004, p. 94.

132 Whites subliminally exposed to black faces. Smith, Pamela K., Dijksterhuis, A., and Chaiken, Shelly. "Subliminal Exposure to Faces and Racial Attitudes: Exposure to Whites Makes Whites Like Blacks Less." *Journal of Experimental Social Psychology* 44, 2008, pp. 50–64.

132 Researchers produced two different versions of a putative campaign advertisement for Barack Obama. From e-mail correspondence with Emory University psychologist Drew Westen. See also "Shades of Prejudice" by Shankar Vedantam, *New York Times*, January 19, 2010, http://www.nytimes.com/2010/01/19/opinion/19vedantam.html?th&emc=th.

132 Darker-skinned African-American defendants are more than twice as likely to get the death penalty. Eberhardt, Jennifer L., Davies, Paul G., Purdie-Vaughns, Valerie J., and Johnson, Sheri Lynn. "Looking Deathworthy: Perceived Stereotypicality of Black Defendants Predicts Capital-Sentencing Outcomes." *Psychological Science* 17, 5, 2006, pp. 383–386.

132 People primed to think about blacks, by reading a list of names regarded as stereotypically African-American . . . Rattan, Aneeta, and Eberhardt, Jennifer L. "The Role of Social Meaning in Inattentional Blindness: When the Gorillas in Our Midst Do *Not* Go Unseen." *Journal of Experimental Social Psychology*, in press.

133 The "Macbeth effect." Zhong, Chen-Bo, and Liljenquist, Katie. "Washing Away Your Sins: Threatened Morality and Physical Cleansing." *Science* 313, 5792, 2006, pp. 1451–1452

133 The simple act of hand cleaning has also been found to wash away regrets about past decisions. Lee, Spike W. S., and Schwarz, Norbert. "Washing Away Postdecisional Dissonance." *Science* 328, 7 May 2010, p. 709.

133 Researchers at the University of Toronto put undergraduates in a brand-new lab . . . Zhong, C. B., Strejcek, B., and Sivanathan, N. "A Clean Self Can Render Harsh Moral Judgment." *Journal of Experimental Social Psychology*, in press.

134 Those exposed to citrus-scented cleaner. Holland, Rob W., Hendriks, Merel, and Aarts, Henk. "Smells Like Clean Spirit: Nonconscious Effects of Scent on Cognition and Behavior." *Psychological Science* 16, 9, 2005, pp. 689–693.

134 Subjects in a room perfumed with citrus-scented Windex. Liljenquist, Katie, Zhong, Chen-Bo, and Galinsky, Adam D. "The Smell of Virtue: Clean Scents Promote Reciprocity and Charity." *Psychological Science* 21, 5, 2010, pp. 381–383.

134 Participants in a dim room cheated more often. Zhong, Chen-Bo, Bohns,

Vanessa K., and Gino, Francesca. "A Good Lamp Is the Best Police: Darkness Increases Dishonesty and Self-Interested Behavior." *Psychological Science*, 2010, in press. Available at SSRN: http://ssrn.com/abstract=1547980.

135 "If thought corrupts language . . ." Orwell, George. "Politics and the English Language." In: *Why I Write*. London: Penguin, 1984, p. 116.

135 Political language is "designed to make lies sound truthful . . ." Ibid., p. 120.

135 "A newly invented metaphor assists thought . . ." Ibid., p. 105–106.

Metaphor and Pleasure
Experience Is a Comb That Nature Gives to Bald Men

138 "When pagan peoples had just embraced civilization . . ." Vico, Giambattista. *New Science*. London: Penguin Classics, 2001, p. 22.

138 "In all languages expressions for inanimate objects . . ." Ibid., pp. 159–160.

138 The "universal principle of etymology . . ." Ibid., p. 97.

139 "Coleridge expanded himself . . ." Cited in: Fisch, M. H. "The Coleridges, Dr. Prati, and Vico." *Modern Philology* 41, 2, 1943, p. 121.

139 "I am more and more delighted with G. B. Vico." Ibid., p. 112.

140 The orator "makes beauty . . ." Cited in: Schaeffer, John D. *Sensus Communis: Vico, Rhetoric, and the Limits of Relativism*. Durham, NC, and London: Duke University Press, 1990, p. 66.

140 "Co-operative act of comprehension." Cohen, Ted. "Metaphor and the Cultivation of Intimacy." In: *On Metaphor*. Sacks, Sheldon, ed. Chicago and London: University of Chicago Press, 1979, p. 7.

141 "Experience is a comb . . ." Cited in: Sommer, Elyse, with Dorrie Weiss. *Metaphors Dictionary*. Canton, MI: Visible Ink Press, 2001.

141 "Like two skeletons copulating . . ." Cited in: Grothe, Mardy. *I Never Metaphor I Didn't Like*. New York: Collins, 2008, p. 83.

141 "She had nostrils like badger-holes." Lee, Laurie. *Cider with Rosie*. London: Vintage Books, 2002, p. 80.

142 Humor and cognitive dissonance. Strick, Madelijn, et al. "Finding Comfort in a Joke: Consolatory Effects of Humor through Cognitive Distraction." *Emotion* 9, 4, 2009, pp. 574–578.

142 Brain scans of people laughing. Mobbs, D., Greicius, M., Abdel-Azim, E., Menon, V., and Reiss, A. "Humor Modulates the Mesolimbic Reward Centers." *Neuron* 40, 5, pp. 1041–1048.

143 Von Economo cells. Watson, Karli K., Matthews, Benjamin J., and Allman, John M. "Brain Activation during Sight Gags and Language-Dependent Humor." *Cerebral Cortex* 17, 2, 2007, pp. 314–324.

143 The ACC and ambiguity and error detection. Hirsh, Jacob B., and Inzlicht, Michael. "Error-related Negativity Predicts Academic Performance." *Psychophysiology* 46, 2009, pp. 1–5.

143 "Above all things, care is to be taken . . ." Quintilian. Institutes, Book 8, Chapter 6, section 50. Available at http://www2.iastate.edu/~honeyl/quintilian/8/chapter6.html#4.

144 The *New Yorker* and "Block That Metaphor." My thanks to Jon Michaud, The *New Yorker*'s head of library, for information on the history of Block That Metaphor. For more information, go to http://emdashes.com/2007/05/ask-the-librarians-v.php.

144 *Step Up to the Plate and Fish or Cut Bait.* Reprinted in the *New Yorker*, January 10, 2000.

144 "The moment that you walk into the bowels of the armpit of the cesspool of crime, you immediately cringe." Reprinted in the *New Yorker*, March 27, 2000.

144 Karyn Hollis's own Block that Metaphor archive. For more howlers, go to http://www19.homepage.villanova.edu/karyn.hollis/prof_academic/Courses/common_files/best_ever_metaphors_and_analogie.htm.

145 Kafka and cognitive dissonance. Proulx, Travis, and Heine, Steven J. "Connections from Kafka: Exposure to Meaning Threats Improves Implicit Learning of an Artificial Grammar." *Psychological Science* 20, 9, 2009, pp. 1125–1131. The stories are available online at http://www.psych.ubc.ca/heine/ImplicitLearningStories.doc.

145 "Devotee of metaphor." Wilson-Quayle, J. "Max Black." *American National Biography 2.* Oxford: Oxford University Press, 1999, pp. 862–864.

146 "What is needed . . ." Black, Max. *Models and Metaphors: Studies in Language and Philosophy.* Ithaca, NY: Cornell University Press, 1962, p. 40.

146–147 "Suppose I look at the night sky . . ." Ibid., p. 41.

147 Donald Leavis as "the George Wallace of Northern Ireland." Tourangeau, Roger. "Metaphor and Cognitive Structure." In: *Metaphor: Problems and Perspectives.* Miall, David S., ed. Brighton, UK: Harvester Press, 1982, pp. 28–29.

148 "Metaphorical terms give people much more pleasure . . ." Cicero. *De Oratore.* Volume 2, pp. 125–127.

149 "Metaphorical force . . ." Goodman, Nelson. *Languages of Art.* Indianapolis: Hackett, 1976, pp. 79–80.

149 "Beautiful like the accidental meeting . . ." Cited in: Arnheim, Rudolf. *Visual Thinking.* London: Faber and Faber, 1970, p. 210.

150 "In using metaphors to give names to nameless things . . ." Aristotle. *The Rhetoric and the Poetics of Aristotle*, p. 170

150 "I constructed it myself . . ." Coleridge, Samuel Taylor. *Biographia Literaria.* London: J. M. Dent and Sons Ltd., 1934, p. 82.

150 "I feel too intensely . . ." Coleridge, Samuel Taylor. *The Notebooks of Samuel Taylor Coleridge.* Volume 2. Coburn, Kathleen, ed. Princeton, NJ: Princeton University Press, 1957, p. 2372.

151 "A few grams of *dantine* . . . have an affair with a goat . . ." Lem, Stanislaw. *The Futurological Congress.* Orlando, FL: Harcourt, Inc., 1974, pp. 80–81.

Metaphor and Children   How Should One Refer to the Sky?

153 "Icicle of blood" and other kennings. Sturluson, Snorri. *The Prose Edda.* Translated with an introduction and notes by Jesse L. Byock. London: Penguin, 2005, p. 124.

153 Kennings for earth. Ibid., p. 112.

153 Kennings for fire. Ibid., p. 113.

154 Bonobos and metaphor. Kenneally, Christine. *The First Word: The Search for the Origins of Language.* New York: Viking Penguin, 2007, pp. 42–43.

154 A flashlight battery and a hairbrush. Gardner, Howard, and Winner, Ellen. "The Development of Metaphoric Competence: Implications for Humanistic Disciplines." In: *On Metaphor.* Sacks, Sheldon, ed. Chicago and London: University of Chicago Press, 1979, p. 132.

155 A comb becomes a centipede . . . Winner, Ellen. *The Point of Words: Children's Understanding of Metaphor and Irony.* Cambridge, MA: Harvard University Press, 1988, p. 90–91.

155 Provide an appropriate simile to end the story. Gibbs, Raymond W., Jr. *The Poetics of Mind: Figurative Thought, Language, and Understanding.* Cambridge: Cambridge University Press, 1994, p. 404–405.

156 The upside-down mop was called "a flower." Winner, Ellen. *The Point of Words: Children's Understanding of Metaphor and Irony,* p. 73.

156 "Sally was a bird flying to her nest." Gentner, D., and Wolff, P. "Metaphor and Knowledge Change." In: *Cognitive Dynamics: Conceptual Change in Humans and Machines.* Districh, E., and Marbnau, A., eds. Mahwah, NJ: Erlbaum, 2000, pp. 314–315.

156 "The prison guard had become a hard rock . . ." Gardner, Howard, and Winner, Ellen. "The Development of Metaphoric Competence: Implications for Humanistic Disciplines," p. 128.

157 The Asch and Nerlove experiments. Asch, S. E., and Nerlove, Harriet. "The Development of Double Function Terms in Children: An Exploratory Investigation." In: *Perspectives in Psychological Theory: Essays in Honor of Heinz Werner.* Kaplan, Bernard, and Wapner, Seymour, eds. New York: International Universities Press, Inc., 1960, pp. 47–60. See also: Winner, Ellen. *The Point of Words: Children's Understanding of Metaphor and Irony,* pp. 38–39 and Gentner, D. "Metaphor as Structure Mapping: The Relational Shift." *Child Development* 59, 1, 1988, pp. 47–59.

158 Piaget and proverbs. Piaget, Jean. *The Language and Thought of the Child.* London: Routledge & Kegan Paul, 1960, pp. 128–135.

159 They did even better, a later study found . . . Honeck, Richard P., Sowry, Brenda M., and Voegtle, Katherine. "Proverbial Understanding in a Pictorial Context." *Child Development* 49, 2, 1978, pp. 327–331.

159 "Nettles." Vernon Scannell's poem is available at http://www.poetry connection.net/poets/Vernon_Scannell/4868.

160   The time line of metaphorical development in young people. Gentner, Dedre. "Metaphor as Structure Mapping: The Relational Shift," pp. 47–59.

161   Gentner and colleagues showed preschoolers a set of pictures, each of which depicted animals in distinct spatial configurations. Christie, S., and Gentner, D. "Where Hypotheses Come From: Learning New Relations by Structural Alignment." *Journal of Cognition and Development,* in press.

162   "Ymir's skull." Sturluson, Snorri. *The Prose Edda,* p. 112.

162   Tamarian kennings from the "Darmok" episode of *Star Trek: The Next Generation.* See: http://memory-alpha.org/wiki/Darmok_%28episode%29.

163   Austria, Sweden, Poland, and Hungary. Tversky, Amos. "Features of Similarity." In: Tversky, Amos. *Preference, Belief, and Similarity: Selected Writings.* Shafir, Eldar, ed. Cambridge, MA: MIT Press, 2004, p. 31.

163–164   "A good metaphor is like a good detective story." Ibid., p. 41.

164   Paintings, billboards, pimples, and warts. Glucksberg, Sam, and Keysar, B. "Understanding Metaphorical Comparisons: Beyond Similarity." *Psychological Review* 97, 1, 1990, pp. 9–10.

164   "The same pair of objects . . ." Tversky, Amos. "Features of Similarity." In: Tversky, Amos. *Preference, Belief, and Similarity: Selected Writings,* p. 41.

164   "No man is an island." Donne, John. *Selected Prose.* London: Penguin, 1987, p. 126.

165   "Like a bear to its floe, I clambered to bed." Cited in: Tourangeau, Roger, and Rips, Lance. "Interpreting and Evaluating Metaphors." *Journal of Memory and Language* 30, 4, 1991, p. 464. For the full poem, see: Jarrell, Randall. *The Complete Poems.* London: Faber and Faber, 1981, pp. 113–114.

166   "The eagle is a lion among birds." Tourangeau, Roger, and Rips, Lance. "Interpreting and Evaluating Metaphors," p. 457.

166   "It would be more illuminating . . . to say . . ." Black, Max. *Models and Metaphors: Studies in Language and Philosophy.* Ithaca, NY: Cornell University Press, 1962, p. 37.

Metaphor and Science   The Earth Is Like a Rice Pudding

167   "As these Flatlanders are to you . . ." Lewis, C. S. "Bluspels and Flalansferes." In: *Rehabilitations and Other Essays.* London: Oxford University Press, 1939, p. 139.

168   Flalansfere "had an air of mystery from the first . . ." Ibid., p. 146.

168   "An hourglass with legs on each side." Glucksberg, Sam. "Metaphors in Conversation: How Are They Understood? Why Are They Used?" *Metaphor and Symbolic Activity* 4, 3, 1989, pp. 125–143.

169   "When we pass beyond pointing to individual sensible objects . . ." Lewis, C. S. "Bluspels and Flalansferes." In: *Rehabilitations and Other Essays,* p. 154.

169   Robert Hooke's "cells." Brown, Theodore L. *Making Truth: Metaphor in Science.* Urbana and Chicago: University of Illinois Press, 2003, p. 146.

169 Jean-Baptiste-Joseph Fourier and the "greenhouse effect." Ibid., p. 168.

170 Max Planck, quantum theory, and vibrating strings. Root-Bernstein, Robert and Michele. *Sparks of Genius: The Thirteen Thinking Tools of the World's Most Creative People*. Boston: Houghton Mifflin, 1999, p. 137.

170 "The words or the language . . ." Cited in: Hadamard, Jacques. *The Mathematician's Mind: The Psychology of Invention in the Mathematical Field*. Princeton, NJ: Princeton University Press, 1996, p. 142.

170 "Language, in its literal capacity . . ." Langer, Suzanne K. *Philosophy in a New Key*. Cambridge, MA: Harvard University Press, 1996, p. 201.

171 Hui Tzu's paradoxes. Cited in: Chuang Tzu. *The Complete Works of Chuang Tzu*. Translated by Burton Watson. New York: Columbia University Press, 1968, pp. 375–377.

171 Hui Tzu "responded without hesitation . . ." Graham, Angus C. *Disputers of the Tao*. Chicago: Open Court Press, 1989, p. 77.

171–172 Hui Tzu and the King of Liang. Cited in: *Mencius*. Translated by D. C. Lau. New York, Penguin, 1970, pp. 262–263. The story is also recounted in: Holyoak, Keith J., and Thagard, Paul. *Mental Leaps: Analogy in Creative Thought*. Cambridge, MA: MIT Press, 1995, p. 183.

172 "Master's metaphor." Lewis, C. S. "Bluspels and Flalansferes." In: *Rehabilitations and Other Essays*, p. 140.

172 "Our thought is independent of the metaphors we employ . . ." Ibid., p. 145.

172 The genie and the jewels. Holyoak, Keith J., and Thagard, Paul. *Mental Leaps: Analogy in Creative Thought*, pp. 75–80.

173 "A kind of teeming . . ." Feynman, Richard. *Six Easy Pieces: The Fundamentals of Physics Explained*. London: Penguin Books, 1995, p. 4.

173 Feynman's explanation of electromagnetic fields. Ibid., p. 31.

174 "When you have satisfied yourself that the theorem is true . . ." Pólya, George. *Mathematics and Plausible Reasoning*. Vol. 1: *Induction and Analogy in Mathematics*. Vol. 2: *Patterns of Plausible Inference*. Oxford: Oxford University Press, 1954, p. 76.

175 Things "do not behave like waves . . ." Feynman, Richard. *Six Easy Pieces: The Fundamentals of Physics Explained*, p. 116–117

175 "There is something it is *like* to be that organism." Nagel, Thomas. "What Is It Like to Be a Bat?" *The Philosophical Review* 83, 1974, p. 323.

176 "I want to know what it is like for a bat to be a bat." Ibid., p. 324.

176–177 "We cannot, coming into something new . . ." Oppenheimer, Robert. "Analogy in Science." *The American Psychologist* 11, 3, 1956, pp. 129–130.

177 Metaphor "plays an essential role . . ." and "Theory change, in particular, is accompanied by a change . . ." Cited in: *Metaphor and Thought*. Ortony, Andrew, ed. Cambridge: Cambridge University Press, 1993, p. 24.

178 "I too play with symbols . . ." Cited in: Gentner, Dedre, and Jeziorski, Michael. "The Shift from Metaphor to Analogy in Western Science." In:

Metaphor and Thought. Ortony, Andrew, ed. Cambridge: Cambridge University Press, 1993, pp. 447–480.

178   A metaphor "is not to be considered as an argument . . ." Cited in: *Philosophical Perspectives on Metaphor.* Johnson, Mark, ed. Minneapolis: University of Minnesota Press, 1981, p. 13.

178   "We are never less the slaves of metaphor . . ." Lewis, C. S. "Bluspels and Flalansferes." In: *Rehabilitations and Other Essays*, p. 155.

178   "If our thinking is ever true . . ." Ibid., p. 158.

Metaphor and Parables and Proverbs   Mighty Darn Good Lies

180   "I was absolute master of my old dressing gown . . ." Diderot, Denis. *Rameau's Nephew and Other Works.* Translated by Jacques Barzun and Ralph H. Bowen with an introduction by Ralph H. Bowen. Indianapolis and Cambridge: Hackett, 2001, pp. 309–310.

181   "An unpleasant peculiarity in his voice . . ." Notice of the death of Edwin Paxton Hood in the *New York Times*, June 24, 1885. Available at http://query.nytimes.com/gst/abstract.html?res=9D07E3DB1439E533A25757C2A9609C94649FD7CF.

181   "Etymologically, [parable] signifies . . ." Hood, Edwin Paxton. *The World of Proverb and Parable.* London: Hodder & Stoughton, 1885, p. 87.

182   When we read a story, our brains plot everything that's going on . . . Speer, Nicole K., et al. "Reading Stories Activates Neural Representations of Visual and Motor Experiences." *Psychological Science* 20, 8, 2009, pp. 989–999.

182   The evolutionary advantage of stories. Dutton, Denis. *The Art Instinct: Beauty, Pleasure and Human Evolution.* New York: Bloomsbury Press, 2009, pp. 117–119.

182   The Managalese. See: McKellin, William H. "Allegory and Inference: Intentional Ambiguity in Managalese Negotiations." In: *Disentangling: Conflict Discourse in Pacific Societies.* Watson-Gegeo, Karen Ann, and White, Geoffrey M., eds. Stanford, CA: Stanford University Press, 1990, pp. 335–363. See also McKellin, William H. "Putting Down Roots: Information in the Language of Managalese Exchange." In: *Dangerous Words: Language and Politics in the Pacific.* Brenneis, Donald Lawrence, and Myers, Fred R., eds. New York: New York University Press, 1984, pp. 108–127.

183   The betel nut parable. Cited in: Holyoak, Keith J., and Thagard, Paul. *Mental Leaps: Analogy in Creative Thought.* Cambridge, MA: MIT Press, 1995, p. 215.

183   "The trial balloons or political Rorschach tests of social relations." McKellin, William H. "Allegory and Inference: Intentional Ambiguity in Managalese Negotiations." In: *Disentangling: Conflict Discourse in Pacific Societies*, p. 336.

184   The boy and the nettles. Aesop. *Aesop's Fables.* Translated by V. S. Vernon Jones. Introduction by G. K. Chesterton. Illustrated by Arthur Rackham. Ware, Hertfordshire: Wordsworth Classics, 1994, p. 66.

184 "The wit of one, the wisdom of many." Cited in: Hood, Edwin Paxton. *The World of Proverb and Parable*, p. 65

185 It is hard to dismount from a tiger. Merwin, W. S. *East Window: The Asian Translations*. Port Townsend, WA: Copper Canyon Press, 1998, p. 134.

185 Chase two hares, both get away. Ibid., p. 96.

185 Ancient Sumerian proverb collections. Gordon, Edmund I. *Sumerian Proverbs: Glimpses of Everyday Life in Ancient Mesopotamia*. Westport, CT: Greenwood Press, 1968, p. 20.

185 Wealth is hard to come by, but poverty is always at hand. Ibid., p 49.

185 Possessions are sparrows in flight that can find no place to alight. Ibid., p 50.

186 "Knowing proverbs and using them appropriately . . ." Penfield, Joyce. *Communicating with Quotes: The Igbo Case*. Westport, CT: Greenwood Press, 1983, p. 70.

186 Proverbs feature prominently in court cases. Finnegan, Ruth. "Proverbs in Africa." In: *The Wisdom of Many: Essays on the Proverb*. Mieder, Wolfgang, and Dundes, Alan, eds. Madison: University of Wisconsin Press, 1994, p. 27.

187 If you visit the home of the toads, stoop. Ibid., p. 28.

187 If something that demands a proverb happens . . . Nwachukwu-Agbada, J. O. J. "The Proverb in the Igbo Milieu." *Anthropos* 89, 1994, p. 197.

187 Psychologist Daniel Stalder asked university students in one study to read stories . . . Stalder, Daniel R. "The Power of Proverbs: Dissonance Reduction through Common Sayings." *Current Research in Social Psychology* 15, 2009, pp. 72-81.

187–188 "The nature of human institutions presupposes a conceptual language . . ." Vico, Giambattista. *New Science*, p. 84.

188 British gardening metaphors and French food metaphors. Cited in: Deignan, Alice. "Corpus Linguistics and Metaphor." In: *The Cambridge Handbook of Metaphor and Thought*. Gibbs, Raymond W., Jr., ed. Cambridge: Cambridge University Press, 2008, p. 289.

188 "Spill the beans" is used metaphorically more than 99 percent of the time. Knowles, Murray, and Moon, Rosamund. *Introducing Metaphor*. London: Routledge, 2006, p. 58. See also: Gibbs, Raymond W., Jr. and O'Brien, Jennifer E. "Idioms and Mental Imagery: The Metaphorical Motivation for Idiomatic Meaning." *Cognition* 36, 1, 1990, pp. 35–68.

188 American and British images of spilled beans. Knowles, Murray, and Moon, Rosamund. *Introducing Metaphor*, p. 49.

189 Pieter Bruegel the Elder's *Netherlandish Proverbs*. Dundes, Alan and Stibbe, Claudia A. "The Art of Mixing Metaphors: A Folkloristic Interpretation of the *Netherlandish Proverbs* by Pieter Bruegel the Elder." *FF Communications* XCVII, 230, 1981, pp. 3–71.

189 Dutch proverbs. See: Stoett, F. A. *Klein Spreekwoordenboek der Nederlandse Taal*. Zutphen, The Netherlands: Thieme-Zutphen, 1984.

190 Dutch and Afrikaans windmill proverbs. Dirven, René. *Metaphor and Nation: Metaphors Afrikaners Live By*. Frankfurt: Peter Lang, 1994, p. 24–25.

191 Dutch foxes (*De vos verliest wel zijn haar, maar niet zijn streken*) and Afrikaans jackals (*Die jakkals verander van haar, maar nie van snaar*). Ibid., p. 26–27.

191 "For a fable, all the persons must be impersonal." Aesop. *Aesop's Fables*, p. 17.

191 The farmer and his prize chickens. Paraphrased from: McPherson, James M. *Abraham Lincoln and the Second American Revolution*. New York and Oxford: Oxford University Press, 1990, pp. 98–99.

192 "Mighty darn good lies." Ibid., p. 100.

192 "No man could tell a story as well as he could." Kaplan, Fred. *Lincoln: The Biography of a Writer*. New York: HarperCollins, 2010, p. 66.

192 "I was not satisfied . . ." McPherson, James M. *Abraham Lincoln and the Second American Revolution*, pp. 97–98.

193 "Whenever Gutei Osho was asked about Zen . . ." Geary, James. *Geary's Guide to the World's Great Aphorists*, p. 258.

193 Nasrudin sometimes took people for trips in his boat. Paraphrased from: Shah, Idries. *The Exploits of the Incomparable Mulla Nasrudin*. London: Picador, 1973, p. 18.

194 The Igbo call proverbs "riddles." Monye, Ambrose Adikamkwu. *Proverbs in African Orature: The Aniocha-Igbo Experience*. Lanham, MD: University Press of America, 1996, p. 41.

195 "Metaphors only seem to describe the outer world of time and place." Campbell, Joseph. *Thou Art That: Transforming Religious Metaphor*. Novato, CA: New World Library, 2001. p. 7.

195 "Bees make honey . . ." Chhandogya Upanishad VI, IX, 1–2. Available at the Vedanta Spiritual Library, http://www.celextel.org/108upanishads/chandogya.html?page=6.

196 "These eastern rivers flow . . ." Ibid., VI, X, 1–2.

196 Uddilaka told Svetaketu to put some salt into water. Ibid., VI, XIII, 1–2.

Metaphor and Innovation Make It Strange

197 "Supersensitive to beauty but . . ." Quoted in: Kermode, Frank. *Wallace Stevens*. London: Faber and Faber, 1989, p. 6.

197 "The creation of resemblance by the imagination." Stevens, Wallace. *The Necessary Angel: Essays on Reality and the Imagination*. New York: Vintage Books, 1951, p. 72.

197 "Its singularity . . ." Ibid., p. 77.

198 "Metaphor creates a new reality . . ." Stevens, Wallace. *Opus Posthumous*. New York: Vintage Books, 1982, p. 169.

198 "We noticed that . . ." Gordon, William J. J. *Synectics: The Development of Creative Capacity*. New York: Harper & Row, 1961, pp. 27–28.

199 "One identifies oneself . . ." Cited in: Raudsepp, Eugene. "Synectics." In: *Metaphor and Metaphorology: A Selective Genealogy of Philosophical and*

Linguistic Conceptions of Metaphor from Aristotle to the 1990s. Taverniers, Miriam, ed. Ghent, Belgium: Academia Press, 2002, p. 143.

199 "Ultimate solutions to problems . . ." Gordon, William J. J. *Synectics*, p. 11.

199 "Strange words simply puzzle us . . ." Aristotle. *The Rhetoric and the Poetics of Aristotle*, p. 186.

200 "Art removes objects from the automatism of perception." Shklovsky, Victor. "Art as Technique." In: *Russian Formalist Criticism: Four Essays.* Translated and with an Introduction by Lee T. Melon and Marion J. Reis. Lincoln/London: University of Nebraska Press, 1965, p. 13.

200 "The technique of art is to make objects 'unfamiliar.'" Ibid., p. 12.

204 "Innovation inspired by nature." See: Benyus, Janine. *Biomimicry: Innovation Inspired by Nature.* New York: Harper Perennial, 2002.

204 "Animals, plants, and microbes are the consummate engineers." See: "What Do You Mean by the Term Biomimicry?" Available at http://www.biomimicryinstitute.org/about-us/what-do-you-mean-by-the-term-biomimicry.html.

204 Sharklet Technologies. See: http://www.sharklet.com/technology.

206 "I follow the way back from the basket to the rib cage . . ." Cited in: Müller, Cornelia. *Metaphors Dead and Alive, Sleeping and Waking: A Dynamic View*, p. 111.

207 "Electrical fluid agrees with lightning . . ." Cited in: Holyoak, Keith J., and Thagard, Paul. *Mental Leaps: Analogy in Creative Thought*, p. 185.

207 "That class of the frightening . . ." Freud, Sigmund. "The 'Uncanny.'" In: *Art and Literature.* London: Penguin, 1990, p. 340.

207 "An uncanny effect . . ." Ibid., p. 367.

Metaphor and Psychology A Little Splash of Color from My Mother

211 "I noticed, if I didn't force people . . ." Tompkins, Penny, and Lawley, James. "And, What Kind of a Man Is David Grove?" *Rapport* 33, 1996. Available at http://www.cleanlanguage.co.uk/articles/articles/37/1/And-what-kind-of-a-man-is-David-Grove/Page1.html.

212 A study of fifty-six patients scheduled for elective cardiac surgery. Juergens, Meike, et al. "Illness Beliefs before Cardiac Surgery Predict Disability, Quality of Life, and Depression 3 Months Later." *Journal of Psychosomatic Research*, in press.

213 Nurses trained in clean language reported that patients felt better understood. Tompkins, Penny, and Lawley, James. "The Mind, Metaphor and Health." Available at http://www.cleanlanguage.co.uk/articles/articles/23/1/The-Mind-Metaphor-and-Health/Page1.html.

213 "Images have a life of their own . . ." Jung, Carl Gustav. *Jung on Active Imagination.* Key Readings Selected and Introduced by Joan Chodorow. London: Routledge, 1997, p. 145.

213–214 "Start with any image . . ." Ibid., p. 164.

214 "Interrogate the metaphor . . ." Cited in a speech by James Lawley, Clean Language Conference, June 21–22, 2008, London.

215 The twelve basic clean questions. Lawley, James, and Tompkins, Penny. *Metaphors in Mind: Transformation through Symbolic Modelling.* London: The Developing Company Press, 2000, p. 54.

216 "Questions couched in 'normal' language . . ." Grove, David J., and Panzer, B. I. *Resolving Traumatic Memories: Metaphors and Symbols in Psychotherapy.* New York: Irvington Publishers, 1989, p. 13.

218 "Our questions will have given a form . . ." Ibid., pp. 10–11.

218 Work is war. Cited in Lawley, James, and Tompkins, Penny. "Coaching with Metaphor." Available at http://www.cleanlanguage.co.uk/articles/articles/127/1/Coaching-with-Metaphor/Page1.html.

219 Working with one teenage boy who had a long history of getting into fist-fights . . . Walker, Caitlin. "Breathing in Blue by Clapton Duck Pond: Facilitating Pattern Detection with 'At-Risk' Teenagers." *Counseling Children and Young People,* 2006.

221 Milton Erickson and the cacti. Battino, Rubin. *Metaphoria: Metaphor and Guided Metaphor for Psychotherapy and Healing.* Carmarthen, Wales: Crown House, 2005, p. 211.

221 "Ambiguous-function assignments." Ibid., p. 211.

221 Researchers in Singapore and Canada devised an ambiguous-function assignment of their own. Li, Xiuping, Wei, Liyuan, and Soman, Dilip. "Sealing the Emotions Genie: The Effects of Physical Enclosure on Psychological Closure." *Psychological Science,* July 9, 2010, doi: 10.1177/0956797610376653.

222 Grove's version of ambiguous-function assignments. Grove, David J., and Panzer, B. I. *Resolving Traumatic Memories: Metaphors and Symbols in Psychotherapy,* pp. 84–86.

Backword The Logic of Metaphor

223 "At Melville's Tomb." Crane, Hart. *The Complete Poems and Selected Letters and Prose of Hart Crane.* Edited with an introduction and notes by Brom Weber. New York: Liveright Publishing Corp., 1966, p. 34.

224 "A sigh is a sword of an Angel King" and "Every street lamp that I pass . . ." Ibid., p. 236.

224 "As a poet I may very possibly be more interested . . ." Ibid., pp. 234–235.

224 The "logic of metaphor." Ibid., p. 221.

225 "This water-course, having divers bridges . . ." Cited in: Barton, Nicholas. *The Lost Rivers of London.* London: Phoenix House Limited/Leicester University Press, 1962, p. 21.

Bibliography

Aaker, J. L. "Dimensions of Brand Personality." *Journal of Marketing Research* 34, 3, 1997, pp. 347–356.

Aarts, H., and Dijksterhuis, A. "The Silence of the Library: Environmental Control over Social Behavior." *Journal of Personality and Social Psychology* 84, 2003, pp. 18–28.

Ackerman, Joshua M., Nocera, Christopher C., and Bargh, John A. "Incidental Haptic Sensations Influence Social Judgments and Decisions." *Science* 328, 5986, 25 June, 2010, pp. 1712–1715.

Addison, Joseph. "Pleasures of the Imagination." *Spectator* 411, 1712, p. 21.

Aesop. *Aesop's Fables.* Translated by V. S. Vernon Jones. Introduction by G. K. Chesterton. Illustrated by Arthur Rackham. Ware, Hertfordshire: Wordsworth Classics, 1994.

Al-Jurjani, Abdalqahir. *The Mysteries of Eloquence.* Hellmut Ritter, ed. Istanbul: Government Press, 1954.

Allbritton, David W., Gerrig, Richard J., and McKoon, Gail. "Metaphor-Based Schemas and Text Representations: Making Connections through Conceptual Metaphors." *Journal of Experimental Psychology: Learning, Memory, and Cognition* 21, 1, 1995, pp. 612–625.

Allman, John M., Watson, Karli K., Tetreault, Nicole A., and Hakeem, Atiya Y. "Intuition and Autism: A Possible Role for Von Economo Neurons." *Trends in Cognitive Sciences* 9, 8, 2005, pp. 367–373.

Andreassen, P. B. "On the Social Psychology of the Stock Market: Aggregate Attributional Effects and the Regressiveness of Prediction." *Journal of Personality and Social Psychology* 53, 1987, pp. 490–496.

Arbib, Michael A. "From Monkey-like Action Recognition to Human Language: An Evolutionary Framework for Neurolinguistics." *Behavioral and Brain Sciences* 28, 2005, pp. 105–167.

Ariely, Dan. *Predictably Irrational: The Hidden Forces That Shape Our Decisions.* London: HarperCollins, 2008.

Aristotle. *The Rhetoric and the Poetics of Aristotle.* Introduction by Edward P. J. Corbett. New York: Modern Library, 1984.

Arnheim, Rudolf. *Visual Thinking.* London: Faber and Faber, 1970.

Asch, S. E. "Forming Impressions of Personality." *Journal of Abnormal and Social Psychology* 41, 1946, pp. 258–290.

————. "The Metaphor: A Psychological Inquiry." In: *Person Perception and Interpersonal Behavior.* R. Taguiri and L. Petrullo, eds. Stanford, CA: Stanford University Press, 1955, pp. 86–94.

Asch, S. E. and Nerlove, Harriet. "The Development of Double Function Terms in Children: An Exploratory Investigation." In: *Perspectives in Psychological Theory: Essays in Honor of Heinz Werner.* Bernard Kaplan and Seymour Wapner, eds. New York: International Universities Press, 1960, pp. 47–60.

Aubrun, Axel, Brown, Andrew, and Grady, Joseph. "Public Structures: A Constructive Model for Government." *Public Briefing,* an occasional white paper series by Demos, March 2006.

Aubrun, Axel, and Grady, Joseph. "Provoking Thought, Changing Talk: Discussing Inequality." In: *You Can Get There from Here . . .* , an occasional paper series from the Social Equity and Opportunity Forum of the College of Urban and Public Affairs at Portland State University, April 2008.

————. " 'Public Structures' as a Simplifying Model for Government." A report commissioned by the FrameWorks Institute on behalf of the Council for Excellence in Government and Demos, October 2005.

Aubusson, P. J., Harrison, A. G., and Ritchie, S. M., eds. *Metaphor and Analogy in Science Education.* Dordrecht, The Netherlands: Springer, 2006.

Avis, Paul. *God and the Creative Imagination: Metaphor, Symbol and Myth in Religion and Theology.* London: Routledge, 1999.

Barcelona, Antonio, ed. *Metaphor and Metonymy at the Crossroads: A Cognitive Perspective.* Berlin and New York: Mouton de Gruyter, 2003.

Barfield, Owen. *History in English Words.* London: Faber and Faber, 1962.

————. *Poetic Diction: A Study in Meaning.* Middletown, CT: Wesleyan University Press, 1973.

Bargary, Gary, et al. "Colored-speech Synaesthesia Is Triggered by Multisensory, Not Unisensory, Preception." *Psychological Science* 20, 5, 2009, pp. 529–533.

Bargh, J. A. "Bypassing the Will: Toward Demystifying Behavioral Priming Effects" In: *The New Unconscious.* Hassin, R., Uleman, J., and Bargh, J., , eds. Oxford: Oxford University Press, 2005, pp. 37–58.

————. "Losing Consciousness: Automatic Influences on Consumer Judgment, Behavior and Motivation." *Journal of Consumer Research* 29, 2, 2002, pp. 280–285.

————. "The Unconscious Mind." *Perspectives on Psychological Science* 3, 2008, pp. 73–79.

Bargh, J. A., and Chartrand, Tanya L. "The Mind in the Middle: A Practical Guide to Priming and Automaticity Research." In: *Handbook of Research Methods in Social and Personality Psychology*. Reis, H. T., and Judd, C. M., eds. New York: Cambridge University Press, 2000, pp. 253–285.

Baron-Cohen, Simon. "The Biology of the Imagination." *Entelechy Journal* 9, Summer/Fall 2007, http://www.entelechyjournal.com/simonbaroncohen.htm.

————. *Mindblindness: An Essay on Autism and Theory of Mind*. Cambridge, MA: MIT Press, 1997.

Barton, Nicholas. *The Lost Rivers of London*. London: Phoenix House Limited/ Leicester University Press, 1962.

Bateson, Gregory. *Mind and Nature: A Necessary Unity*. New York: Bantam Books, 1980.

Battino, Rubin. *Metaphoria: Metaphor and Guided Metaphor for Psychotherapy and Healing*. Carmarthen, Wales: Crown House, 2005.

Battino, Rubin, and South, Thomas L. *Ericksonian Approaches: A Comprehensive Manual*. Carmarthern, Wales: Crown House, 2005.

Beardsley, Monroe C. *The Aesthetic Point of View: Selected Essays*. Michael J. Wreen and Donald M. Callen, eds. Ithaca, NY, and London: Cornell University Press, 1982.

Beattie, Geoffrey. *Visible Thought: The New Psychology of Body Language*. London: Routledge, 2003.

Bechara, Antoine, and Damasio, Antonio R. "The Somatic Marker Hypothesis: A Neural Theory of Economic Decision-making." *Games and Economic Behavior* 52, 2005, p. 336–372.

Beer, Francis A., and De Landtsheer, Christ'l. *Metaphorical World Politics*. East Lansing: Michigan State University Press, 2004.

Belsky, Gary, and Gilovich, Thomas. *Why Smart People Make Big Money Mistakes and How to Correct Them*. New York: Simon and Schuster, 1999.

Benczes, Réka. "Analysing Metonymical Noun-Noun Compounds: The Case of Freedom Fries." In: *The Metaphors of Sixty: Papers Presented on the Occasion of the 60th Birthday of Zoltán Kövecses*. Réka Benczes and Szilvia Csábi, eds. Budapest: Eötvös Loránd University, 2006, pp. 46–54.

Benyus, Janine. *Biomimicry: Innovation Inspired by Nature*. New York: Harper Perennial, 2002.

Berggren, Douglas. "The Use and Abuse of Metaphor." *Review of Metaphysics* 16, 1962, pp. 237–258.

Bicchieri, Cristina. "Should a Scientist Abstain from Metaphor?" In: *The Consequences of Economic Rhetoric*. Arjo Klamer, D. N. McCloskey, and Robert M. Solow, eds. New York: Cambridge University Press, 1988, pp. 100–114.

Black, Max. *Models and Metaphors: Studies in Language and Philosophy*. Ithaca, NY: Cornell University Press, 1962.

Borges, Jorge Luis. *Historia de la eternidad*. Buenos Aires: Emecé, 1953.

———. *This Craft of Verse*. Cambridge, MA: Harvard University Press, 2000.

Boroditsky, L. "Comparison and the Development of Knowledge." *Cognition* 102, 1, 2007, pp. 118–128.

———. "Does Language Shape Thought? English and Mandarin Speakers' Conceptions of Time." *Cognitive Psychology* 43, 1, 2001, pp. 1–22.

———. "Metaphoric Structuring: Understanding Time through Spatial Metaphors." *Cognition* 75, 1, 2000, pp. 1–28.

Boroditsky, L., and Ramscar, M. "The Roles of Body and Mind in Abstract Thought." *Psychological Science* 13, 2, 2002, pp. 185–188.

Bowdle, Brian F., and Gentner, Dedre. "The Career of Metaphor." *Psychological Review* 112, 1, 2005, pp. 193–216.

Bowdle, Brian F., and Gentner, D., Wolff, P., and Boronat, C. "Metaphor Is like Analogy." In: *The Analogical Mind: Perspectives from Cognitive Science*. D. Gentner, K. J. Holyoak, and B. N. Kokinov, eds. Cambridge, MA: MIT Press, 2001, pp. 199–253.

Brewer, E. Cobham. *The Dictionary of Phrase & Fable*. New York: Avenel Books, 1978.

Brooke-Rose, Christine. *A Grammar of Metaphor*. London: Secker and Warburg, 1958.

Brown, Theodore L. *Making Truth: Metaphor in Science*. Urbana and Chicago: University of Illinois Press, 2003.

Brumbaugh, Robert S. *The Philosophers of Greece*. Albany: State University of New York Press, 1981.

Burgess, C., and Chiarello, C. "Neurocognitive Mechanisms Underlying Metaphor Comprehension and Other Figurative Language." *Metaphor and Symbolic Activity* 11, 1, 1996, pp. 67–84.

Burke, Kenneth. *A Grammar of Motives*. Berkeley and Los Angeles: University of California Press, 1969.

Cacciari, Cristina. "Crossing the Senses in Metaphorical Language." In: *The Cambridge Handbook of Metaphor and Thought*. Raymond W. Gibbs Jr., ed. Cambridge: Cambridge University Press, 2008, pp. 425–446.

Cacciari, Cristina, and Tabossi, P., eds. *Idioms: Processing, Structure and Interpretation*. Hillsdale, NJ: Erlbaum, 1993.

Call, Josep, and Tomasello, Michael. "Does The Chimpanzee Have a Theory of Mind? 30 Years Later." *Trends in Cognitive Sciences* 12, 5, 2008, pp. 187–192.

Camac, M., and Glucksberg, S. "Metaphors Do Not Use Associations between

Concepts, They Are Used to Create Them." *Journal of Psycholinguistic Research* 13, 1984, pp. 443–455.

Cameron, Lynne. "Metaphor and Talk." In: *The Cambridge Handbook of Metaphor and Thought.* Raymond W. Gibbs Jr., ed. Cambridge: Cambridge University Press, 2008.

———. "Patterns of Metaphor Use in Reconciliation Talk." *Discourse and Society* 18, 3, 2007, pp. 197–222.

——— and Low, Graham, eds. *Researching and Applying Metaphor.* Cambridge: Cambridge University Press, 1999.

Campbell, Joseph. *The Inner Reaches of Outer Space: Metaphor as Myth and as Religion.* Novato, CA: New World Library, 2002.

———. *Thou Art That: Transforming Religious Metaphor.* Novato, CA: New World Library, 2001.

Carey, John. *John Donne: Life, Mind, Art.* London: Faber and Faber, 1990.

Cary, Mark S. "Ad Strategy and the Stone Age Brain." *Journal of Advertising Research* 40, 1/2, 2000, pp. 103–106.

Casasanto, Daniel, and Boroditsky, L. "Time in the Mind: Using Space to Think about Time." *Cognition* 106, 2008, pp. 579–593.

Casasanto, Daniel, and Dijkstra, Katinka. "Motor Action and Emotional Memory." *Cognition* 115, 2010, pp. 179–185.

Chapman, Gretchen B., and Johnson, Eric J. "Incorporating the Irrelevant: Anchors in Judgments of Belief and Value." In: *Heuristics and Biases: The Psychology of Intuitive Judgment.* Thomas Gilovich, Dale Griffin, and Daniel Kahneman, eds. Cambridge: Cambridge University Press, 2002, pp. 120–138.

Charteris-Black, Jonathan. *Corpus Approaches to Critical Metaphor Analysis.* Basingstoke, Hampshire: Palgrave Macmillan, 2004.

———. "Metaphor and Vocabulary Teaching in ESP Economics." *English for Specific Purposes* 19, 2000, pp. 149–165.

———. *Politicans and Rhetoric: The Persuasive Power of Metaphor.* New York: Palgrave Macmillan, 2005.

Christie, S., and Gentner, D. "Where Hypotheses Come From: Learning New Relations by Structural Alignment." *Journal of Cognition and Development,* in press.

Chuang Tzu. *The Complete Works of Chuang Tzu.* Translated by Burton Watson. New York: Columbia University Press, 1968.

Cicero. *De Oratore.* Volume 2. Translated by H. Rackham. London: William Heinemann, 1942.

Cicone, M., Gardner, H., and Winner, E. "Understanding the Psychology in Psychological Metaphors." *Journal of Child Language* 8, 1, 1981, pp. 213–216.

Cienki, Alan. "Metaphoric Gestures and Some of Their Relations to Verbal Metaphoric Expressions." In: *Discourse and Cognition: Bridging the Gap.* Jean-Pierre Kōnig, ed. Stanford, CA: CSLI Publications, 1998, pp. 189–204.

Cienki, Alan, and Müller, Cornelia. "The Application of Conceptual Metaphor Theory to Political Discourse: Methodological Questions and Some Possible Solutions." In: *Political Language and Metaphor: Interpreting and Changing the World*. Terrell Carver and Jernej Pikalo, eds. London and New York: Routledge, 2008, pp. 241–256.

———. "Metaphor, Gesture, and Thought." In: *The Cambridge Handbook of Metaphor and Thought*. Raymond W. Gibbs Jr., ed. Cambridge: Cambridge University Press, 2008, pp. 483–501.

Cila, Nazil. "Understanding Product Metaphors." Eighth International Conference on Researching and Applying Metaphor, July 2010, Amsterdam.

Clark, H. H. "Space, Time, Semantics, and the Child." In: *Cognitive Development and the Acquisition of Language*. T. E. Moore, ed. New York: Academic Press, 1973, pp. 27–63.

Clason, George S. *The Richest Man in Babylon*. New York: Signet, 1988.

Cohen, Ted. "Figurative Speech and Figurative Acts." *Journal of Philosophy* 72, 19, 1975, pp. 669–684.

———. "Metaphor and the Cultivation of Intimacy." In: *On Metaphor*. Sheldon Sacks, ed. Chicago and London: University of Chicago Press, 1979.

———. "Notes on Metaphor." *Journal of Aesthetics and Art Criticism* 34, 3, 1976, pp. 249–259.

———. *Thinking of Others: On the Talent for Metaphor*. Princeton, NJ, and Oxford: Princeton University Press, 2008.

Coleridge, Samuel Taylor. *Biographia Literaria*. London: J. M. Dent and Sons, 1934.

———. *The Notebooks of Samuel Taylor Coleridge*. Volume 2. Kathleen Coburn, ed. Princeton, NJ: Princeton University Press, 1957.

Coulehan, Jack. "Metaphor and Medicine: Narrative in Clinical Practice." *Yale Journal of Biology and Medicine* 76, 2003, pp. 87–95.

Coulson, Seana. "Metaphor Comprehension and the Brain." In: *The Cambridge Handbook of Metaphor and Thought*. Raymond W. Gibbs Jr., ed. Cambridge: Cambridge University Press, 2008, pp. 177–196.

Cozens, Alexander. "A New Method of Assisting the Invention in Drawing Original Compositions of Landscape." In: Oppé, A. P. *Alexander and John Robert Cozens*. London: Adam and Charles Black, 1952.

Crane, Hart. *The Complete Poems and Selected Letters and Prose of Hart Crane*. Edited with an introduction and notes by Brom Weber. New York: Liveright Publishing Corp., 1966.

Crisp, Peter. "Allegory: Conceptual Metaphor in History." *Language and Literature* 10, 1, 2001, pp. 5–20.

———. "Allegory, Maps, and Modernity: Cognitive Change from Bunyan to Forster." *Mosaic* 36, 4, 2003, pp. 49–64.

Dapretto, Mirella, et al. "Understanding Emotions in Others: Mirror Neuron Dysfunction in Children with Autism Spectrum Disorders." *Nature Neuroscience* 9, 2006, pp. 28–30.

Da Vinci, Leonardo. *The Notebooks of Leonardo da Vinci.* Selected and Edited by Irma A. Richter. Oxford: Oxford University Press, 1998.

De Bonis, M., Epelbaum, C., Deffez, V., and Féline, A. "The Comprehension of Metaphors in Schizophrenia." *Psychopathology* 30, 3, 1997, pp. 149–154.

Decety, Jean, and Grezes, Julie. "The Power of Simulation: Imagining One's Own and Other's Behavior." *Brain Research* 1079, 2006, pp. 4–14.

Dehaene, Stanislas. *Reading in the Brain: The Science of Evolution of a Human Invention.* New York: Viking, 2009.

Deignan, Alice. "Corpus-based Research into Metaphor." In: *Researching and Applying Metaphor.* Lynne Cameron and Graham Low, eds. Cambridge: Cambridge University Press, 1999, pp. 177–199.

Diderot, Denis. *Rameau's Nephew and Other Works.* Translated by Jacques Barzun and Ralph H. Bowen with an introduction by Ralph H. Bowen. Indianapolis and Cambridge: Hackett Publishing Company, Inc., 2001.

DiFonzo, N., and Bordia, P. "Rumor and Prediction: Making Sense (but Losing Dollars) in the Stock Market." *Organizational Behavior and Human Decision Processes* 71, 1997, pp. 329–353.

Dilts, Robert Brian. *Roots of Neuro-Linguistic Programming.* Cupertino, CA: Meta Publications, 1983.

Dirven, René. *Metaphor and Nation: Metaphors Afrikaners Live By.* Frankfurt: Peter Lang, 1994.

Dirven, René, and Porings, Ralf, eds. *Metaphor and Metonymy in Comparison and Contrast.* Berlin: de Gruyter, 2002.

Domino, George, et al. "Assessing the Imagery of Cancer: The Cancer Metaphors Test." *Journal of Psychosocial Oncology* 9, 4, 1991, pp. 103–121.

Donne, John. *Selected Prose.* London: Penguin Books, 1987.

Duckworth, Kenneth, et al. "Use of Schizophrenia as a Metaphor in U.S. Newspapers." *Psychiatric Services* 54, 2003, pp. 1402–1404.

Dundes, Alan, and Stibbe, Claudia A. "The Art of Mixing Metaphors: A Folkloristic Interpretation of the *Netherlandish Proverbs* by Pieter Bruegel the Elder." *FF Communications* XCVII, 230, 1981, pp. 3–71.

Dutton, Denis. *The Art Instinct: Beauty, Pleasure and Human Evolution.* New York: Bloomsbury Press, 2009.

Dyson, George. "Economic Dis-Equilibrium: Can You Have Your House and Spend It Too?" The Edge Web site, http://edge.org/3rd_culture/dysong08.1/dysong08.1_index.html.

Eberhardt, Jennifer L., Davies, Paul G., Purdie-Vaughns, Valerie J., and Johnson, Sheri Lynn. "Looking Deathworthy: Perceived Stereotypicality of Black Defendants Predicts Capital-Sentencing Outcomes." *Psychological Science* 17, 5, 2006, pp. 383–386.

Edelman, Gerald M. *Bright Air, Brilliant Fire: On the Matter of the Mind.* London: Penguin Books, 1994.

————. *Second Nature: Brain Science and Human Knowledge.* New Haven and London: Yale University Press, 2006.

Edelman, Gerald M., and Tononi, Giulio. *Consciousness: How Matter Becomes Imagination.* London: Allen Lane, 2000.

Eliot, T. S. *Selected Essays.* London: Faber and Faber, 1972.

Emerson, Ralph Waldo. *Selected Prose and Poetry.* New York: Holt, Rinehart and Winston, 1969.

Empson, William. *Seven Types of Ambiguity.* London: Pimlico, 2004.

Epley, Nicholas, and Gilovich, Thomas. "Putting Adjustment Back in the Anchoring and Adjustment Heuristic." In: *Heuristics and Biases: The Psychology of Intuitive Judgment.* Thomas Gilovich, Dale Griffin, and Daniel Kahneman, eds. Cambridge: Cambridge University Press, 2002, pp. 139–149.

Erickson, Milton H. *My Voice Will Go with You: The Teaching Tales of Milton H. Erickson.* Edited and with commentary by Sidney Rosen. New York and London: W. W. Norton & Company, 1982.

Eubanks, Philip. *A War of Words in the Discourse of Trade: The Rhetorical Constitution of Metaphor.* Carbondale and Edwardsville: Southern Illinois University Press, 2000.

Evans, Roberta D., and Evans, Gerald E. "Cognitive Mechanisms in Learning from Metaphors." *Journal of Experimental Education* 58, 1, 1989, pp. 5–19.

Fauconier, Gilles, and Turner, Mark. *The Way We Think: Conceptual Blending and the Mind's Hidden Complexities.* New York: Basic Books, 2002.

Feldman, Jerome A. *From Molecule to Metaphor: A Neural Theory of Language.* Cambridge, MA: MIT Press, 2006.

Feynman, Richard. *Six Easy Pieces: The Fundamentals of Physics Explained.* London: Penguin Books, 1995.

Finke, Ronald A., Ward, Thomas B., and Smith, Steven M. *Creative Cognition: Theory, Research, and Applications.* Cambridge, MA: MIT Press, 1992.

Finnegan, Ruth. *Oral Literature in Africa.* Oxford: Clarendon Press, 1970.

————. "Proverbs in Africa." In: *The Wisdom of Many: Essays on the Proverb.* Wolfgang Mieder and Alan Dundes, eds. Madison: University of Wisconsin Press, 1994, pp. 10–42.

Finucane, M. L., Alhakami, A., Slovic, P., and Johnson, S. M. "The Affect Heuristic in Judgments of Risks and Benefits." *Journal of Behavioral Decision Making* 13, 2000, p. 1–17.

Fisch, M. H. "The Coleridges, Dr. Prati, and Vico." *Modern Philology* 41, 2, 1943, pp. 111–122.

Fiske, Susan T., Cuddy, Amy J. C., and Glick, Peter. "A Model of (Often Mixed) Stereotype Content: Competence and Warmth Respectively Follow from Perceived Status and Competition." *Journal of Personality and Social Psychology* 82, 6, 2002, pp. 878–902.

Fogelin, Robert J. *Figuratively Speaking.* New Haven and London: Yale University Press, 1988.

Forceville, Charles. "Metaphor in Pictures and Multimodal Representations." In: *The Cambridge Handbook of Metaphor and Thought.* Raymond W. Gibbs Jr., ed. Cambridge: Cambridge University Press, 2008, pp. 462–482.

————. *Pictorial Metaphor in Advertising.* London and New York: Routledge, 1996.

Foroni, Francesco, and Semin, Gun R. "Language That Puts You in Touch with Your Bodily Feelings." *Psychological Science* 20, 8, 2009, pp. 974–980.

Frank, M. G., and Gilovich, T. "The Dark Side of Self and Social Perception: Black Uniforms and Aggression in Professional Sports." *Journal of Personality and Social Psychology* 54, 1988, pp. 74–85.

Fraser, Deborah F. G. "From the Playful to the Profound: What Metaphors Tell Us about Gifted Children." *Roeper Review* 25, 4, 2003, pp. 180–184.

Freud, Sigmund. "The 'Uncanny.'" In: *Art and Literature.* London: Penguin Books, 1990.

Frisson, Steven, and Pickering, Martin J. "The Processing of Metonymy: Evidence from Eye Movements." *Journal of Experimental Psychology: Learning, Memory, and Cognition* 25, 6, 1999, pp. 1366–1383.

Frith, Chris. *Making Up the Mind: How the Brain Creates Our Mental World.* Oxford: Blackwell Publishing, 2007.

Frith, Uta. "Mindblindness and the Brain in Autism." *Neuron* 32, 2001, pp. 969–979.

Frost, Robert. "Education by Metaphor." Available at http://www.en.utexas.edu/amlit/amlitprivate/scans/edbypo.html.

Frye, Northrop. *Myth and Metaphor: Selected Essays, 1974–1988.* Charlottesville and London: University Press of Virginia, 1990.

Galinsky, Adam, and Glucksberg, Sam. "Inhibition of the Literal: Metaphors and Idioms as Judgmental Primes." *Social Cognition* 18, 1, 2000, pp. 35–54.

Gallagher, Helen L., and Frith, Christopher D. "Functional Imaging of 'Theory of Mind.'" *Trends in Cognitive Sciences* 7, 2, 2003, pp. 77–83.

Gamow, George. *Thirty Years That Shook Physics: The Story of Quantum Theory.* New York: Dover, 1966.

Gannon, Martin J. *Cultural Metaphors: Readings, Research Translations, and Commentary.* Thousand Oaks, CA: Sage Publications, 2001.

Gardner, Howard. "Metaphors and Modalities: How Children Project Polar Adjectives onto Diverse Domains." *Child Development* 45, 1, 1974, pp. 84–91.

Gardner, Howard, and Winner, Ellen. "The Development of Metaphoric Competence: Implications for Humanistic Disciplines." In: *On Metaphor.* Sheldon Sacks, ed. Chicago and London: University of Chicago Press, 1979, pp. 121–139.

————. "Metaphor and Irony: Two Levels of Understanding." In: *Metaphor and Thought.* Andrew Ortony, ed. Cambridge: Cambridge University Press, 1993, pp. 425–443.

Gardner, John. *On Moral Fiction.* New York: Basic Books, 2000.

Gavins, Joanna, and Steen, Gerard. *Cognitive Poetics in Practice.* London and New York: Routledge, 2003.

Geary, James. *Geary's Guide to the World's Great Aphorists.* New York: Bloomsbury USA, 2007.

———. *The World in a Phrase: A Brief History of the Aphorism.* New York: Bloomsbury USA, 2005.

Gentner, Dedre. "The Evolution of Mental Metaphors in Psychology: A 90-Year Retrospective." *American Psychologist* 40, 2, 1985, pp. 181–192.

———. "Metaphor as Structure Mapping: The Relational Shift." *Child Development* 59, 1, 1988, pp. 47–59.

———. "Structure-mapping: A Theoretical Framework for Analogy." *Cognitive Science* 7, 1983, pp. 155–170.

Gentner, Dedre, Anggoro, F. K., and Klibanoff, R. S. "Structure-mapping and Relational Language Support Children's Learning of Relational Categories." *Child Development*, in press.

Gentner, Dedre, and Bowdle, Brian. "The Psychology of Metaphor Processing." In: *Encyclopedia of Cognitive Science.* London: Nature Publishing Group, 2002, p. 21.

Gentner, Dedre, Holyoak, K. J., and Kokinov, B. N., eds. *The Analogical Mind: Perspectives from Cognitive Science.* Cambridge, MA: MIT Press, 2001.

Gentner, Dedre, and Imai, Mutsumi. "Is The Future Always Ahead? Evidence for System-mappings in Understanding Space-Time Metaphors." In: *Proceedings of the 14th Annual Conference of the Cognitive Science Society.* Bloomington, 1992, pp. 510–515.

Gentner, Dedre, Imai, M., and Boroditsky, L. "As Time Goes By: Evidence for Two Systems in Processing Space Time Metaphors." *Language and Cognitive Processes* 17, 5, 2002, pp. 537–565.

Gentner, Dedre, and Jeziorski, Michael. "The Shift from Metaphor to Analogy in Western Science." In: *Metaphor and Thought.* Andrew Ortony, ed. Cambridge: Cambridge University Press, 1993, pp. 447–480.

Gentner, Dedre, and Wolff, P. "Metaphor and Knowledge Change." In: *Cognitive Dynamics: Conceptual Change in Humans and Machines.* E. Districh and A. Marbnau, eds. Mahwah, NJ: Erlbaum, 2000, pp. 295–342.

Ghiselin, Brewster. *The Creative Process.* New York: New American Library, 1952.

Gibbs, Raymond W., Jr., ed. *The Cambridge Handbook of Metaphor and Thought.* Cambridge: Cambridge University Press, 2008.

———. "Categorization and Metaphor Understanding." *Psychological Review* 99, 3, 1992, pp. 572–577.

———. *Embodiment and Cognitive Science.* Cambridge: Cambridge University Press, 2006.

————. "How Context Makes Metaphor Comprehension Seem 'Special.'" *Metaphor and Symbolic Activity* 4, 3, 1989, pp. 145–158.

————. "Linguistic Factors in Children's Understanding of Idioms." *Journal of Child Language* 14, 3, 1987, pp. 569–586.

————. *The Poetics of Mind: Figurative Thought, Language, and Understanding.* New York: Cambridge University Press, 1994.

————. "Why Idioms Are Not Dead Metaphors." In: *Idioms: Processing, Structure and Interpretation.* C. Cacciari and P. Tabossi, eds. Hillsdale, NJ: Erlbaum, 1993, pp. 57–78.

————. "Why Many Concepts are Metaphorical." *Cognition* 61, 3, 1996, pp. 309–319.

Gibbs, Raymond W., Jr., Bogdanovich, J. M., Sykes, J. R., and Barr, D. J. "Metaphor in Idiom Comprehension." *Journal of Memory and Language* 37, 1997, pp. 141–154.

Gibbs, Raymond W., Jr., and Matlock, Teenie. "Metaphor, Imagination, and Simulation: Psycholinguistic Evidence." In: *The Cambridge Handbook of Metaphor and Thought.* Raymond W. Gibbs Jr., ed. Cambridge: Cambridge University Press, 2008, pp. 161–176.

Gibbs, Raymond W., Jr., and O'Brien, Jennifer E. "Idioms and Mental Imagery: The Metaphorical Motivation for Idiomatic Meaning." *Cognition* 36, 1, 1990, pp. 35–68.

Gibbs, Raymond W., Jr., and Steen, Gerard J, eds. *Metaphor in Cognitive Linguistics.* Selected Papers from the Fifth International Cognitive Linguistics Conference, Amsterdam, July 1997. Amsterdam: John Benjamins, 1999.

Giessner, Steven R., and Schubert, Thomas W. "High in the Hierarchy: How Vertical Location and Judgments of Leaders' Power Are Interrelated." *Organizational Behavior and Human Decision Processes* 100, 2006, pp. 160–176.

Gillan, D. J., Premack, D., and Woodruff, G. "Reasoning in the Chimpanzee 1: Analogical Reasoning." *Journal of Experimental Psychology–Animal Behavior Processes* 7, 1, 1981, pp. 1–17.

Gilovich, T. "Seeing the Past in the Present: The Effects of Associations to Familiar Events on Judgments and Decisions." *Journal of Personality and Social Psychology* 40, 7, 1981, pp. 797–808.

Gilovich, T., Vallone, R., and Tversky, A. "The Hot Hand in Basketball: On the Misperception of Random Sequences." *Cognitive Psychology* 17, 1985, pp. 295–314.

Glucksberg, Sam. "Beyond Literal Meanings: The Psychology of Allusion." *Psychological Science* 2, 3, 1991, pp. 146–152.

————. "Metaphors in Conversation: How Are They Understood? Why Are They Used?" *Metaphor and Symbolic Activity* 4, 3, 1989, pp. 125–143.

————. "The Psycholinguistics of Metaphor." *Trends in Cognitive Science* 7, 2, 2003, pp. 92–96.

Glucksberg, Sam, and Cacciari, Cristina. "Understanding Idiomatic Expressions: The Contribution of Word Meanings." In: *Understanding Word and*

Sentence. Greg B. Simpson, ed. Amsterdam: Elsevier Science Publishers, 1991, pp. 217–240.

Glucksberg, Sam, and Galinsky, A. D. "Inhibition of the Literal: Metaphors and Idioms as Judgmental Primes." *Social Cognition* 18, 2000, pp. 35–54.

Glucksberg, Sam, Gildea, P., and Bookin, H. B. "On Understanding Nonliteral Speech: Can People Ignore Metaphors?" *Journal of Verbal Learning and Verbal Behavior* 21, 1, 1982, pp. 85–98.

Glucksberg, Sam, and Keysar, Boaz. "Understanding Metaphorical Comparisons: Beyond Similarity." *Psychological Review* 97, 1, 1990, pp. 3–18.

Glucksberg, Sam, Keysar, Boaz, and McGlone, Matthew S. "Metaphor Understanding and Accessing Conceptual Schema: Reply to Gibbs." *Psychological Review* 99, 3, 1992, pp. 578–581.

Glucksberg, Sam, and McGlone, Matthew S. *Understanding Figurative Language: From Metaphors to Idioms.* New York: Oxford University Press, 2001.

———. "When Love Is Not a Journey: What Metaphors Mean." *Journal of Pragmatics* 31, 12, 1999, pp. 1541–1558.

Goatly, A. *The Language of Metaphors.* London: Routledge, 1997.

Goldin-Meadow, Susan, et al. "Gesturing Gives Children New Ideas about Math." *Psychological Science* 20, 2009, pp. 267–272.

———. *Hearing Gesture: How Our Hands Help Us Think.* Cambridge, MA: Harvard University Press, 2003.

Goldman, Alvin I. "Simulation Theory and Mental Concepts." In: *Simulation and Knowledge of Action.* Jerome Dokic and Joelle Proust, eds. Amsterdam and Philadelphia: John Benjamins, 2002, pp. 1–20.

Goodman, Nelson. *Languages of Art.* Indianapolis: Hackett Publishing Company, Inc., 1976.

———. *Ways of Worldmaking.* Indianapolis: Hackett Publishing Company, Inc., 1981.

Gordon, David. *Therapeutic Metaphors: Helping Others through the Looking Glass.* Cupertino, CA: META Publications, 1978.

Gordon, Edmund I. *Sumerian Proverbs: Glimpses of Everyday Life in Ancient Mesopotamia.* New York: Greenwood Press, 1968.

Gordon, William J. J. *Synectics: The Development of Creative Capacity.* New York: Harper & Row, 1961.

Gozzi, Raymond, Jr. *The Power of Metaphor in the Age of Electronic Media.* Cresskill, NJ: Hampton Press, Inc., 1999.

———. "Races You Might Not Want to Win: The Technological Race as Metaphor." *A Review of General Semantics* 55, 1, 1998, pp. 91–105.

Grady, Joseph. "Cross-linguistic Regularities in Metaphorical Extension." A talk delivered at the Linguistic Society of America Annual Meeting, Los Angeles, January 9, 1999.

Grady, Joseph E. "A Typology of Motivation for Conceptual Metaphor: Correlation vs. Resemblance." In: *Metaphor in Cognitive Linguistics*. Selected Papers from the Fifth International Cognitive Linguistics Conference, Amsterdam, July 1997. Raymond W. Gibbs Jr. and Gerard J. Steen, eds. Amsterdam: John Benjamins, 1999, pp. 79–100.

Graham, Angus C. *Disputers of the Tao*. Chicago: Open Court Press, 1989.

Graham, Benjamin. *The Intelligent Investor: A Book of Practical Counsel*. Updated with new commentary by Jason Zweig. Preface and appendix by Warren E. Buffett. New York: Collins Business Essentials, 2006.

Grothe, Mardy. *I Never Metaphor I Didn't Like*. New York: Collins, 2008.

Grove, David. "The Philosophy and Principles of Clean Language." Edited by James Lawley from a talk given at Clean Language Research Day, 13 November, 1998, London. Available at http://www.cleanlanguage.co.uk/articles/articles/38/1/The-Philosophy-And-Principles-Of-Clean-Language/Page1.html.

———. "Problem Domains and Non-Traumatic Resolution through Metaphor Therapy." Edited from notes provided by David Grove and partially written by Rob McGavock. Available at http://www.cleanlanguage.co.uk/articles/articles/4/1/Problem-Domains-And-Non-Traumatic-Resolution-Through-Metaphor-Therapy/Page1.html.

Grove, David, and Panzer, B. I. *Resolving Traumatic Memories: Metaphors and Symbols in Psychotherapy*. New York: Irvington Publishers, Inc., 1989.

Guttenplan, Samuel. *Objects of Metaphor*. Oxford: Clarendon Press, 2005.

Hadamard, Jacques. *The Mathematician's Mind: The Psychology of Invention in the Mathematical Field*. Princeton, NJ: Princeton University Press, 1996.

Haddon, Mark. *The Curious Incident of the Dog in the Night-time*. London: Vintage, 2004.

Halford, G. *Children's Understanding: The Development of Mental Models*. Hillsdale, NJ: Erlbaum, 1991.

Hanne, M., and Hawken, S. J. "Metaphors for Illness in Contemporary Media." *Journal of Medical Ethics* 33, 2007, pp. 93–99.

Happé, Francesca, et al. "'Theory of Mind' in the Brain: Evidence from a PET Scan Study of Asperger Syndrome." *NeuroReport* 8, 1996, p. 198.

Haraway, Donna Jeanne. *Crystals, Fabrics, and Fields: Metaphors of Organicism in Twentieth-Century Developmental Biology*. New Haven and London: Yale University Press, 1976.

Harlow, Harry. "The Nature of Love." *American Psychologist* 13, 1958, pp. 673–685.

Harris, J. L., Bargh, J. A., and Brownell, K. D. "Priming Effects of Television Food Advertising on Eating Behavior." *Health Psychology* 28, 2009, pp. 404–413.

Havelock, Eric A. *The Greek Concept of Justice from Its Shadow in Homer to Its Substance in Plato*. Cambridge, MA: Harvard University Press, 1978.

———. *The Literate Revolution in Greece and Its Cultural Consequences*. Princeton, NJ: Princeton University Press, 1982.

Heberlein, Andrea S., and Adolphs, Ralph. "Impaired Spontaneous Anthropomorphizing Despite Intact Perception and Social Knowledge." *Proceedings of the National Academy of Sciences* 101, 19, 2004, pp. 7487–7491.

Heider, F., and Simmel, M. "An Experimental Study of Apparent Behaviour." *American Journal of Psychology* 57, 1944, pp. 243–259.

Henle, Paul, ed. *Language, Thought, and Culture*. Ann Arbor: University of Michigan Press, 1958.

Herbeck, Dale A. "Sports Metaphors and Public Policy: The Football Theme in Desert Storm Discourse." In: *Metaphorical World Politics*. Francis A. Beer and Christ'l De Landtsheer, eds. East Lansing: Michigan State University Press, 2004, pp. 121–139.

Hesse, Mary B. *Models and Analogies in Science*. Notre Dame, IN: University of Notre Dame Press, 1970.

Heyes, C. M. "Theory of Mind in Non-human Primates." *Behavioral and Brain Sciences* 21, 1, 1998, pp. 101–134.

Hintikka, Jaakko, ed. *Aspects of Metaphor*. Dordrecht, The Netherlands: Kluwer Academic Publishers, 1994.

Hirsh, Jacob B., and Inzlicht, Michael. "Error-related Negativity Predicts Academic Performance." *Psychophysiology* 46, 2009, pp. 1–5.

Hobbes, Thomas. *Leviathan*. Oxford: Oxford University Press, 1998.

Holland, Rob W., Hendriks, Merel, and Aarts, Henk. "Smells Like Clean Spirit: Nonconscious Effects of Scent on Cognition and Behavior." *Psychological Science* 16, 9, 2005, pp. 689–693.

Holmes, Richard. *Coleridge: Darker Reflections*. London: HarperCollins, 1998.

Holyoak, Keith J., and Thagard, Paul. *Mental Leaps: Analogy in Creative Thought*. Cambridge, MA: MIT Press, 1995.

Honeck, Richard P. *A Proverb in Mind: The Cognitive Science of Proverbial Wit and Wisdom*. Mahwah, NJ: Erlbaum, 1997.

Honeck, Richard P., and Hoffman, Robert R., eds. *Cognition and Figurative Language*. Hillsdale, NJ: Erlbaum, 1980.

Honeck, Richard P., Sowry, B. M., and Voegtle, K. "Proverbial Understanding in a Pictorial Context." *Child Development* 49, 2, 1978, pp. 327–331.

Hood, Edwin Paxton. *The World of Proverb and Parable*. London: Hodder & Stoughton, 1885.

Hubbard, Edward, and Ramachandran, Vilayanur S. "Neurocognitive Mechanisms of Synesthesia." *Neuron* 48, 3, 2005, pp. 509–520.

Huettel, Scott A., et al. "Perceiving Patterns in Random Series: Dynamic Processing of Sequence in The Prefrontal Cortex." *Nature Neuroscience* 5, 5, 2002, pp. 485–490.

Humphrey, Nicholas. *The Inner Eye: Social Intelligence in Evolution*. Oxford: Oxford University Press, 2002.

————. *Seeing Red: A Study in Consciousness.* Cambridge, MA: The Belknap Press of Harvard University Press, 2006.

Hunt, Patrick. *Poetry in the Song of Songs: A Literary Analysis.* Frankfurt: Peter Lang, 2008.

Ibarretxe-Antunano, Iraide. "Metaphorical Mappings in the Sense of Smell." In: *Metaphor in Cognitive Linguistics.* Selected Papers from the Fifth International Cognitive Linguistics Conference, Amsterdam, July 1997. Raymond W. Gibbs Jr. and Gerard J. Steen, eds. Amsterdam: John Benjamins, 1999, pp. 29–45.

Jakobson, Roman. "Two Aspects of Language and Two Types of Aphasic Disturbances." In: Jakobson, Roman, and Halle, Morris. *Fundamentals of Language.* The Hague: Mouton, 1956.

Jarrell, Randall. *The Complete Poems.* London: Faber and Faber, 1981.

Johnson, Mark, ed. *Philosophical Perspectives on Metaphor.* Minneapolis: University of Minnesota Press, 1981.

Jones, W. T. *A History of Western Philosophy: The Classical Mind.* New York: Harcourt Brace Jovanovich, 1970.

Jostmann, Nils B., Lakens, Daniel, and Schubert, Thomas W. "Weight as an Embodiment of Importance." *Psychological Science* 20, 9, 2009, pp. 1169–1174.

Juergens, Meike, et al. "Illness Beliefs before Cardiac Surgery Predict Disability, Quality of Life, and Depression 3 Months Later." *Journal of Psychosomatic Research,* in press.

Jung, Carl Gustav. *Jung on Active Imagination.* Key Readings Selected and Introduced by Joan Chodorow. London: Routledge, 1997.

————. "The Transcendent Function." In: Miller, Jeffrey C. *The Transcendent Function: Jung's Model of Psychological Growth through Dialogue with the Unconscious.* Albany: State University of New York Press, 2004.

Kadosh, Roi Cohen, et al. "Induced Cross-modal Synaesthetic Experience without Abnormal Neuronal Connections." *Psychological Science* 20, 2, 2009, pp. 258–265.

Kafka, Franz. *The Great Wall of China and Other Short Works.* London: Penguin, 2002.

Kaplan, Fred. *Lincoln: The Biography of a Writer.* New York: HarperCollins, 2010.

Kassler, Jamie C., ed. *Metaphor: A Musical Dimension.* Sydney: Currency Press, 1991.

Katz, Albert N., Cacciari, Cristina, Gibbs, Raymond W., Jr., and Turner, Mark. *Figurative Language and Thought.* Oxford: Oxford University Press, 1998.

Kay, Aaron C., et al. "Material Priming: The Influence of Mundane Physical Objects on Situational Construal and Competitive Behaviour Choice." *Organizational Behavior and Human Decision Processes* 95, 2004, pp. 83–96.

Kelly, Michael H., and Keil, Frank C. "Metaphor Comprehension and Knowledge of Semantic Domains." *Metaphor and Symbolic Activity* 2, 1, 1987, pp. 33–52.

Kenneally, Christine. *The First Word: The Search for the Origins of Language.* New York: Viking, 2007.

Kennedy, George A. "Fenollosa, Pound and the Chinese Character." *Yale Literary Magazine* 126, 5, 1958, pp. 24–36.

Kennedy, John M. "Metaphor in Pictures." *Perception* 11, 5, 1982, pp. 589–605.

Kermode, Frank. *Wallace Stevens.* London: Faber and Faber, 1989.

Keysar, B., and Glucksberg, S. "Metaphor and Communication. "*Poetics Today* 13, 4, 1992, pp. 633–658.

Keysar, B., Shen, Y., Glucksberg, S., and Horton, W. S. "Conventional Language: How Metaphorical Is It?" *Journal of Memory and Language* 43, 2000, pp. 576–593.

Kilner, J. M., et al. "An Interference Effect of Observed Biological Movement on Action." *Current Biology* 13, 6, 2003, pp. 522–525.

Kittay, Eva Feder. *Metaphor: Its Cognitive Force and Linguistic Structure.* Oxford: Clarendon Press, 1987.

Klamer, Arjo, and McCloskey, D. N. "One Quarter of GDP Is Persuasion." *American Economic Review* 92, 1995, pp. 191–195.

Kleparski, Grzegorz A. "Hot Pants, Cold Fish and Cool Customers: The Search for Historical Metaphorical Extensions in the Realm of Temperature Terms." *Studia Anglica Resoviensia* 4, 2007, pp. 100–118.

Knowles, Murray, and Moon, Rosamund. *Introducing Metaphor.* London and New York: Routledge, 2006.

Koestler, Arthur. *The Act of Creation.* London: Arkana, 1989.

Kogan, Nathan, Connor, Kathleen, Gross, Augusta, and Fava, Donald. "Understanding Visual Metaphor: Developmental and Individual Differences." *Monographs of the Society for Research in Child Development* 45, 1, Serial No. 183, 1980.

Koller, V. " 'A Shotgun Wedding': Co-occurrence of War and Marriage Metaphors in Mergers and Acquisitions Discourse." *Metaphor and Symbol* 1, 7, 2003, pp. 179 –203.

Kopp, Richard R. *Metaphor Therapy: Using Client-Generated Metaphors in Psychotherapy.* London: Routledge, 1995.

Kosslyn, Stephen M., Ganis, G., and Thompson, W. L. "Neural Foundations of Imagery." *Nature Reviews Neuroscience* 2, 2001, pp. 635–642.

Kosslyn, Stephen M., and Thompson, William L. "Shared Mechanisms in Visual Imagery and Visual Perception: Insights from Cognitive Neuroscience." In: *The New Cognitive Neurosciences.* Michael S. Gazzaniga, editor in chief. Cambridge, MA: MIT Press, 2000, pp. 975–985.

Kovecses, Zoltan. *Metaphor: A Practical Introduction.* Oxford: Oxford University Press, 2002.

Kreitman, Norman. *The Roots of Metaphor: A Multidisciplinary Study in Aesthetics.* Aldershot, UK: Ashgate, 1999.

Krennmayr, Tina. "When Do People Think Metaphorically?" The Eighth International Conference on Researching and Applying Metaphor, July 2010, Amsterdam.

Kristiansen, Gitte, Achard, Michel, Dirven, René, and Ruiz de Mendoza Ibáñez, Francisco J. *Cognitive Linguistics: Current Applications and Future Perspectives*. Berlin: de Gruyter, 2006.

Kuhn, Thomas S. *The Structure of Scientific Revolutions*. Chicago: University of Chicago Press, 1970.

Kurath, Hans. *The Semantic Sources of the Words for the Emotions in Sanskrit, Greek, Latin and the Germanic Languages*. Menasha, WI: George Banta Publishing Co., 1921.

Lakoff, George. "The Contemporary Theory of Metaphor." In: *Metaphor and Thought*. Andrew Ortony, ed. Cambridge: Cambridge University Press, 1993, pp. 202–251.

———. "Metaphor and War: The Metaphor System Used to Justify War in the Gulf." Available at http://www2.iath.virginia.edu/sixties/HTML_docs/Texts/Scholarly/Lakoff_Gulf_Metaphor_1.html.

———. "Metaphor, Morality, and Politics: Or, Why Conservatives Have Left Liberals In the Dust." *Social Research* 62, 2, 1995, pp. 177–214.

———. "Metaphors of Terror." *In These Times*, 2001. Available at http://www.press.uchicago.edu/News/911lakoff.html.

———. *Moral Politics: How Liberals and Conservatives Think*. Chicago: University of Chicago Press, 2002.

Lakoff, George, and Johnson, Mark. *Metaphors We Live By*. Chicago: University of Chicago Press, 2003.

———. *Philosophy in the Flesh: The Embodied Mind and Its Challenge to Western Thought*. New York: Basic Books, 1999.

Lakoff, George, and Nunez, Rafael E. *Where Mathematics Comes From: How the Embodied Mind Brings Mathematics into Being*. New York: Basic Books, 2000.

Lakoff, George, and Turner, Mark. *More than Cool Reason: A Field Guide to Poetic Metaphor*. Chicago: University of Chicago Press, 1989.

Landau, Mark J., et al. "Evidence that Self-Relevant Motives and Metaphoric Framing Interact to Influence Political and Social Attitudes." *Psychological Science* 20, 11, 2009, pp. 1421–1427.

Langer, Suzanne K. *Philosophy in a New Key*. Cambridge, MA: Harvard University Press, 1996.

Lankton, Carol H., and Lankton, Stephen R. *Enchantment and Intervention in Family Therapy*. New York: Brunner/Mazel, 1986.

———. *Tales of Enchantment: Goal-Oriented Metaphors for Adults and Children in Therapy*. New York: Brunner/Mazel, 1989.

Lautréamont, Comte de. *Les Chants du Maldoror*. New York: New Directions, 1966.

Lawley, James, and Tompkins, Penny. "Coaching with Metaphor." Available at http://www.cleanlanguage.co.uk/articles/articles/127/1/Coaching-with-Metaphor/Page1.html.

———. *Metaphors in Mind: Transformation through Symbolic Modelling*. London: Developing Company Press, 2000.

Leary, David E., ed. *Metaphors in the History of Psychology*. Cambridge: Cambridge University Press, 1990.

Leatherdale, W. H. *The Role of Analogy, Model and Metaphor in Science*. Amsterdam: North Holland Publishing Company, 1974.

Lee, Laurie. *Cider with Rosie*. London: Vintage Books, 2002.

Lee, Spike W. S., and Schwarz, Norbert. "Washing Away Postdecisional Dissonance." *Science* 328, 7 May 2010, p. 709.

Lem, Stanislaw. *The Futurological Congress*. Orlando, FL: Harcourt, Inc., 1974.

Leslie, A. M. "Pretense and Representation: The Origins of 'Theory of Mind.'" *Psychological Review* 94, 1987, pp. 412–426.

Lettvin, J. Y., Maturana, H. R., McCulloch, W. S., and Pitts, W. H. "What the Frog's Eye Tells the Frog's Brain." *Proceedings of the IRE* 47, 11, 1959, pp. 1940–1959.

Levav, Jonathan, and Fitzsimons, Gavan J. "When Questions Change Behavior: The Role of Ease of Representation." *Psychological Science* 17, 3, 2006, pp. 207–213.

Lévi-Strauss, Claude. *The Savage Mind*. London: Weidenfeld and Nicolson, 1962.

Lewis, C. S. "Bluspels and Flalansferes." In: *Rehabilitations and Other Essays*. London: Oxford University Press, 1939, pp. 135–158.

Li, Xiuping, Wei, Liyuan, and Soman, Dilip. "Sealing the Emotions Genie: The Effects of Physical Enclosure on Psychological Closure." *Psychological Science*, July 9, 2010, doi: 10.1177/0956797610376653.

Liljenquist, Katie, Zhong, Chen-Bo, and Galinsky, Adam D. "The Smell of Virtue: Clean Scents Promote Reciprocity and Charity." *Psychological Science* 21, 5, 2010, pp. 381–383.

Locke, John. *An Essay Concerning Human Understanding*. Available at http://oregonstate.edu/instruct/phl302/texts/locke/locke1/Essay_contents.html.

Lodge, David. *The Modes of Modern Writing: Metaphor, Metonymy, and the Typology of Modern Literature*. London: Edward Arnold, 1977.

Loetscher, T., et al. "Eye Position Predicts What Number You Have in Mind." *Current Biology* 20, 6, pp. 264–265.

Loue, Sana. *The Transformative Power of Metaphor in Therapy*. New York: Springer, 2008.

Lucretius. *On the Nature of the Universe*. Available at http://classics.mit.edu/Carus/nature_things.html.

MacCormac, Earl. *A Cognitive Theory of Metaphor*. Cambridge, MA: MIT Press, 1985.

MacGregor, D. G., Slovic, P., Dreman, D., and Berry, M. "Imagery, Affect, and Financial Judgment." *Journal of Psychology and Financial Markets* 1, 2, 2000, pp. 104–110.

MacNiece, Louis. *Varieties of Parable.* Cambridge: Cambridge University Press, 1965.

Malgady, R. G. "Children's Interpretation and Appreciation of Similes." *Child Development* 48, 4, 1977, pp. 1734–1738.

Marcus, Solomon. "Fifty-two Oppositions between Scientific and Poetic Communication." In: *Pragmatic Aspects of Human Communication.* C. Cherry, ed. Dordrecht, The Netherlands: Reidel, 1974, pp. 83–96.

Mark, Margaret, and Pearson, Carol S. *The Hero and the Outlaw: Building Extraordinary Brands through the Power of Archetypes.* New York: McGraw-Hill, 2001.

Marks, Lawrence E. "Bright Sneezes and Dark Coughs, Loud Sunlight and Soft Moonlight." *Journal of Experimental Psychology: Human Perception and Performance* 8, 2, 1982, pp. 177–193.

———. "On Associations of Light and Sound: The Mediation of Brightness, Pitch, and Loudness." *American Journal of Psychology* 87, 1/2, 1974, pp. 173–188.

———. "On Perceptual Metaphors." *Metaphor and Symbolic Activity* 11, 1, 1996, pp. 39–66.

———, et al. "Perceiving Similarity and Comprehending Metaphor." *Monographs of the Society for Research in Child Development* 52, 1, 1987, pp. 1–100.

Martin, Emily. *The Woman in the Body: A Cultural Analysis of Reproduction.* Boston: Beacon Press, 1992.

Matlock, T., Ramscar, M., and Boroditsky, L. "On the Experiential Link Between Spatial and Temporal Language." *Cognitive Science* 29, 2005, pp. 655–664.

Matsuki, Keiko. "Metaphors of Anger in Japanese." In: *Language and the Cognitive Construal of the World.* John R. Taylor and Robert E. MacLaury, eds. Berlin: de Gruyter, 1995, pp. 137–151.

Maturana, Humberto R., and Varela, Francisco J. *The Tree of Knowledge: The Biological Roots of Human Understanding.* Boston: Shambhala, 1998.

McCloskey, Deirdre N. "Metaphors Economists Live By." *Social Research* 62, 2, 1995, pp. 215–237.

———. *The Rhetoric of Economics.* Second edition. Madison: University of Wisconsin Press, 1998.

McCulloch, K. C., Ferguson, M. J., Kawada, C. C. K., and Bargh, J. A. "Taking a Closer Look: On the Operation of Nonconscious Impression Formation." *Journal of Experimental Social Psychology* 44, 2008, pp. 614–623.

McCulloch, Warren S. *Embodiments of Mind.* Cambridge, MA: MIT Press, 1965.

McCune-Nicolich, Lorraine. "Toward Symbolic Functioning: Structure of Early Pretend Games and Potential Parallels with Language." *Child Development* 52, 3, 1981, pp. 785–797.

McFague, Sallie. *Metaphorical Theology: Models of God in Religious Language.* Philadelphia: Fortress Press, 1982.

———. *Speaking in Parables: A Study in Metaphor and Theology.* London: SCM Press, 2002.

McGeoch, Paul D., Brang, David, and Ramachandran, V. S. "Apraxia, Metaphor, and Mirror Neurons." *Medical Hypotheses* 69, 2007, pp. 1165–1168.

McGlone, M. S. "Conceptual Metaphors and Figurative Language Understanding." *Journal of Memory and Language* 35, 4, 1996, pp. 544–565.

McKellin, William H. "Allegory and Inference: Intentional Ambiguity in Managalese Negotiations." In: *Disentangling: Conflict Discourse in Pacific Societies.* Karen Ann Watson-Gegeo and Geoffrey M. White, eds. Stanford, CA: Stanford University Press, 1990, pp. 335–363.

———. "Putting Down Roots: Information in the Language of Managalese Exchange." In: *Dangerous Words: Language and Politics in the Pacific.* Donald Lawrence Brenneis and Fred R. Myers, eds. New York: New York University Press, 1984, pp. 108–127.

McMullen, Linda M. "Metaphor and Psychotherapy." In: *The Cambridge Handbook of Metaphor and Thought.* Raymond W. Gibbs Jr., ed. Cambridge: Cambridge University Press, 2008, p. 397–411.

McNeill, David. *Gesture and Thought.* Chicago and London: University of Chicago Press, 2005.

———. *Hand and Mind: What Gestures Reveal about Thought.* Chicago and London: University of Chicago Press, 1992.

McPherson, James M. *Abraham Lincoln and the Second American Revolution.* New York and Oxford: Oxford University Press, 1990.

McQuarrie, Edward F., and Mick, David Glen. "Figures of Rhetoric in Advertising Language." *Journal of Consumer Research* 22, 4, 1996, pp. 424–438.

Meier, Brian P., et al. "What's 'Up' with God? Vertical Space as a Representation of the Divine." *Journal of Personality and Social Psychology* 93, 5, 2007, pp. 699–710.

Meier, Brian P., and Dionne, Darah. "Downright Sexy: Verticality, Implicit Power, and Perceived Physical Attractiveness." *Social Cognition* 27, 6, 2009, pp. 883–892.

Meier, Brian P., and Robinson, Michael D. "Does 'Feeling Down' Mean Seeing Down? Depressive Symptoms and Vertical Selective Attention." *Journal of Research in Personality* 40, 2006, pp. 451–461.

———. "The Metaphorical Representation of Affect." *Metaphor and Symbol* 20, 4, 2005, pp. 239–257.

———. "Why the Sunny Side Is Up: Associations Between Affect and Vertical Position." *Psychological Science* 15, 2004, pp. 243–247.

Meier, Brian P., Robinson, Michael D., and Caven, Andrew J. "Why a Big Mac Is a Good Mac: Associations Between Affect and Size." *Basic and Applied Social Psychology* 30, 2008, pp. 46–55.

Meier, Brian P., Robinson, Michael D., and Clore, Gerald L. "Why Good Guys Wear White: Automatic Inferences about Stimulus Valence Based on Brightness." *Psychological Science* 15, 2, 2004, pp. 82–87.

Mencius. *Mencius.* Translated by D. C. Lau. New York: Penguin, 1970.

Merwin, W. S. *East Window: The Asian Translations.* Port Townsend, WA: Copper Canyon Press, 1998.

Miall, David S., ed. *Metaphor: Problems and Perspectives.* Brighton, UK: Harvester Press, 1982.

Mieder, Wolfgang. *Yes We Can: Barack Obama's Proverbial Rhetoric.* New York: Peter Lang, 2009.

Mieder, Wolfgang, and Dundes, Alan, eds. *The Wisdom of Many: Essays on the Proverb.* Madison: University of Wisconsin Press, 1994.

Miles, Lynden K., Nind, Louise K., and Macrae, C. Neil. "Moving through Time." *Psychological Science* 21, 1, 2010, pp. 1–2.

Miller, Jeffrey C. *The Transcendent Function: Jung's Model of Psychological Growth through Dialogue with the Unconscious.* Albany: State University of New York Press, 2004

Mobbs, D., Greicius, M., Abdel-Azim, E., Menon, V., and Reiss, A. "Humor Modulates the Mesolimbic Reward Centers." *Neuron* 40, 5, pp. 1041–1048.

Moll, J., et al. "The Moral Affiliations of Disgust: A Functional MRI Study." *Cognitive and Behavioral Neurology* 18, 1, 2005, pp. 68–78.

Monye, Ambrose Adikamkwu. *Proverbs in African Orature: The Aniocha-Igbo Experience.* Lanham, MD: University Press of America, 1996.

Mooij, J. J. A. *A Study of Metaphor: On the Nature of Metaphorical Expressions, with Special Reference to Their Reference.* Amsterdam: North Holland Publishing Company, 1976.

Morgan, Gareth. *Images of Organization.* Beverly Hills, CA: Sage Publications, 1986.

————. *Imaginization: New Mindsets for Seeing, Organizing, and Managing.* Thousand Oaks, CA: Sage Publications, 1997.

Morris, Michael W., Sheldon, Oliver J., Ames, Daniel R., and Young, Maia J. "Metaphors and the Market: Consequences and Preconditions of Agent and Object Metaphors in Stock Market Commentary." *Organizational Behavior and Human Decision Processes* 102, 2, 2007, pp. 174–192.

Morris, William, and Morris, Mary. *Dictionary of Word and Phrase Origins.* New York: HarperCollins, 1988.

Morse, Samuel French. *Wallace Stevens: Life as Poetry.* New York: Pegasus, 1970.

Morwitze, V. G., Johnson, Eric, and Schmittlein, David. "Does Measuring Intent Change Behavior?" *Journal of Consumer Research* 20, 1993, pp. 46–61

Müller, Cornelia. *Metaphors Dead and Alive, Sleeping and Waking: A Dynamic View.* Chicago: University of Chicago Press, 2008.

Mussweiler, Thomas, and Strack, Fritz. "Comparing Is Believing: A Selective Accessibility Model of Judgmental Anchoring." In: *European Review of Social Psychology* 10, 1999, pp. 135–167.

————. "Hypothesis-Consistent Testing and Semantic Priming in the Anchoring Paradigm: A Selective Accessibility Model." *Journal of Experimental Social Psychology* 35, 1999, pp. 136–164.

Nagel, Thomas. "What Is It Like to Be a Bat?" *Philosophical Review* 83, 1974, pp. 435–450.

Napier, John. *Hands.* Revised by Russell H. Tuttle. Princeton, NJ: Princeton University Press, 1993.

Newman, James R., ed. *The World of Mathematics.* Volume 2. Mineola, NY: Dover, 2000.

Nietzsche, Friedrich. "On Truth and Falsity in Their Ultramoral Sense." In: *The Complete Works of Friedrich Nietzsche.* Oscar Levy, ed. New York: MacMillan, 1911, pp. 183–184.

Nolan, Vincent. *The Innovator's Handbook.* London: Sphere Books Ltd., 1990.

Noveck, Ira A. "The Costs and Benefits of Metaphor." *Metaphor and Symbol* 16, 1/2, 2001, pp. 109–121.

Nwachukwu-Agbada, J. O. J. "The Proverb in the Igbo Milieu." *Anthropos* 89, 1994, pp. 194–200.

Nyce, James M., and Kahn, Paul, eds. *From Memex to Hypertext: Vannevar Bush and the Mind's Machine.* Boston: Academic Press, 1991.

O'Brien, Gerald V. "Indigestible Food, Conquering Hordes, and Waste Materials: Metaphors of Immigrants and the Early Immigration Restriction Debate in the United States." *Metaphor and Symbol* 18, 1, 2003, pp. 33–47.

Oden, D. L., Thompson, R. K. R., and Premack, D. "Infant Chimpanzees Spontaneously Perceive Both Concrete and Abstract Same/Different Relations." *Child Development* 61, 3, 1990, pp. 621–631.

Olson, J., Waltersdorff, K., and Forr, J. "Incorporating Deep Customer Insights in the Innovation Process." Available online.

Oppenheimer, Robert. "Analogy in Science." *American Psychologist* 11, 3, 1956, pp. 127–135.

Ortony, Andrew, ed. "Beyond Literal Similarity." *Psychological Review* 86, 3, 1979, pp. 161–180.

————. *Metaphor and Thought.* Cambridge: Cambridge University Press, 1993.

————. "Why Metaphors Are Necessary and Not Just Nice." *Educational Theory* 25, 1, 1975, pp. 45–53.

Ortony, Andrew, and Fainsilber, Lynn. "The Role of Metaphors in Descriptions of Emotions." In: *Theoretical Issues in Natural Language Processing.* Proceedings of the 1987 Workshop on Theoretical Issues in Natural Language Processing, 1986, pp. 181–184.

Ortony, Andrew, et al. "Metaphor: Theoretical and Empirical Research." Cambridge, MA: Bolt, Beranek and Newman, Inc., Technical Report No. 27, 1977.

Orwell, George. "Politics and the English Language." In: *Why I Write*. London: Penguin Books, 1984.

Osborn, Alex F. *Applied Imagination: Principles and Procedures of Creative Problem-Solving*. New York: Charles Scribner's Sons, 1963.

Parini, Jay. *Robert Frost: A Life*. London: Pimlico, 2001.

———. *Why Poetry Matters*. New Haven and London: Yale University Press, 2008.

Penfield, Joyce, and Duru, Mary. *Communicating with Quotes: The Igbo Case*. Westport, CT: Greenwood Press, 1983.

———. "Proverbs: Metaphors that Teach." *Anthropological Quarterly* 61, 3, 1988, pp. 119–128.

Penn, David. "Getting Animated About Emotion." A talk delivered at the European Society for Opinion and Marketing Research Congress 2008, Montreal, September 22, 2008.

Piaget, Jean. *The Language and Thought of the Child*. London: Routledge & Kegan Paul, 1960.

———. *Play, Dreams and Imitation in Childhood*. London: Routledge & Kegan Paul, 1962.

Piller, Ingrid. "Extended Metaphor in Automobile Fan Discourse." *Poetics Today* 20, 3, 1999, pp. 483–498.

Pinker, Steven. *How the Mind Works*. London: Allen Lane, 1998.

———. *The Stuff of Thought*. London: Allen Lane, 2007.

Poincaré, Henri. *The Foundations of Science*. Lancaster, PA: The Science Press, 1946.

Polya, George. *How to Solve It*. London: Penguin Books, 1990.

———. *Mathematics and Plausible Reasoning*. Vol. 1: *Induction and Analogy in Mathematics*. Vol. 2: *Patterns of Plausible Inference*. Oxford: Oxford University Press, 1954.

Pragglejaz Group. "A Practical and Flexible Method for Identifying Metaphorically Used Words in Discourse." *Metaphor and Symbol* 22, 1, 2007, pp. 1–39.

Premack, D., and Woodruff, G. "Does the Chimpanzee Have a Theory of Mind?" *Behavioral and Brain Sciences* 4, 1978, pp. 515–526.

Prince, George. *The Practice of Creativity: A Manual for Dynamic Group Problem Solving*. New York: Harper & Row, 1970.

Proulx, Travis, and Heine, Steven J. "Connections from Kafka: Exposure to Meaning Threats Improves Implicit Learning of an Artificial Grammar." *Psychological Science* 20, 9, 2009, pp. 1125–1131.

Punter, David. *Metaphor*. London: Routledge, 2007.

Quian Quiroga, R., et al. "Invariant Visual Representation by Single Neurons in the Human Brain." *Nature* 435, 2005, pp. 1102–1107.

Quintilian. *The Institutes.* Available at http://www2.iastate.edu/~honeyl/quintilian/8/chapter6.html#4.

Quong, Rose. *Chinese Written Characters: Their Wit and Wisdom.* Boston: Beacon Press, 1973.

Ramachandran, Vilayanur S. "Broken Mirrors: A Theory of Autism." *Scientific American,* November 2006, pp. 62–69.

Ramachandran, Vilayanur S., and Hubbard, Edward M. "Hearing Colors, Tasting Shapes." *Scientific American,* May 2003, pp.17–23.

———. "Neural Cross Wiring and Synesthesia." *Journal of Vision* 1, 3, 2001. http://www.journalofvision.org/content/1/3/67.

———. "Synesthesia: A Window into Perception, Thought, and Language." *Journal of Consciousness Studies* 8, 12, 2001, pp. 3–34.

Rapp, Alexander M., et al. "Neural Correlates of Metaphor Processing." *Cognitive Brain Research* 20, 2004, pp. 395–402.

Rattan, Aneeta, and Eberhardt, Jennifer L. "The Role of Social Meaning in Inattentional Blindness: When the Gorillas in Our Midst Do *Not* Go Unseen." *Journal of Experimental Social Psychology,* in press.

Raudsepp, Eugene. "Synectics." In: *Metaphor and Metaphorology: A Selective Genealogy of Philosophical and Linguistic Conceptions of Metaphor from Aristotle to the 1990s.* Miriam Taverniers, ed. Ghent, Belgium: Academia Press, 2002.

Reddy, M. J. "The Conduit Metaphor: A Case of Frame Conflict in Our Language about Language." In: *Metaphor and Thought.* Second edition. A. Ortony, ed. Cambridge: Cambridge University Press, 1993, pp. 164–201.

Rehder, Robert. *Stevens, Williams, Crane and the Motive for Metaphor.* Hampshire, UK: Palgrave MacMillan, 2005.

Richards, I. A. *The Philosophy of Rhetoric.* Oxford: Oxford University Press, 1965.

Ricoeur, Paul. *The Rule of Metaphor.* London: Routledge & Kegan Paul, 2004.

Rimbaud, Arthur. *Complete Works.* Translated by Paul Schmidt. New York: Harper Colophon Books, 1976.

Rizzolatti, Giacomo, and Arbib, Michael A. "Language Within Our Grasp." *Trends in Neuroscience* 21, 1998, pp. 188–194.

Rizzolatti, Giacomo, and Craighero, L. "The Mirror-Neuron System." *Annual Review of Neuroscience* 27, 2004, pp. 169–192.

Rizzolatti, Giacomo, Fogassi, L., and Gallese, V. "Mirror Neurons in the Mind." *Scientific American,* November 2006, pp. 54–69.

Robb, Graham. *Rimbaud.* London: Picador, 2000.

Roberts, Richard M., and Kreuz, Roger J. "Why Do People Use Figurative Language?" *Psychological Science* 5, 1994, pp. 159–163.

Rogers, James. *The Dictionary of Clichés.* New York: Ballantine Books, 1987.

Rogers, Tim B. "Proverbs as Psychological Theories . . . Or Is It the Other Way Around?" *Canadian Psychology* 31, 3, 1990, pp. 195–207.

Root-Bernstein, Robert, and Root-Bernstein, Michele. *Sparks of Genius: The Thirteen Thinking Tools of the World's Most Creative People.* Boston: Houghton Mifflin, 1999.

Rothbart, Daniel. *Explaining the Growth of Scientific Knowledge: Metaphors, Models, and Meanings.* Lewiston, NY: Edwin Mellen Press, 1997.

Russell, Bertrand. *The Scientific Outlook.* London: Routledge, 2009.

Rutchick, Abraham M., Slepian, Michael L., and Ferris, Bennett D. "The Pen Is Mightier than the Word: Object Priming of Evaluative Standards." *European Journal of Social Psychology* 40, 5, 2010, pp. 704–708.

Sacks, Sheldon, ed. *On Metaphor.* Chicago and London: University of Chicago Press, 1979.

Sakamoto, Maki, and Utsumi, Akira. "Cognitive Effects of Synesthetic Metaphors Evoked by the Semantic Interaction." *Proceedings of the 31st Annual Meeting of the Cognitive Science Society,* 2009, pp. 1593–1598.

Scannell, Vernon. *Collected Poems, 1950–1993.* London: Faber and Faber, 2010.

Schaeffer, John D. *Sensus Communis: Vico, Rhetoric, and the Limits of Relativism.* Durham, NC, and London: Duke University Press, 1990.

Schmidt, Christopher M. "Metaphor and Cognition: A Cross-Cultural Study of Indigenous and Universal Constructs in Stock Exchange Reports." *Intercultural Communication* 5, 2002. http://www.immi.se/intercultural.

Scholes, Robert, Comley, Nancy R., and Ulmer, Gregory L. *Text Book: An Introduction to Literary Language.* New York: St. Martin's Press, 1988.

Scholl, B. J., and Tremoulet, P. D. "Perceptual Causality and Animacy." *Trends in Cognitive Sciences* 4, 8, 2000, pp. 299–309.

Schorn, Robert, Tappeiner, Gottfried, and Walde, Janette. "Analyzing 'Spooky Action at a Distance' Concerning Brand Logos." *Innovative Marketing* 2, 1, 2006, pp. 45–60.

Schubert, Thomas W. "The Power in Your Hand: Gender Differences in Bodily Feedback from Making a Fist." *Personality and Social Psychology Bulletin* 30, 6, 2004, pp. 757–769.

———. "Your Highness: Vertical Positions as Perceptual Symbols of Power." *Journal of Personality and Social Psychology* 89, 2005, pp. 1–21.

Schubert, Thomas W., and Kooleb, Sander L. "The Embodied Self: Making a Fist Enhances Men's Power-related Self-conceptions." *Journal of Experimental Social Psychology* 45, 2009, pp. 828–834.

Scitovsky, Tibor. *The Joyless Economy: The Psychology of Human Satisfaction.* Oxford: Oxford University Press, 1992.

Scruton, Roger. *The Aesthetics of Music.* Oxford: Oxford University Press, 1999.

Seitz, Jay A. "The Development of Metaphoric Understanding: Implications for a Theory of Creativity." *Creativity Research Journal* 10, 4, 1997, pp. 347–353.

Semino, E. "A Sturdy Baby or a Derailing Train? Metaphorical Representations of the Euro in British and Italian Newspapers." *Text* 22, 1, 2002, pp. 107–139.

Sewell, Elizabeth. *The Human Metaphor*. Notre Dame, IN: University of Notre Dame Press, 1964.

Shah, Idries. *The Exploits of the Incomparable Mulla Nasrudin*. London: Picador, 1973.

Sheehy, Noel, Chapman, Antony J., and Conroy, Wendy A. *Biographical Dictionary of Psychology*. London: Taylor & Francis, 1997.

Shelley, Percy Bysshe. "In Defence of Poetry." In: *Political Tracts of Wordsworth, Coleridge and Shelley*. R. J. White, ed. Cambridge: Cambridge University Press, 1953.

Shen, Yeshayahu. "Cognitive Aspects of Metaphor Comprehension: An Introduction." *Poetics Today* 13, 4, 1992, pp. 567–574.

Shen, Yeshayahu, and Cohen, Michael. "How Come Silence Is Sweet but Sweetness Is Not Silent: A Cognitive Account of Directionality in Poetic Synesthesia." *Language and Literature* 7, 2, 1998, pp. 123–140.

Shen, Yeshayahu, and Eisenamn, Ravid. "Heard Melodies Are Sweet, but Those Unheard Are Sweeter: Synaesthesia and Cognition." *Language and Literature* 17, 2, 2008, pp. 101–121.

Sherman, Gary D., and Clore, Gerald L. "The Color of Sin: White and Black Are Perceptual Symbols of Moral Purity and Pollution." *Psychological Science* 20, 8, 2009, pp. 1019–1025.

Shibata, M., Abe, J., Terao, A., and Miyamoto, T. "Neural Mechanisms Involved in the Comprehension of Metaphoric and Literal Sentences: An fMRI Study." *Brain Research* 1166, 2007, pp. 92–102.

Shibles, Warren. *Essays on Metaphor*. Whitewater, WI: The Language Press, 1972.

Shklovsky, Victor. "Art as Technique." In: *Russian Formalist Criticism: Four Essays*. Translated and with an Introduction by Lee T. Melon and Marion J. Reis. Lincoln and London: University of Nebraska Press, 1965.

Siegelman, Ellen Y. *Metaphor and Meaning in Psychotherapy*. New York and London: Guilford Press, 1990.

Siler, Todd. *Think like a Genius: Use Your Creativity in Ways That Will Enrich Your Life*. London: Bantam Press, 1996.

Skeat, Walter W. *Concise Dictionary of English Etymology*. London: Wordsworth Reference, 2007.

Skelton J. R., et al. "A Concordance-based Study of Metaphoric Expressions Used by General Practitioners and Patients in Consultation." *British Journal of General Practice* 52, 475, 2002, pp. 114–118.

Skorczynska, H., and Deignan, A. "Readership and Purpose in the Choice of Economics Metaphor." *Metaphor and Symbol* 21, 2, 2006, pp. 87–104.

Slepian, M. L., Weisbuch, M., Rutchick, A. M., Newman, L.S., and Ambady, N. "Shedding Light on Insight: Priming Bright Ideas." *Journal of Experimental Social Psychology* 46, 2010, pp. 696–700.

Smith, G. P. "How High Can a Dead Cat Bounce?: Metaphor and the Hong Kong Stock Market." *Organizational Behavior and Human Decision Processes* 18, 1995, pp. 43–57.

Smith, J. W. A. "Children's Comprehension of Metaphor: A Piagetian Interpretation." *Language and Speech* 19, 3, 1976, pp. 236–243.

Smith, P. K., Dijksterhuis, A., and Chaiken, S. "Subliminal Exposure to Faces and Racial Attitudes: Exposure to Whites Makes Whites Like Blacks Less." *Journal of Experimental Social Psychology* 44, 2008, pp. 50–64.

Sommer, Elyse, with Dorrie Weiss. *Metaphors Dictionary.* Canton, MI: Visible Ink Press, 2001.

Sontag, Susan. *AIDS and Its Metaphors.* New York: Farrar, Straus and Giroux, 1989.

———. *Illness as Metaphor.* New York: Random House, 1983.

Soskice, Janet Martin. *Metaphor and Religious Language.* Oxford: Clarendon Press, 1987.

Spall B., et al. "Metaphor: Exploring Its Origins and Therapeutic Use in Death, Dying and Bereavement." *International Journal of Palliative Nursing* 7, 7, 2001, pp. 345–353.

Speer, Nicole K., et al. "Reading Stories Activates Neural Representations of Visual and Motor Experiences." *Psychological Science* 20, 8, 2009, pp. 989–999.

Spitzer, Michael. *Metaphor and Musical Thought.* Chicago: University of Chicago Press, 2004.

Stalder, Daniel R. "The Power of Proverbs: Dissonance Reduction through Common Sayings." *Current Research in Social Psychology* 15, 2009, pp. 72–81.

Stapledon, Olaf. *Star Maker.* London: Victor Gollancz Books, 2001.

Steen, G. J. "What Counts as a Metaphorically Used Word? The Pragglejaz Experience." In: *The Literal and Nonliteral in Language and Thought.* Seanna Coulson and Barbara Lewandowska-Tomasczyk, eds. Berlin: Peter Lang, 2005, pp. 299–322.

Stepper, S., and Strack, F. "Proprioceptive Determinants of Emotional and Nonemotional Feelings." *Journal of Personality and Social Psychology,* 64, 1993, pp. 211–220.

Stern, Josef. *Metaphor in Context.* Cambridge, MA: MIT Press, 2000.

Stevens, Wallace. *The Necessary Angel: Essays on Reality and the Imagination.* New York: Vintage Books, 1951.

———. *Opus Posthumous.* New York: Vintage Books, 1982.

Stoett, F. A. *Klein Spreekwoordenboek der Nederlandse Taal.* Zutphen, The Netherlands: Thieme-Zutphen, 1984.

Strack, F., Martin, L. L., and Schwarz, N. "Priming and Communication: Social Determinants of Information Use in Judgments of Life Satisfaction." *European Journal of Social Psychology* 18, 1988, pp. 429–442.

Strick, Madelijn, et al. "Finding Comfort in a Joke: Consolatory Effects of Humor through Cognitive Distraction." *Emotion* 9, 4, 2009, pp. 574–578.

Stroop, J. Ridley. "Studies of Interference in Serial Verbal Reactions." *Journal of Experimental Psychology* 18, 1935, pp. 643–662.

Stuart-Hamilton, Ian. *An Asperger Dictionary of Everyday Expressions*. London and Philadelphia: Jessica Kingsley Publishers, 2007.

Stubbs, John. *Donne: The Reformed Soul*. London: Penguin, 2006.

Sturluson, Snorri. *The Prose Edda*. Translated with an Introduction and Notes by Jesse L. Byock. London: Penguin, 2005.

Sullivan, Wendy, and Rees, Judy. *Clean Language: Revealing Metaphors and Opening Minds*. Carmarthen, Wales: Crown House Publishing, 2008.

Sweetser, Eve. *From Etymology to Pragmatics: Metaphorical and Cultural Aspects of Semantic Structure*. Cambridge: Cambridge University Press, 1990.

Tammet, Daniel. *Born on a Blue Day: A Memoir of Asperger's and an Extraordinary Mind*. London: Hodder & Stoughton, 2007.

———. *Embracing the Wide Sky: A Tour Across the Horizons of the Mind*. London: Hodder & Stoughton Ltd, 2009.

Taub, Sarah F. *Language from the Body: Iconicity and Metaphor in American Sign Language*. Cambridge: Cambridge University Press, 2004.

Taverniers, Miriam. *Metaphor and Metaphorology: A Selective Genealogy of Philosophical and Linguistic Conceptions of Metaphor from Aristotle to the 1990s*. Ghent, Belgium: Academia Press, 2002.

Thaler, Richard H., and Sunstein, Cass R. *Nudge: Improving Decisions about Health, Wealth and Happiness*. New Haven and London: Yale University Press, 2008.

Thompson, Philip, and Davenport, Peter. *The Dictionary of Visual Language*. London: Penguin, 1982.

Tompkins, Penny, and Lawley, James. "And, What Kind of a Man Is David Grove?" *Rapport* 33, 1996. Available at www.cleanlanguage.co.uk/articles/articles/37/1/And-what-kind-of-a-man-is-David-Grove/Page1.html.

———. "The Mind, Metaphor and Health." Available at http://www.cleanlanguage.co.uk/articles/articles/23/1/The-Mind-Metaphor-and-Health/Page1.html.

Torralboa, Ana, Santiago, Julio, and Lupiáñez, Juan. "Flexible Conceptual Projection of Time onto Spatial Frames of Reference." *Cognitive Science* 30, 2006, pp. 745–757.

Tourangeau, Roger. "Metaphor and Cognitive Structure." In: *Metaphor: Problems and Perspectives*. David S. Miall, ed. Brighton, UK: The Harvester Press, 1982, pp. 28–31.

Tourangeau, Roger, and Rips, Lance. "Interpreting and Evaluating Metaphors." *Journal of Memory and Language* 30, 4, 1991, pp. 452–472.

Tourangeau, Roger, and Sternberg, Robert J. "Understanding and Appreciating Metaphors." *Cognition* 11, 3, 1982, pp. 203–244.

Turbayne, Colin Murray. *The Myth of Metaphor*. Columbia: University of South Carolina Press, 1970.

Turner, Mark. *The Literary Mind*. Oxford: Oxford University Press, 1998.

Tversky, Amos. "Features of Similarity." In: Tversky, Amos. *Preference, Belief, and Similarity: Selected Writings*. Eldar Shafir, ed. Cambridge, MA: MIT Press, 2004.

Upanishads. The text of the Chhandogya Upanishad is at the Vedanta Spiritual Library: http://www.celextel.org/108upanishads/chandogya.html?page=6.

Valenzuela, Javier, and Soriano, Cristina. "Cognitive Metaphor and Empirical Methods." *Barcelona English Language and Literature Studies* 14, 2005, pp. 1–19.

———. "Looking at Metaphors: A Picture-Word Priming Task as a Test for the Existence of Conceptual Metaphor." Fifth Annual AELCO/SCOLA Conference, University of Zaragoza, Spain, 2004.

———. "Reading Anger Stories: A Lexical Decision Task as a Test for the Existence of Metaphorical Representation." In: *Language, Mind and the Lexicon*. I. Ibarretxe-Antunano, C. Inchaurralde, and J.-M. Sanchez-Garcia, eds. Frankfurt: Peter Lang, 2007, pp. 281–303.

Van Teeffelen, Toine. "(Ex)communicating Palestine: From Best-Selling Terrorist Fiction to Real-Life Personal Accounts." *Studies in the Novel* 36, 3, 2004, pp. 438–459.

———. "Racism and Metaphor: The Palestinian-Israeli Conflict in Popular Literature." *Discourse & Society* 5, 3, 1994, pp. 381–405.

Vickers, Brian, ed. *Occult and Scientific Mentalities in the Renaissance*. Cambridge: Cambridge University press, 1984.

Vico, Giambattista. *The Art of Rhetoric (Institutiones Oratoriae)*. Giorgio A. Pinton and Arthur W. Shippee, translators and editors. Amsterdam: Rodopi, 1996.

———. *New Science*. London: Penguin Classics, 2001.

Vieilledent, Stephane, Kosslyn, Stephen M., Berthoz, Alain, and Giraudo, Marie Dominique. "Does Mental Simulation of Following a Path Improve Navigation Performance Without Vision?" *Cognitive Brain Research* 16, 2003, pp. 238–249.

Von Ghyczy, Tihamer. "The Fruitful Flaws of Strategy Metaphors." *Harvard Business Review*, September 2003, pp. 86–93.

Vosniadou, Stella. "Children and Metaphors." *Child Development* 58, 1987, pp. 870–885.

———. "The Emergence of the Literal-Metaphorical-Anomalous Distinction in Young Children." *Child Development* 54, 1983, pp. 154–161.

Vosniadou, Stella, and Ortony, Andrew, eds. *Similarity and Analogical Reasoning*. Cambridge: Cambridge University Press, 1989.

Vosniadou, Stella, Ortony, A., Reynolds, R. E., and Wilson, P. T. "Sources of Difficulty in Children's Comprehension of Metaphorical Language." *Child Development* 55, 1984, pp. 1588–1607.

Vygotsky, Lev Semenovich. *Thought and Language*. Translated by Eugenia Hanf-mann and Gertrude Vakar. Cambridge, MA: MIT Press, 1972.

Wagner, Sheldon, et al. " 'Metaphorical' Mapping in Human Infants." *Child Development* 52, 2, 1981, pp. 728–731.

Walker, Caitlin. "Breathing in Blue by Clapton Duck Pond: Facilitating Pattern Detection with 'At-Risk' Teenagers." *Counselling Children and Young People*, 2006.

Wallas, Graham. *The Art of Thought*. London: Watts & Co., 1949.

Watson, Karli K., Matthews, Benjamin J., and Allman, John M. "Brain Activation during Sight Gags and Language-Dependent Humor." *Cerebral Cortex* 17, 2, 2007, pp. 314–324.

Whaley, Bryan B. "When 'Try, Try Again' Turns to 'You're Beating a Dead Horse': The Rhetorical Characteristics of Proverbs and their Potential for Influencing Therapeutic Change." *Metaphor and Symbolic Activity* 8, 2, 1993, pp. 127–139.

Wheelwright, Philip. *The Burning Fountain: A Study in the Language of Symbolism*. Bloomington and London: Indiana University Press, 1968.

———. *Metaphor and Reality*. Bloomington: Indiana University Press, 1964.

White, Michael. "The Use of Metaphor in Reporting Financial Market Transactions." *Cuadernos de Filología Inglesa* 612, 1997, pp. 233–245.

White, Roger M. *The Structure of Metaphor: The Way the Language of Metaphor Works*. Cambridge, MA: Blackwell, 1996.

Whitworth, Michael H. *Einstein's Wake: Relativity, Metaphor, and Modernist Literature*. Oxford: Oxford University Press, 2001.

Wilkowski, Benjamin M., et al. "Hot-Headed Is More Than an Expression: The Embodied Representation of Anger in Terms of Heat." *Emotion* 9, 4, 2009, pp. 464–477.

Williams, J. "Synaesthetic Adjectives: A Possible Law of Semantic Change." *Language* 52, 2, 1976, pp. 461–478.

Williams, James G. *Those Who Ponder Proverbs: Aphoristic Thinking and Biblical Literature*. Sheffield, UK: Almond Press, 1981.

Williams, Lawrence, and Bargh, J. A. "Experiencing Physical Warmth Promotes Interpersonal Warmth." *Science* 322, 2008, pp. 606–607.

Williams, Lawrence, Huang, Julie Y., and Bargh, John A. "The Scaffolded Mind: Higher Mental Processes Are Grounded in Early Experience of the Physical World." *European Journal of Social Psychology* 39, 2009, pp. 1257–1267.

Williamson, Judith. *Consuming Passions: The Dynamics of Popular Culture*. London and New York: Marion Boyars, 1986.

———. *Decoding Advertisements: Ideology and Meaning in Advertising*. London and New York: Marion Boyars, 1985.

Wilson-Quayle, J. Max Black. *American National Biography* Vol. 2. Oxford: Oxford University Press, 1999.

Winawer, J., Huk, A., and Boroditsky, L. "A Motion Aftereffect from Still Photographs Depicting Motion." *Psychological Science* 19, 3, 2008, pp. 276–283.

Winner, Ellen. *The Point of Words: Children's Understanding of Metaphor and Irony.* Cambridge, MA: Harvard University Press, 1988.

Winner, Ellen, Levy, J., Kaplan, J., and Rosenblatt, E. "Children's Understanding of Nonliteral Language." *Journal of Aesthetic Education* 22, 1, 1988, pp. 51–63.

Wisniewski, Edward J., and Gentner, Dedre. "On the Combinatorial Semantics of Noun Pairs: Minor and Major Adjustments to Meaning." In: *Understanding Word and Sentence.* Greg B. Simpson, ed. Amsterdam: Elsevier Science Publishers, 1991, pp. 241–284.

Witkoski, Michael. "The Bottle That Isn't There and the Duck That Can't Be Heard: The 'Subjective Correlative' in Commercial Messages." *Studies in Media & Information Literacy Education* 3, 3, 2003, pp. 1–11.

Wolford, George, et al. "The Left Hemisphere's Role in Hypothesis Formation." *Journal of Neuroscience* 20, 2000, pp. 1–4.

Wraga, Matyjane, and Kosslyn, Stephen M. "Imagery." In: *Encyclopedia of Cognitive Science.* Lynn Nadel, editor in chief. London: Nature Publishing Group, 2003, pp. 466–470.

Yu, Ning. *The Contemporary Theory of Metaphor: A Perspective from Chinese.* Amsterdam: John Benjamins, 1998.

———. "Metaphorical Expressions of Anger and Happiness in English and Chinese." *Metaphor and Symbolic Activity* 10, 1995, pp. 59–92.

Zaltman, Gerald, and Zaltman, Lindsay. *Marketing Metaphoria: What Deep Metaphors Reveal about the Minds of Consumers.* Boston: Harvard Business Press, 2008.

Zharikov, S., and Gentner, D. "Why Do Metaphors Seem Deeper than Similes?" In: *Proceedings of the Twenty-Fourth Annual Conference of the Cognitive Science Society.* W. D. Gray and C. D. Schunn, eds. Fairfax, VA: George Mason University, 2002, pp. 976–981.

Zhong, Chen-Bo, Bohns, Vanessa K., and Gino, Francesca. "A Good Lamp Is the Best Police: Darkness Increases Dishonesty and Self-Interested Behavior." *Psychological Science,* 2010, in press. Available at SSRN: http://ssrn.com/abstract=1547980.

Zhong, Chen-Bo, and DeVoe, Sanford E. "You Are How You Eat: Fast Food and Impatience." *Psychological Science* 21, 3, 2010, pp. 1–4.

Zhong, Chen-Bo, and Leonardelli, Geoffrey J. "Cold and Lonely: Does Social Exclusion Literally Feel Cold?" *Psychological Science* 19, 9, 2008, pp. 838–842.

Zhong, Chen-Bo, and Liljenquist, Katie. "Washing Away Your Sins: Threatened Morality and Physical Cleansing." *Science* 313, 5792, 2006, pp. 1451–1452.

Zhong, Chen-Bo, Strejcek, B., and Sivanathan, N. "A Clean Self Can Render Harsh Moral Judgment." *Journal of Experimental Social Psychology,* in press.

Zweig, Jason. *Your Money and Your Brain.* London: Souvenir Press, 2007.

Index